RAZOR SHARP

DREW SHARP

Detroit Free Press

The talented editors and copy editors of the Detroit Free Press have made me look good for 20 years. A tall order, indeed, but they went beyond the extra mile in the development of this project.

I'm extremely appreciative of book editor Tom Panzenhagen's yeoman effort. That he never once retreated from his computer screaming after reviewing my multiple attacks on the Lions and Michigan basketball is a testament to his tolerance.

Thanks to assistant book editor Maureen Ground, production editor Bob Ellis, cover illustrator Rick Nease and photographers J. Kyle Keener and Kirthmon F. Dozier, copy editors Terrance Collins and Bill Collison, proofreaders Alison Boyce Cotsonika, Tim Marcinkoski and Carlos Monarrez, and to technical assistant Alice Pepper.

Special thanks to Free Press publisher Heath Meriwether, executive editor Carole Leigh Hutton, deputy managing editor Dave Robinson, sports editor Gene Myers and deputy sports editor Owen Davis, and to the real boss of the office, secretary Laurie Delves, for dealing with five years of irate reader calls and e-mails.

And my enduring gratitude goes to the late Bob McGruder.

DREW SHARP

To Dad, for encouraging a 6-year-old to dream.
To my wife, Karen, for pushing me to pursue a dream.

Detroit Free Press

Printed in the United States of America
ISBN 0-937247-41-3

OTHER RECENT BOOKS BY THE FREE PRESS:

Fishing Michigan
Hang 10
Time Frames
The Detroit Almanac
Ernie Harwell: Stories From My Life in Baseball
HeartSmart Kids Cookbook
State of Glory
Corner to Copa
The Corner
Century of Champions
PC@Home
Yaklennium
Believe!
Stanleytown

To order any of these title, please call 800-245-5082
or go to **www.freep.com/bookstore**

Foreword

First and foremost, I'm a sports fan. I've always followed sports closely, and as a retired professional athlete, I've gained a certain perspective. I feel like I know what I'm looking for and, more important, what a good sports writer should look for.

Drew Sharp is an insightful sports journalist who knows what he should look for — whether it's tackling issues or taking issue. Drew isn't bashful about telling you what he thinks.

I may not always agree with what Drew writes — but to me, that's the mark of a good columnist. It's not about having everyone agree with what you write, but rather having people respect what you write.

Drew doesn't hide behind his column, a common complaint of athletes and coaches. He'll criticize, but he'll make sure he's at the next practice or the next game in the locker room.

And if you asked sports fans in Detroit, they would all say that although they may not always agree with Drew, they respect what he has to say — and how he says it — making Drew one of the must-reads when you wake up and want to get a look at what's going on behind the scenes.

I've known Drew a very long time, from back when he was the Pistons beat writer during our back-to-back NBA championship run. He understands the dynamics and complexities of sports and athletes, making him uniquely qualified to convey his thoughts and opinions.

If I didn't respect his work ethic, his fairness, his passion and his ability to get the story right, I would not have agreed to participate in this book.

Most athletes can quickly see through the fakes in the media — and when they do, they don't bother dealing with them. So when you see how Drew has access to all the top sports figures, you know that Drew is real.

You may not always like what he has to say, but you look forward to what he has to say.

JOE DUMARS

Introduction

Ever since I was 6, I wanted to be a newsman.

The seed was planted as I lay in the intensive care unit at Children's Hospital in Detroit, recovering from open-heart surgery and watching Walter Cronkite anchor the evening news.

It's a revelation that to this day amazes many — including me.

How many 6-year-olds are more interested in the news than cartoons?

When I got out of the hospital, my father got me a "news desk" and a typewriter, and I spent my recuperation writing stories for my evening report at the dinner table. And what's a news desk without a microphone? It's easily assembled. Just take the cardboard spool from a roll of paper towels, attach a crude replica of the CBS eye, and you're ready to broadcast.

Love is like a perfectly fluid golf swing. You don't find it so much as it finds you, and you have to be ready to take advantage. I've always believed that everyone is blessed with at least one special gift, and when it emerges, the luckiest are those who find a path to develop that interest.

Journalism's intoxicant is the emotional spontaneity of the moment, the adrenaline rush that occurs when something unexpected unfolds before your eyes.

I was too young to realize it then, but my hospital-bed career decision was an immediate and impulsive reaction to learning from my doctors that my medical condition excluded me from a normal childhood of Little League and high school football.

Sports aren't an option, so what do you do?

You react and then go along for the ride.

And what a ride it has been.

The more memorable moments are those when you ride along with a breaking news story. And unfortunately, more often than not, those occasions have tragic underpinnings.

I'll never forget that February afternoon at Daytona when Dale Earnhardt's Monte Carlo rather innocently hit the wall at Turn 4 on the last lap of the 2001 Daytona 500. No big deal. He's done it dozens of times, and he'll pop out of the car with barely a scratch.

But seconds turned into minutes, and the unthinkable became undeniable.

NASCAR's silence when asked repeatedly about Earnhardt's condition was deafening. He was gone. Everyone knew it, but we waited and waited and waited for official word.

And as I stood in a tiny infield press room jammed with twice its capacity to receive confirmation of Earnhardt's death, I envisioned that cramped room at Parkland Hospital in Dallas on Nov. 22, 1963, when President Kennedy's assassination was confirmed.

And that tuning fork deep inside goes off, reminding you of the alluring occupational drama when history walks lockstep with fate.

You react and then go along for the ride — even when it collides with popular opinion.

A columnist's life isn't for the insecure. You're revered one second and reviled the next — opinionated to some, a pinhead to others. It comes with the terrain, and five years of pointed commentary have toughened my hide and stiffened my resolve to tell it like it is.

If I've learned anything through my share of peaks and valleys, it is that you have to be true to your voice, regardless of how long it takes you to find it or how coarse it might occasionally sound to some.

I owe it to that 6-year-old with the cardboard microphone.

DREW SHARP

Table of contents

CHAPTER 3:
TWO LIONS WALK INTO A BAR 85

CHAPTER 4:
THERE MUST BE A PAINLESS WAY TO TURN THIS HEART BACK TO STONE 125

CHAPTER 6:

ST. PATRICK IN GAME 7, EH, YOU #@&%! GENIUS! 203

CHAPTER 7:

WHERE'S THE SOFA? WHERE ARE THE MATCHES? 227

CHAPTER ONE

You can't be from Detroit, you negative #@&%!

APRIL 11, 1997

Follow your dream no matter what

Telephone messages were stacked high on Scott Perry's desk in the Michigan basketball office, with precious little time to answer them. He had gotten little sleep in the last 48 hours. And now he had to make sure the sports coat he would wear at his introductory news conference matched the school color — maroon.

Such are the demands when you're about to take your first head-coaching job, but Perry loved every minute of it. He had lived for this moment almost his entire life.

Perry, a U-M assistant for four seasons, was about to be introduced as Eastern Kentucky's head coach. At 33, he would be one of the youngest major-college head coaches in the country, a distinction that may have raised concerns.

But he had heard the doubters before: "Too young to be playing with the big boys, Scott."

Nestled in Richmond, Ky., Eastern is only 20 miles from Lexington, home of the sacrosanct Kentucky Wildcats. But in terms of tradition and sheer reverence, the Colonels aren't even on the map. Nurturing a successful team in Kentucky's dominating shadow can be intimidating, but Perry relished the prospect.

"It's exciting to coach in such a basketball-crazy state like Kentucky," said Perry, who got a five-year contract. "We'll be in Kentucky's shadow here, but that's no reason why we can't develop a consistently winning program. It's a matter of having a plan that you believe in and sticking with it."

It's nothing unusual for an assistant to get his first head-coaching job, but personal pride swells with this particular story. I could see this day developing for 25 years.

You see, Scott Perry is my cousin.

We grew up a block from each other in Detroit with a mutual obsession for sports. That meant summers filled with basketball and Wiffle ball in my backyard. Since my parents decided not to rebuild our garage, my brothers turned the freshly poured concrete floor into the biggest court in the neighborhood.

Aptly named Sharp Square Garden, it was a magnet to everyone who thought he had a game. Fully understanding that I didn't, I usually watched from what history will record as the first stadium luxury box — my upstairs balcony.

But there was Scott, an 8-year-old determined to compete with players six years older and a couple of feet taller. As expected, he was humored but not taken seriously, frustrated occasionally to the point of tears.

But Scott kept coming back and back and back again.

You couldn't have realized it then, but Scott was developing the attitude that he wouldn't back down from seemingly insurmountable challenges, whether it was beating your older brother in a pickup game or beating the odds at a school that hadn't played in the NCAA tournament in 18 years.

If it's true the directions we follow as adults are largely predicated on the paths taken when we were young, then Scott's success comes as no surprise. What little boy doesn't dream of a life in sports? But the key is keeping the dream alive when doors are slammed in your face.

JULY 6, 1999

Senseless death a reminder: Never forget who you are

As gutless in death as he allegedly was in the last 48 hours of his life, avowed white supremacist Benjamin Smith took the easy way out, killing himself rather than facing his accusers and three innocent children who want to know why their father was taken from them.

As more light is shed on Smith's dark inner depths, it increasingly appears that this 21-year-old cut a bloody swath of racial and ethnic hatred through Illinois and Indiana under the guise of perverse political expression. Just as the Columbine High killers used Adolf Hitler's birthday as the backdrop for their carnage, Smith allegedly used the Independence Day weekend as the forum for his demented statement.

Ricky Byrdsong's senseless murder, plus the death of a Korean college student and the wounding of six Orthodox Jews, once again leaves us stunned and looking for answers. But one searing question is what do you tell Byrdsong's 8-year-old son, who saw his father shot in the back as the assailant sped away? What can you tell him?

This tragedy leaves a personal scar. Byrdsong and his wife, Sherialyn, were family friends of mine. When he was the head basketball coach at Detroit Mercy, Byrdsong hired my cousin, Scott Perry, as an assistant. It was Scott's first full-time coaching position, and it started him on the road that eventually took him to Eastern Kentucky, where he became one of the youngest Division I head coaches in 1997.

Byrdsong often attended family gatherings and was so easily engaging it was as though he were another member of the family. And that didn't change when he moved to Northwestern. Our career paths occasionally crossed, and Byrdsong, a deeply spiritual man, often told me to never forget that "God don't make junk."

But garbage is created somehow, some way.

Byrdsong's murder reminded me of a discussion my late father and I had in 1982, as I approached my college graduation and prepared to embark on what I hoped would be a prosperous and fulfilling career. My rather affable, non-threatening personality made it much easier for me to blend in socially with those from various ethnic and cultural backgrounds, thus making me less susceptible to racism's wrath, right?

My father spoke of the virtues of working hard and working well with others. But he finished by telling me never to forget that I'm a black man because if I do, somebody will remind me of that fact regardless of my professional or financial standing.

And such reminders have come, whether it's the inability to get a cab from Madison Square Garden at 1 in the morning following an NBA Finals game while others had no difficulty, or an e-mail from a reader who couldn't accept seeing a black face attached to a hockey column and who envisioned tying me to his truck bumper and dragging me through the dirt paths of northern Michigan (similar to a recent hate crime in Jasper, Texas).

"The only reason why Ricky's not still with us today," said Northwestern athletic director Rick Taylor, "is because a black man couldn't walk the streets in Chicago — and that's wrong."

His shooting was a most extreme reminder of why a color-blind society is a myth. It's an unattainable panacea, a cultural fallacy increasingly invoked by conservative ideologues often seeking political gain or public motivation to reverse the modest strides we've taken as a society to level a radically tilted playing surface.

We're missing the point. Our diversity should be embraced. It's not a question of teaching ourselves not to see different ethnicities, but to see beyond them before rendering judgment.

"All men are created equal" doesn't mean there aren't differences but that our physical or religious distinctions do not make us any better or worse than the next person. Countries far, far older than ours, and often divided by ethnic or religious differences, still haven't grasped that concept. So what makes you think we hold the recipe for complete racial and ethnic tranquillity?

"This isn't a gun problem," Sherialyn Byrdsong said. "This is a heart problem."

Or a lack thereof.

Independence Day is a celebration of freedom and the birth of the "great American melting pot." But the irony is that some families changed their names when they arrived in the United States, and some changed their appearances to attain a more ethnic ambiguity and make melting into the mix that much easier. But this deadly spree through the Midwest cruelly reminds us that no amount of affluence, education or compassionate civility can conceal who you are if somebody's bent on not looking beyond the exterior.

Perhaps that's what you tell Ricky Jr.

Embrace what God intended us to be. Love and respect yourself and others as your father did. Understand that the only limitations to how high you can soar are the ones you set yourself. But never forget that you'll grow up to be a black man.

MAY 1, 1999

Looking for heroes? Look across the breakfast table

The horizon appears vacant, bereft of stars who capture the imaginations of those who thirst for lasting sports heroes. With the recent retirement of three sports icons — Michael Jordan, Wayne Gretzky and John Elway — many in our business wonder, "Where do we go now for heroes?" As usual, our fixation on the surface blinds us from the deeper message.

An athlete's greatest heroics come when the cheers end and the bright lights dim. The loudest applause should come for what an athlete has done after he has taken his last bow on the competitive stage. Let me tell you about such a man. His name is Lowell Perry.

Perry was an All-America end at Michigan and played less than one season in the NFL for the Pittsburgh Steelers. But unlike many of today's athletes, who are rudderless upon premature retirement, Perry rechanneled his ambition, daring to advance through doors previously shut for blacks.

He was the first black coach in the modern era of the NFL when the Steelers named him receivers coach in 1957.

He was the first black NFL broadcaster when CBS hired him for game analysis in 1966.

He was the first black to become a manager at an American automotive plant when Chrysler picked him in 1973 to run one of its Detroit gear and axle operations, overseeing more than 3,800 employees.

He was one of the first African Americans to head a major government agency when President Gerald Ford appointed him chairman of the U.S. Equal Employment Opportunity Commission in 1975.

Now I have to confess I'm more than a little biased here. Lowell Perry is my uncle.

I'm as guilty as anybody in blurring priorities. When I've talked about my uncle to others, the conversation usually revolved around a football career that abruptly ended when a crushing Rosey Grier tackle broke his pelvis and hip, hospitalizing him for 13 weeks. Playing in the Rose Bowl is more spellbinding a story than standing in the White House Rose Garden during a swearing-in ceremony.

Yet his eminence actually grew the further he moved from his football days. But to his nephews and nieces, he always has been Uncle Lodi, an honorable yet unpretentious man who made time for, and placed a high priority on, family, whether it was assisting in landing a summer job, offering an ear, a wise word or, more important, laying out the road map for my generation to follow.

Perry, 66, is retiring after nearly 40 years of accomplishments and contributions in the public and private sector, spending the past nine years working in Gov. John Engler's administration. But the story won't make ESPN's "SportsCenter," as will Elway's farewell Sunday in Denver.

Many of Perry's family and friends will gather in Ypsilanti to give tribute to a remarkable life. The evening's theme, "Reaching Back," accurately reflects the path of a man who never forgot to extend a caring and helpful hand and was strong enough to pull others in his direction.

Perry strongly believes that education is the strongest helping hand we can provide, which is why, in lieu of gifts, donations in his name will go to the Perry Child Developmental Center in Ypsilanti. The center, named after my grandfather, has gained national attention for giving kindergartners an academic head start.

Perry's story is a reminder that when we're looking for inspiration, perhaps we should drop the sports page and merely look across the breakfast table. True sports heroes aren't necessarily All-Americas or professional all-stars. They could be those who never played a minute beyond high school but dedicated their lives to the non-headline-grabbing tasks of instilling a work ethic in their children, giving them a foundation so they grow up respectful of others despite their differences.

That's the only game that matters. That's the biggest pass my uncle ever caught.

Finding inspiration isn't as hard as you might think. Similar people are right under your nose. There were many who steered my life, but those with the greatest influence were the four closest to me — a quietly strong father, a tough-as-nails mother and two older brothers who set the right standard to emulate.

The landscape isn't as barren as you think. Trust me, there are plenty of real sports heroes remaining. We're just too busy looking for them in the wrong places.

JAN. 9, 2001

Thank you for caring

Never one for overstatement, Lowell Perry always embraced the quick quote. One favorite came from Winston Churchill.

"You make a living out of what you do, but you make a life out of what you give."

If so, my uncle had a wonderful life.

Perry died the same as he lived — with a quiet, unpretentious dignity that symbolized a man who never imposed his burdens on others while devoting his energies to lifting the weight from their shoulders. A brief, yet valiant battle with cancer silenced the roar of a lion but not the force of his heart, which will beat for years to come in those he touched. And there were many.

I wrote about my uncle once before, upon his retirement after 40 years of historical benchmarks, public service and private commitment. He was a sports pioneer, but his contributions went well beyond that. His death is another occasion to celebrate his life.

I'm sure he's up there cringing at the thought, bellowing that there's far better use of newspaper space than to share his legacy with others. But he's going to get what he deserved in the fashion he would have desired.

A simple thank you.

Thank you for blazing the trail for my generation to follow.

Thank you for setting a standard predicated on deeds rather than words.

Thank you for a genuine sincerity that made you more special than you would ever admit.

Leaving us after only 68 years was much too soon, but after we reflect upon your diverse catalog of accomplishments, it's hard to imagine a fuller life. Perry remains an important history lesson, a hard-fought chronicle of staring down obstacles and tearing down barriers.

He was never hesitant in using his influence to help but ever hesitant in accepting gratitude.

"The NFL has lost a loyal and trusted member with the death of Lowell Perry," NFL commissioner Paul Tagliabue said. "He was unselfish in his dedication to NFL Charities and contributed an enormous amount of time and energy to helping those in need through our charitable foundation. His leadership and, just as importantly, his friendship will be missed."

Perry was a charter member of NFL Charities, the benevolent brainchild of Lions owner William Clay Ford, Steelers owner Art Rooney and then-league commissioner Pete Rozelle in 1974. It has raised millions of dollars, and Perry sat on the board of directors with such league icons as Kansas City Chiefs owner Lamar Hunt and former New York Giants owner Wellington Mara.

But the greatest act of charity is taking the time to care, and this was my uncle's greatest gift. He once sponsored a recreation basketball team at Detroit's famed St. Cecilia gym. One of his players was a former Pershing High star who often sought my uncle's counsel. Once again, he served as mentor, providing a beacon of hope to someone too casually tossed aside as hopeless.

Sadly, the young man didn't heed the advice and eventually found himself flirting with the wrong side of the law. Nobody had heard much from him in years, but there he was at the hospital after hearing my uncle was gravely ill. And he stayed there for hours with one simple purpose.

He just wanted to say thank you for trying. Thank you for caring.

There aren't four better words to describe Uncle Lodi.

DEC. 17, 2002

Good health is the heart of the matter

Joey Harrington was hooked up to heart monitors in a cardiac intensive care unit, no longer a quarterback expected to excite a football-fixated city. Instead, he was a son and nephew diagnosed with an affliction shared by other members of his family — an irregular heartbeat.

The Lions reported that Harrington was doing fine the day after he was forced to leave the game at Ford Field, and that was of primary importance. It was also important that tests at Henry Ford Hospital did not reveal any structural abnormalities to his heart.

But whether Harrington would ever take another snap as an NFL quarterback was not so important.

Harrington's season ended prematurely because nobody wanted to take unnecessary chances with his arrhythmia. It was the right decision. It was the only decision.

Based on discussions with team physicians, coach Marty Mornhinweg confidently assured reporters that Harrington's irregular heartbeat wasn't "career-threatening."

Irregular heartbeats are common and, most often, easily treatable, but they shouldn't be as casually dismissed as a twisted knee or a pulled groin. Roughly one of five Americans is afflicted with some variation of cardiac arrhythmia.

I'm one of them.

A heart murmur detected when I was 5 revealed a congenital heart defect that required two open-heart operations before my eighth birthday, forever silencing those childhood hopes of growing up to become the Tigers' second baseman.

While the other neighborhood kids played basketball in our backyard, I sat to the side, writing stories on my little typewriter, blasting the players' incompetence for bricking easy jump shots, insisting they should be fired.

And a future columnist was born.

Heart palpitations, a rapid fluttering in the rhythm, have become an occasional nuisance, usually serving as a reminder that more than the customary stress has built up or perhaps I shouldn't have had that second cup of coffee.

As I learned through a life of frequent medical questions and concerns, my case was one of those rare instances when one's life was changed dramatically. That didn't appear to be the case with Harrington.

Mornhinweg said he has coached about a half-dozen players with irregular heartbeats. "They got it corrected," he said. "They got it fixed, and they were fine."

Mornhinweg is one of those who can find the bright side even on the darkest day, an essential attribute for a Lions coach. Panic is such an intrinsic emotion with this franchise that you can't blame the Lions for trying to paint as positive a picture as possible.

Harrington was their most important investment in years, and he was as much a symbol of hope as the team's sparkling new downtown stadium. Nobody wanted to entertain the notion that an organization tormented with misfortune could be devastated once again.

Yet Harrington, 24, must be watched closely. His problem likely is something he will deal with the rest of his life, regardless of his occupation. It's important that everyone look at this apart from the context of a rookie quarterback whose season ended earlier than expected.

It was not most important that Harrington stay healthy enough to lead the Lions, but rather that he stay healthy, period.

JAN. 3, 2000

Bowlmania: Two big games in one day

JUST ABOUT EVERYWHERE IN FLORIDA — "So did you enjoy the game, Drew?" said the person seated next to me on the plane.

"Excuse me?"

"That's your name, isn't it? It says so on your name tag there."

Oh, my goodness. I had just spent the last 45 minutes at Orlando International Airport with a Citrus Bowl press credential dangling from my neck, looking like some confused idiot for all to see.

I felt like a 6-year-old going on my first-grade field trip, walking around with the obligatory note that your mother pinned on you just in case you got lost and needed help.

But this time the note read: This is a wandering — though basically harmless — sports writer. Do not feed him or provide him beer. Just deliver him to the nearest bowl game.

Many questioned the wisdom of an adventurous soul attempting the ultimate bowl adventure — two games in one day: Michigan State vs. Florida at the Citrus Bowl in Orlando, followed by Michigan vs. Alabama at the Orange Bowl in Miami.

Correction. They questioned the sanity.

But the plan appeared perfect. A 6:10 p.m. flight from Orlando to Miami. A 7:30 arrival. A 45-minute trip from the airport to Pro Player Stadium. An estimated time of arrival at my seat in the press box of 8:25 — 10 minutes before kickoff.

But there was one crucial flaw. I didn't plan on a Florida quarterback not completing a pass. Twenty-six incomplete Doug Johnson tosses coupled with what seemed like 26 unsportsmanlike-conduct penalties dragged the first game to nearly four hours before Michigan State kicker Paul Edinger mercifully ended my torture by ending the game by 5 p.m.

So much for the 6:10 flight. As that plane embarked for Miami, I was just leaving the Citrus Bowl.

Ah, but perpetrating such madness always requires a backup plan. There was a 7:25 p.m. flight to Miami, which would put me in my Orange Bowl seat a little after 9.

No problem. The Spartans' victory was certainly going to be the more compelling story of the two games, so it really wouldn't matter if I missed much of Michigan's first half.

Problem.

Traffic was horrendous getting out of the stadium, requiring alternate routes and scaring the Metamucil out of several silver-haired drivers. Finally, I got to the gate at 7:20 for that 7:25 flight, then arrived outside Pro Player Stadium in Miami about 9:15, with a boring first quarter about to conclude.

Problem.

All the parking lots were closed and a rather belligerent Miami-Dade police officer told me I couldn't get in because it was 30 minutes after kickoff. But I would not be denied after coming this close.

I got out of my car — a risky proposition this time of evening in Miami — and removed two of the barricade cones right in front of another police car. At this point, I didn't care.

And apparently that particular police officer didn't care, either. I finally got to my seat in the press box at 9:51 p.m., just in time to see Tom Brady put Michigan on the scoreboard for the first time — a bellwether of things to come, as this turned out to be the most impressive bowl day ever for the state of Michigan.

Both teams entered their games as underdogs, both needed comebacks to emerge victorious, and both would finish the season among the nation's top seven teams for the first time (U-M at No. 5, MSU at No. 7).

All right, so the Wolverines won on a fluke — a missed extra point in overtime. It was an appropriate finish to a wild day — a New Year's Day that featured a triple-header among Big Ten and Southeastern Conference schools.

And after Purdue choked on a 25-0 lead at the Outback Bowl in Tampa — ultimately losing to Georgia, 28-25 — Big Ten critics sharpened their talons, ready to strike.

The final tally? Big Ten 2, SEC 1. But the real winners were those fortunate enough to experience the games firsthand.

Too bad there wasn't a way I could've squeezed in that third one.

APRIL 10, 2001

At Augusta, playing a round is daunting business

AUGUSTA, Ga. – Perhaps it's but another form of Southern graciousness, but the golf balls at Augusta National are extremely polite. Should you not strike them well enough when chipping to the greens, they will roll back to the precise spot of the original shot. You don't have to move one inch to take another whack. Isn't that considerate?

Such cruel twists of destiny are somehow more easily forgiven when they occur here, golf's national cathedral. Your heart skips, your breath quickens when you traverse such monuments as the Ben Hogan Bridge, which carries you to the 12th green and is Augusta's picture postcard.

You feel humbled when walking these fairways, appreciating the honor of tracing footsteps of golf's royal lineage. The names associated with Augusta roll off the tongue.

Jones, Nicklaus, Woods . . . SHARP?

Someone call security.

Who dares desecrate this precious gem with his wicked slice? The privilege of playing Augusta, barely 14 hours after Tiger Woods placed his historical stamp on it, introduced me to a new dimension of fear. I was trembling the moment I found out that I was one of the chosen few, one of 20 media representatives selected in a lottery every year.

The course was set up the same as it was for the final round of the Masters. The pins were positioned in corners among unforgiving undulations guarded by bunkers. Whom was I kidding? I put the "Ha" in hack. My game's a joke.

Interestingly, another writer told me about how one previous lottery winner thought of selling the club's letter of admittance on eBay for a tidy sum, thinking that an aficionado would pay any last-minute airfare in a heartbeat for the chance to play at Augusta. I kept telling myself that it's not important how I play but that I'm playing.

My golf-crazed father could peer down from heaven and see his son walk where few of color have had the opportunity. That settled me. Until I got to my first hole at 7:45 a.m.

I'm not a deeply religious person, and certainly God has more important tasks than catering to the concerns of a squeamish high handicapper, but I prayed as I took a few practice swings. "Oh, please, just keep it in the fairway for just this first hole. I'll do anything. I'll even say something nice about the Lions."

My foursome included ESPN golf host Mike Tirico, Orlando Sentinel columnist David Whitley and Knight Ridder/Tribune editor Tom Peterson. They all are excellent golfers. And here was I, the house hack. My caddie, 19-year-old Todd Pitcher, assured me I wasn't alone in my trepidation. And the tension eased when the first hitter from the foursome ahead swung mightily and sent his first shot rocketing a solid two feet. Yes, I was in my element after all.

I stepped up and sliced a driver, a shot that went about 110 yards, deep into the pine bark to the right of the fairway. And I walked off the tee with the biggest smile on my face.

You cannot truly appreciate the difficulty of this course until you face it head-on. It's not terribly challenging from tee to green. My driving and three-woods from the fairways were pretty consistent, not too long, but straight and in the short stuff. But those greens! Is it any wonder that David Duval and Phil Mickelson left screaming about their missed three-foot putts in the Masters?

Judging speeds on such multiplateaued, waxy-slick surfaces is a harrowing test. As for my final tally: 35-over-par 107, 13 three-putt holes, two balls lost in the water, no greens reached in regulation and no curse words.

Well, there was that one or maybe two. Oh, yeah, and there was that third one, when I hit that pathetic little tree that had no business on a course where a president has a huge oak named after him.

There's the Eisenhower Tree at 17. And now there's the Boodini Sapling at 5.

But the experience was worth the occasional embarrassment. Once you've won the media lottery, you don't get another chance, so it's a moment to cherish. I left Augusta with fond memories. And also a divot I snatched from Amen Corner.

No matter what I could get for it on eBay, it wouldn't be enough.

AUG. 6, 2002

Oakland Hills: No place for an amateur

The only place where they've had no trouble growing grass this dry summer is Oakland Hills Country Club.

It's growing and growing, and before the best amateur golfers in the country take aim at the course Ben Hogan called "the Monster" in two weeks, it's going to grow a couple inches more. Yet already it's green, lush and capable of ripping a seven-iron out of your hands.

"Nice (friendly) rough," shouted another victim (and I'm paraphrasing there) to one of the club members who joined us masochistic media members who had been invited to test the trail that will host the U.S. Amateur Championship.

And, naturally, in order for me to get first-hand knowledge of what these talented men will endure, I felt it important to play Oakland Hills from the tall stuff. This was journalistic research.

It's boring playing fairway golf and keeping the ball long and straight. Bottle the testosterone and dribble it short and crooked. That's the true measure of a man's character.

You're not buying it, are you? OK, so I gave it a shot. Which is more than I could say about my game off the tee during the media outing.

But I shot 81.

OK, so it was through 13 holes.

The thrill remains just being there, retracing the steps of many of the game's legends who conceded that Oakland Hills mercilessly brought them to their knees on a number of occasions.

This course bearhugged me to the ground, rubbed my face in the rough, lifted it up for a little air and then rubbed it in again for good measure.

The rough was four inches tall this day. For the tournament, the primary rough will be 3½ inches, and farther off the fairway the grass will grow to six inches, meeting the USGA's demanding (demeaning might be a better word) standards.

This was as close as any of us would ever get to playing on a U.S. Open course setup, and I found everything buried in that rough but my ball.

"Is that you down there, Mr. Hoffa?"

"The setup is basically the same for the Amateur as it is for the U.S. Open," USGA official Tom Meeks said. "The same green speed, the same narrowed fairways and the same rough."

Ah, yes, the rough. Pardon me while I release a little frustration. AAAARRRGGGGHHHH!!!!

Golf's intoxicant is the torture. It's the only game that allows you to beat yourself up and seem perfectly natural in the process. You're always trying to find that shot. But the trick we hackers are always told is letting the shot find you. Who knows when it's going to happen?

My shot found me on the par-three 13th hole. It was about 138 yards to the pin. I used a six-iron. Before I went to golf instruction boot camp at Boyne Mountain a month earlier, I would have used a three-wood in that situation.

Relaxed and smooth, my swing put the clubface perfectly on the ball, which flew to the green, landing above the hole and rolling back, back, back, finally coming to rest.

One foot from the hole.

Twelve inches from a hole-in-one on the Monster. That's why you put up with unsuccessful hunts through unrelenting rough.

OK, so I choked on the birdie putt.

JAN. 5, 1999

It's not all fun and games

ORLANDO, Fla. — Temperatures were expected to dip below freezing in Orlando, but some Michigan football fans discovered that cold is a relative term. At least they weren't battling snow-covered streets back home.

"It could be a lot worse," said Anita Bershoff, who had been trying to get a flight out of Orlando since the Wolverines beat Arkansas in the Citrus Bowl on New Year's Day. "There are worse places to be stranded than Orlando. As frustrating as this has been, I should count my blessings because there are others who are being affected much worse."

Thousands of fans were left stranded at Orlando International Airport by the snowstorm in Michigan. Northwest Airlines officials said about 4,000 passengers were unable to get a flight back to Detroit as of Monday morning. Some had been told they couldn't get a confirmed seat before Thursday.

Flights left on schedule Monday afternoon, but only one Northwest plane departed Orlando in the 48 hours that stretched from 1 p.m. Saturday to 1 p.m. Monday. The problem was finding room on overbooked flights.

Members of the Michigan Alumni Club and the university marching band returned Monday to Detroit when they finally got a chartered flight out of Orlando.

Those who had booked commercial flights continued to wait and hope.

Laura Vamplew of Belleville, who said she was "29 and holding," hadn't missed a Michigan game in more than 10 years. When she arrived at the airport Sunday afternoon, she quickly realized she wasn't going anywhere. As a Northwest customer service agent at Metro Airport for 15 years, she knew the signs of chaos.

But rather than worry about her own inconvenience, she volunteered to help behind the ticket and gate counters, much to the gratitude of the frazzled Northwest employees.

"I went to the supervisor and said I worked in Detroit and asked if I could help," Vamplew said. "I barely got the words out of my mouth before they brought me back there and put me to work. I could understand what the people here were going through, so I helped check people in, book other flights and answer questions. It's just in my nature to try and help.'

But helplessness was the overriding feeling among those stuck at the airport or at the crowded hotels.

"The timing couldn't have been worse," said airport spokeswoman Carolyn Fennell. "Orlando is the most popular family destination during Christmas vacation, and our busiest travel days of the year are the first weekend after New Year's Day.

"Most of the travelers are coming from the Midwest, and then the worst storm in 25 years paralyzes two of our biggest destinations — Chicago and Detroit. Unfortunately, some people might not be getting back to Detroit for at least another couple of days."

Of course, some Michigan fans weren't in a hurry to go anywhere.

Bob Silvernail, 56, of Des Moines, Iowa, a retired senior vice president of Norwest Corp., had been stranded since Sunday.

"The ticketing agent told me that I may have to wait until Thursday to get out of Orlando," Silvernail said, "and I told her I could last until April 1."

Like Vamplew, Silvernail hadn't missed a Michigan road game in years. His plan for Monday night? Hang out at his hotel's bar, watch the Fiesta Bowl and talk football with Gary, the night bartender, an Ohio State fan.

That might've stirred heavier winds than the snowstorm.

DEC. 25, 2001

The Columnist Who Stole Christmas

'Twas Christmas Day, and all through the city,
The discouraged and disconsolate wallowed in self-pity.

The calendar grew gray, as well as their spirits,
A sporting year somberly grim would beget another season hopelessly dim.

The thirst for holiday cheer brought them all together,
Convened at a popular watering hole in the hope of breaking the gloomy weather.

A dark cloud had pitched itself overhead and refused to leave,
Giving us 12 months of damning the heavens with more than enough embarrassment to grieve.

But in sauntered a vision in solitary black, emotionless except for a sinister leer.
He gauged the depth of the overall depression and offered to pay for everyone's beer.

Who was this benevolent soul, they wondered. Perhaps an angel from above?
Whatever the reasoning, it was impossible to reject this act of seasonal charity and love.

But off to the side of the bar, one man raised his head from behind his morning news.
The stranger's face in the doorway suddenly gained familiarity, and he wasn't terribly amused.

He vented his outrage at the magnanimous gesture, pushing aside his drink and grabbing his coat.
"I'm not taking any drinks from him!" he hiccuped. "It's the Columnist Who Stole Christmas, and he's coming here to gloat!"

A horrified gasp stopped the room.
They had heard about this heretic and how he always predicted doom.

They had heard his soul was hollow, his heart removed at birth.
They had heard the comments from coach after coach that he was the most mean-spirited person on the face of the earth.

He was not a brainwashed advocate for the home cause, much to his shame.
And since it's irrational to fault those actually accountable, we'll hold him to blame.

The Columnist Who Stole Christmas must have been in his glory in 2001 as Detroit took it on the chin.
An inglorious sports year by any standard, but where do you begin?

There was plenty to make everyone frown.
The Lions and Tigers actually occupied first place, if you had your newspaper upside down.

The Wings let a first-round playoff series get away from them, much to our disbelief,
Wheezing through the last games, hopelessly looking for their missing offense and oxygen tanks, as well as their false teeth.

The Pistons went with the customary approach:
Merely continue losing and bring in another new coach.

"Be gone, blasphemer!" the patrons cried. "You're not welcome here!"
But they let him stick around after he offered to buy a second round of beer.

"What about Michigan State basketball?" one countered. "They went to their third straight Final Four!"
Need we remind you of that semifinal game and its final score?

Michigan once again wasted its immense football wealth, and from all we could tell,
The talent they accrue never reaches its potential until it gets to the NFL.

Michigan State once again sings the praises of a mediocre season,
Extending contracts and offering raises for no particular reason.

And backward up the field, it's yardage the Lions yield.
The only one willing to embrace this injury-riddled mess is Blue Cross and Blue Shield.

Chapter 1

Randy Smith, George Irvine, Marty Mornhinweg, Phil Garner, Brian Ellerbe,

The ineptitude in leadership spread about as far as the eye could see.

"Away with your cynicism," they yelled as they waved their shiny crucifixes in his face.

"You are partners in an unholy alliance, spewing the refuse of a sacrilegious disgrace."

But wait, there's more. The Grand Prix sped away from the city, taking the Gold Cup with it.

And the only way you knew the names of Michigan's basketball players was through their traffic tickets.

Drew Henson traded maize-and-blue wings for Yankee pinstripes, while Jason Richardson and Zach Randolph opted for a different shade of green.

The idea of teenagers becoming Fortune 500 companies bordered on the obscene.

Comerica Park was desolate and joy-bereft,

Success coming only to those named Gonzalez, who were once Tigers but gladly left.

The fences too far, the pocketbook strings too tight,

Thousands of fans disguised as empty seats became the most common sight.

A new attitude blew into town, but it soon became clear,

It's not so important that the bar be high, but that the bar be near.

The Lions' only consistency was their inconsistency, not a game going by without repeated snags,

Linemen, offensive and defensive alike, wondering what nice Christmas handkerchief gifts they could give with all those cute yellow flags.

But as the circus leaves, so does the residual bitterness, a lesson that we in this city never seem to learn,

The more we leave ourselves vulnerable to these teams, the more we get burned.

What once was a screaming pitch had mellowed into whimpering. "Enough, enough," the barflies softly and defeatedly pattered.

The Columnist Who Stole Christmas knew he had beaten them

down, stripping them of the blind, unwavering devotion that most mattered.

With swollen eyes and sunken faces, they solemnly stared, wondering what impish creation could possess such fiendish power,

And then two people snuck up from behind and doused the columnist with a Gatorade shower.

The crowd roared its approval as their nemesis shriveled, shrinking before their eyes.

"No, no, there's nothing to celebrate," he cried, "only further cause to despise."

His pessimism proving no match for the indomitable will of the perpetually hopeful, the Columnist Who Stole Christmas turned to leave.

One-and-13 records, last-place finishes and neither the money nor interest in free agency are quickly forgiven because of this insatiable capacity to believe.

Though they bow to victorious gullibility this time, the doubters vow to once again have their say.

But every year the best Christmas gift for the Detroit sports fan is that next year is only a week away.

DEC. 25, 2002

2002 in review: It's not a wonderful life

My sound sleep was interrupted by the stinging, wafting aroma of a low-brow cigar combined with a guttural cackling that steadily grew in resonance. I awakened to a horrifying image slowly crystallizing before my startled eyes.

It was a jovial gentleman riding in a golf cart that bore 10-point antlers on its hood. He carried the appearance of someone living large with the physical dimensions to match. He possessed a coast-to-coast smile that suggested the Mickey Mouse ears on his head were just a tad too snug.

Oh, my god. It was Wayne Fontes!

Chapter 1

"Boooooooo-dini, Boooooooo-dini," he howled. "I know you didn't expect to see me, did you? I'm here as a favor for Mistah Ford. You know that I'd do anything for Mistah Ford."

"This is certainly an argument for sobriety," I responded. "What are you doing here? Don't you know there's a standing warrant for your arrest the next time you step foot in the state of Michigan for grand larceny for the money you stole masquerading as a head coach before you were fired?"

"Fired? What do you mean fired?" he said, laughing. "Don't you recognize me? I'm the ghost of Lions coaches past. I'm the spirit of the glory days of 8-8. Believe it or not, I'm here because I'm a guardian angel who's waiting to get his wings. Word has it that you've grown so disillusioned with your constant badgering and bashing of the local sports teams that you're actually contemplating leaving town to work elsewhere."

"Look, Wayne-o, I'm familiar with this holiday tale," I replied. "I've seen 'It's a Wonderful Life' a number of times. You're here to show me how the sports life would be in this town if I were writing in another city, and how much my literary presence really enhances the experience here rather than detracts from it."

"No, I'm here to make sure you get to the airport and get the hell out of town. Hop into the cart!" he said.

"I thought you said you were my guardian angel," I said.

"No, I'm the guardian angel for the sports fans," he said. "I'm trying to protect them from you."

Fontes explained that every time a local team loses or embarrasses itself, an angel loses its wings. Although 2002 was more upbeat than 2001, it nonetheless maintained a basically discouraging tone.

The Tigers bounced their manager and general manager just six games into the season.

The University of Michigan sacrificed its saintly image — as well as more than 100 basketball games — in the face of one of the worst scandals in NCAA history.

Michigan State solidified its hold as a national football mockery, embarrassing itself throughout the season and with its search for a new coach.

And the Lions were, well, the Lions.

"What are you afraid of?" the Big Buck asked. "Why not take a little trip back with me and experience 2002 without your acidic pen."

"Why not? What have I got to lose? But I'm not going anywhere with you until you get rid of that powdery substance that's on the passenger seat."

"Don't worry about that," he said. "It's my son's."

We cruised into a blinding light and soon emerged into what appeared to be a festive scene. It was a downtown parade with thousands of wildly enthused fans lining the streets. As the guests of honor made their way down Woodward Avenue, many fans rushed to the cars to get a closer glimpse of their heroes, and a few even fainted at the rapture of the moment.

"Wayne-o, I already saw this," I said. "This is the Wings' Stanley Cup championship parade last summer."

"Ah, check the calendar, my brother," he said.

"It's October," I discovered. "That doesn't make any sense. What would anyone celebrate here in October? Did Marty finally win a road game?"

"No, the Tigers stunned the baseball world with an 81-81 season. They believed in themselves because nobody constantly reminded them that they weren't any good. Cynics thought baseball was dead in this city, but look at those happy, smiling faces. This is evidence of the power of positive thinking. But it was only possible once your dark cloud passed through."

"Really?"

"Still don't believe me?" Fontes asked. "Check out the front page of this morning's Free Press. See that headline? It says, 'Barry closes in on record.' How about that?"

"It must be a slow news day if we're following Jon Barry's exploits," I responded.

"It's not that Barry," Fontes said, smirking.

"Get out of here! You must have something else rolled up in that stogie you're puffing. There's no way Barry Sanders would come back. The Lions' ineptitude had beaten him down."

"But when you left town, you took the curse of the Lions with you. Barry stunned everyone, came back and gained more than 200 yards in each of the Lions' first four games. Take a look at the standings. They're unbeaten and sitting in first place."

"I thought I had the paper upside down," I said.

"It's difficult to accept, isn't it, my brother," Fontes said, "but it should be pretty apparent to even you that the Detroit sports world would be better off if you worked somewhere else. I was sent down to appeal to whatever sense of community remains within you. See all the smiling faces about you? Don't you want to give the sports fans the best Christmas present imaginable?"

"These people are happy, optimistic and blindly supportive of everything their beloved teams do," I said.

"WHY ON EARTH WOULD I WANT THAT? WHY SHOULD I BESTOW A BREAK UPON THEM WHEN I'VE HAD TO SUFFER THROUGH THIS IDIOCY YEAR AFTER YEAR? I'M NOT GOING ANYWHERE. I DON'T WANT TO LEAVE, WAYNE! I DON'T WANT TO LEAVE! I DON'T WANT TO LEAVE!"

Sweating profusely, I awakened. I raced downstairs to get my Morning Friendly and nervously searched for the sports section. I let out a sigh of relief. The Lions were in last place.

And all was right with the world.

CHAPTER TWO

Keep telling it like it is

AUG. 5, 2002

Please don't shoot the messenger

Why waste time? Let's begin with a blanket apology for what follows.

To (your name):

I regret any perceived impropriety or insensitivity per my commentary in today's Free Press. There was no malice intended, merely the free exchange of individual opinions for the purpose of stimulating thought and discussion.

I apologize if anyone was offended by how those opinions were expressed.

Sincerely, Drew Sharp

Is everyone pacified now? Speaking the unfiltered truth these days means always having to say you're sorry. So why not just get it out of the way?

Cincinnati Reds general manager Jim Bowden recently apologized for putting his foot in his mouth. Tigers president Dave Dombrowski recently apologized for putting his foot in his players' backsides.

Their comments struck two vastly different chords. Dombrowski's words stayed well within the confines of his baseball team. Bowden's comments stretched to Ground Zero and the grieving survivors of the thousands killed Sept. 11, 2001.

We demand bluntness from our sports executives rather than the customary hedging. After all, it's only sports, right? What's the big deal? Yet when we get a frank assessment, we demand a retraction because someone's feelings were trampled.

Baseball fined Bowden an unspecified amount for what it called his "insensitive and inappropriate" comparison of a possible work stoppage with the 9/11 terrorist attacks. Bowden's indiscretion was this analogy: "Let (union leader) Donald Fehr drive the plane into the building."

That clearly crossed the line of good judgment and taste. Fine him. Fire him. Whatever. He has to be accountable for his actions.

But Bowden was right in the overall theme of his comments, suggesting that the approaching one-year commemoration of the terrorist attacks — anyone who refers to it as an "anniversary" is more guilty of insensitivity than Bowden —weighs heavily on the minds of both owners and players during these negotiations.

There's speculation that, should the players' union set a strike date, it would come shortly after Sept. 11 because the image of millionaires picketing and complaining of unfair working practices on that day of solemn remembrance might come across as a shade disrespectful.

Gee, you think?

And shutting down the game four days later would be more appropriate?

Those outraged by Bowden's "insensitivity" need to be reminded that sports was basically inconsequential before 9/11, and that didn't change in the wake of the attacks. But our 24/7 media saturation is gradually de-sensitizing us to the magnitude of that terrible day's shock and horror, and Bowden's misplaced "plane in the building" comment was a product of that anesthesia.

We mourn, but we move on. There's no alternative.

After 9/11, it supposedly was going to be difficult for America to laugh again, but it didn't take long for the late-night comics to lace their monologues with al Qaeda and Osama bin Laden punch lines. And audiences chortled.

Where's their written apology for insensitive and inappropriate conduct?

If players and owners want to show the proper respect to the memory of 9/11, they should accept the relative meaningless of their quibbles over revenue sharing and freezing salaries, and they should strike a deal.

If Bowden's bluntness moves two equally stubborn opponents a little closer to a rational resolution, baseball fans should write the Reds GM letters of thanks rather than demanding his head on a platter.

Baseball commissioner Bud Selig has gotten so much negative exposure in recent months that he thought it better to cut his public relations losses and force Bowden to say he was wrong and that he was sorry.

So what if Bowden's assessment was basically correct?

JULY 12, 1999

Hooray for U.S. women, but not for World Cup hype

What comes first? The hype or the history? Maybe I'm missing something here, but I didn't sense the pulsating frenzy that allegedly had overtaken the nation as the U.S. women's soccer team sought its second World Cup championship in three tries.

It was seared into our heads through days of unrelenting hype that we were on the brink of one of the defining athletic episodes of our time. And that the World Cup final attracted the biggest audience ever to watch a soccer game on U.S. network television is more a result of the media's vast power to market and manipulate than it is a historical testament.

No event is monumental simply because the media tell you it is. Its historical significance is measured by the public's reaction and willingness to embrace the accomplishment, and that comes only through time. It's gauged by its residual impact months and years later.

Hype didn't create Super Bowl Sunday, but rather Super Bowl Sunday spawned hype.

Mia Mania was lost on those, like me, who spent Saturday afternoon on the golf course. The course was packed. Where were all the World Cup parties? Wasn't everyone supposed to be glued to the television?

You didn't get any "Have you heard a score?" queries or "Do you know how many corner kicks I'm missing because of your slow play?" laments from trailing foursomes.

There wasn't a crowd around the television in the pro shop lounge. In fact, there was only one person watching, and his interest was somewhat muted.

Here you had the world championship of women's soccer, coming down to sudden-death overtime — a supposed watershed moment that was promoted all week as appointment television — yet it wasn't dramatic enough to lure inside for a firsthand glimpse the two dozen or so golfers on the patio deck.

Apparently, this tiny snapshot didn't reflect the national mood, but keep the numbers in perspective. That more people watched the World Cup than some games of the NBA Finals shouldn't stun anyone. The 0-0 deadlock provided only slightly less scoring than a typical NBA game this season.

The United States won the Cup on penalty kicks, 5-4, and the team's achievements are worth celebrating. You can't help but find positives out of anything that promotes opportunity and encourages hope. It's fantastic that little girls — and boys — can point to Mia Hamm as perhaps this country's finest soccer player, period, without qualifying the claim by gender.

But when we try to make more of something than what it is, comparing it with other achievements, we risk diminishing its importance.

It's an insult to equate this with Jackie Robinson's smashing another barrier more than 50 years ago, as some would do. I'm sure these women encountered narrow-mindedness for simply wanting the chance to express themselves athletically, but I doubt that death threats were one of the obstacles they cleared.

Let this victory stand on its own impressive merits and be judged accordingly. Don't force a perception of greatness down our throats masked as political correctness.

Part of the national team's attraction is that soccer might be the appropriate athletic venue for women to stand alone and ahead of their male counterparts. If so, that's fabulous. But I'm afraid the greatest obstacle facing women's soccer is the sport itself. American men could have been playing for the World Cup title, and it would have been difficult to hold interest through a 0-0 game.

The opportunity existed for memorable drama, but FIFA, the sport's governing body, kicked the ball out of bounds with its inane shoot-out rule. If a game tied following 90 minutes of play stays deadlocked following another 30 minutes of overtime, the outcome is determined by five shooters from each team who take aim from close range at a defenseless goalie.

Ask yourself how you'd feel if Game 7 of the Stanley Cup finals went into sudden death — and rather than let the drama and tension unfold at their own pace, the NHL decided to use an Olympic-style shoot-out.

You'd probably feel cheated.

Soccer is supposed to be the new American sport of the new millennium. And although its popularity continues to ascend, it will never captivate the masses and command the attention that football, basketball and baseball enjoy.

And when we overly hype to create an imaginary air of importance, we risk eroding the splendor of the achievement. Give the U.S. women their due for a job well done, but only time — not the size of headlines or television ratings — will determine whether their world soccer supremacy will live on as one of the great sports moments of this century.

TIGERS, TAKE ONE: SEPT. 28, 1999

Not everyone mourns passing of The Corner

The deeply rooted animosity has long since passed, the cultural sins of Ty Cobb and Walter Briggs long since buried. But forgiveness stopped short of absolution, stalling instead at indifference.

Saying good-bye to Tiger Stadium didn't bring universal tears in Detroit, despite all the buildup and contrived sentimentality. Many couldn't have cared less.

The Tigers never connected as well as they should have with the black community, which largely defined this city in the last half of the 20th Century. The team left a growing, influential segment feeling unwanted, and the stadium served as a symbol of that exclusion.

"The city has come a long way, and this team has come a long way back from when I used to sneak inside the stadium when I was 12," said Willie Horton, one of the Tigers' first black players. "But I guess some memories are still too deep for some to put aside.

"I'm still a proud part of my old neighborhood, but I haven't had a lot of people in my neighborhood come up to me and tell me how much they're going to miss this old ballpark."

That probably was a common reaction in many neighborhoods.

It would be hypocritical for me to shed crocodile tears, disingenuous to wax poetically about a close family member lost.

The old ballpark's mortar is mixed with memories. It is a time machine, a vehicle for reflecting upon the snapshots of our lives. Walking through the park one final time evoked memories of the Opening Days my father and I skipped work to share, providing a small measure of comfort as I approached the second anniversary of losing him.

It is history molded in crumbling concrete and draped with rusty steel and chipped paint.

But to properly evaluate its place in the city's evolution of the last 87 years, we must remember the entire history lesson. We must recognize the echoes that others prefer to ignore.

Recall the acidic rhetoric of Briggs, whose family owned the Tigers in 1920-56 and who swore that a black man would never grace the Olde English D as long as he had breath remaining in his body. Hear the numerous tales of elders about how those of color rarely felt welcome at Briggs Stadium in the 1940s and '50s, regularly banished to the leftfield seats.

And hear the stories of little boys who grew up in the 1960s envisioning a career with the home team, only to draw scorn from others for displaying allegiance to an organization that didn't care about them.

So why should those who were ignored suddenly care now?

"I have nothing but fond memories of my experiences with these guys and this organization," said Gates Brown, "but I can certainly understand why a lot of people don't look upon this stadium as fondly as others. And the Tigers have only themselves to blame for that. They missed the chance to create that connection with the city. Maybe they can make up for that with the new park."

Brown, another of the Tigers' early black players, was a celebrated pinch-hitter during his 13 seasons in Detroit — 1963-75. He also was the batting coach when the team won the 1984 World Series.

Horton, who signed with the Tigers out of Northwestern High in 1961, found a sad day a little more solemn as he gazed at the dozens who stood outside Tiger Plaza. They were catching a sentimental glimpse of baseball and personal lives turned gray, but Horton couldn't find one black face in the crowd. He shook his head in disappointment.

"That '68 team has always been credited with helping bring the races together in the city the year after the riots," Horton said. "That might be one of the proudest achievements I ever had during my Tiger career. That might have been the first time the Tigers ever made that connection with the black community."

But the organization allowed the bridge to crack, wasting away to the point that few blacks apparently cared if another was built. If there were a lottery to win the first swing of the wrecking ball to the old gray park, there would be a long line of Detroiters with fists full of dollars for tickets.

Tiger Stadium had long since outlived its usefulness. Knowing that Babe Ruth once grazed the hallowed terrain didn't make fans feel any safer walking down dimly lit streets to distant parking spaces. Understanding that deathly ill Lou Gehrig's last major league appearance came at Michigan and Trumbull didn't lessen the interminable wait at concession stands and rest rooms during the times when the ballpark swelled to capacity.

And appreciating Cobb's unparalleled skill between the white lines at Navin Field still can't rationalize his incorrigible conduct away from the diamond.

"It's not that folks are mad over stuff that happened 50 or so years ago," said former Tiger and Detroit native Ron LeFlore, "but it's that they just don't care because they probably think the team doesn't care. And that's probably even sadder. Some wounds take longer to heal than others."

People forgive, but they never forget. And Tiger Stadium's legacy suffers in the process.

Firing Larry Parrish both right and wrong

What does it tell you about an organization when it doesn't have the guts to fire a manager before hiring his successor? It tells you it's as clueless as the players on the field.

What did they do? Leave a message on Larry Parrish's voice mail?

"Hey, L.P., this is Randy Smith. Remember when we told you last week that the little pink slip in your next check was a wallpaper swatch? Well, don't worry, we're still redecorating your office. But we're starting with the guy sitting in your chair."

If this is how Mike Ilitch treats those who work for him, how can the average fan expect to be treated with any respect? And why should anyone think the Tigers finally have found the right answer in Phil Garner, their third manager in three years?

Garner's reputation is certainly much stronger than his unimpressive record in nearly eight years with Milwaukee. He will bring a credibility to the clubhouse that Parrish couldn't because of his inexperience. But same as with the Brewers, Garner will be only as effective as the talent Smith procures for him.

The pressure is on Smith. He finally has the manager he wanted to hire last year, and he was determined not to lose him to other bidders. But by moving quickly, Smith thumbed his nose at the commissioner's edict to recruit qualified minority candidates for managerial openings or risk punitive action.

It's clear Parrish was never the man the Tigers wanted, so they threw him into a sure-to-fail situation as a first-time manager with a novice coaching staff.

Ilitch has always had the benefit of the doubt with Tigers fans because of his success with the Red Wings. But management has lost that blanket of trust with the way this managerial merry-go-round was handled.

Parrish didn't deserve to return, but he deserved better treatment. The questions about his ability to guide a team in the proper direction were justified.

But considering how management also bungled the change in command, similar questions about its aptitude are justified, as well.

Team makes a mockery of affirmative action

Let's adjust the hue of this picture, shall we? Let's say Phil Garner was a black man with a strong baseball reputation despite a resume of seven consecutive losing seasons and no playoff experience. And he was the only candidate interviewed despite the presence of perhaps more qualified white candidates whose credentials included back-to-back World Series championships and a wild-card berth for a third-year expansion team.

Many would assail Garner's hiring, accusing the Tigers of pandering to league-imposed diversity mandates. Lost would be a perfectly justifiable motive — providing an opportunity for someone to compete on a level playing field.

Performed with typical comedic flair, the Tigers actually practiced the basic principles of affirmative action in the Garner hiring process. They balanced inequities when determining the value of one's qualifications, arguing that Garner could win a World Series with a higher payroll, as Cito Gaston did with Toronto in 1992 and '93, or a playoff berth, as Don Baylor did with Colorado in 1995.

They offered one example of providing opportunity but, sadly, at the expense of another.

The Tigers have the right to hire whomever they desire, but their flat rejection of the commissioner's-office edict to actively recruit qualified minority candidates speaks volumes.

What's personally irritating is why anyone should have faith in an organization that hired its third manager in three years. How could you know whether a potentially better fit than Garner was out there if you didn't look?

Team president John McHale initially said the Tigers couldn't have contacted Baylor because he was under contract with Atlanta, serving as the Braves' hitting coach. But when reminded that the Chicago Cubs sought permission from the Braves to speak with Baylor about their managerial opening, McHale added that the Tigers had read stories that Baylor wasn't interested in the Detroit job.

Read stories? You didn't ask him in person?

Perception often evolves into reality. McHale, owner Mike Ilitch and general manager Randy Smith understood that all too clearly, which explains their rather nervous explanations as to why they handled Garner's hiring as amateurishly as they did.

Ilitch even took a page from the Bill Clinton book of semantics by suggesting that Larry Parrish wasn't fired, because he was offered another job within the organization.

"There isn't a legal obligation to adhere to any directives from the commissioner's office," McHale said. "Hiring practices should entirely be up to the discretion of the individual clubs."

But isn't there a moral obligation to advance diversity whenever possible?

"Well, er, yeah," McHale answered.

Well, er, yeah, there is. The Tigers leveled the playing field to rationalize hiring Garner. Balancing the inequities of baseball: Hmm, what an interesting concept.

TIGERS, TAKE FOUR: APRIL 6, 2002

Bad start a bad omen for manager Phil Garner

Losing requires an explanation. Embarrassment demands a scapegoat.

The season is only four games old, but Tigers fans sent a strong and decisive message at the home opener. They were cold. They were mad. And they were ready to bail on this team before the winless Tigers had taken one turn through the starting rotation.

Understandably, manager Phil Garner has become the most convenient target. He was booed when he was introduced during pregame ceremonies, uncharacteristic for a home opener. Fans are trying to attach a face to their frustration over another season that's seemingly over before it's a week old.

The lone compelling interest now is can the Tigers match the Lions' 0-12 start? And if they do, who might be managing them then?

This was team president Dave Dombrowski's home debut, as well. The new man in charge of this wayward franchise couldn't have liked what he saw and heard — a stream of fans heading for the exits after the second inning with the Tigers trailing, 6-0, and derisive sarcasm from those who remained in the blustery cold.

Except for the 12-inning loss in their second game, each Tigers performance has been progressively worse. Should the poor start continue, Dombrowski might have no alternative but to fire Garner before the end of April.

"I certainly didn't expect this kind of a start," Dombrowski said. "It's disappointing that our last two games have been blowouts. And I can certainly understand the frustrations of those who've had to endure the disappointment of past history. But I'm just starting to get my arms around this thing myself."

But how long will it be before he feels like wrapping his hands around some throats?

The Tigers blew their chance to create a decent first impression for the home folks with a 10-1 loss. People want to believe. The television ratings for the season opener at Tampa Bay were tremendous, evidence of a hopeful curiosity that greets the birth of a season. But the way the Tigers have lost — no timely hitting, no middle relief and no fundamental clue about how the game is played —doesn't breed confidence.

Eight straight losing seasons have drained Detroit's level of tolerance, shortening the window of opportunity for a team to sell itself. The Tigers will not get a two-month grace period before fans render judgment. They will be lucky if they get two weeks.

Is it fair? No. Is it fact? Yes.

It's a reality of the Tigers' dwindling place in the local sports conscience. Few will care what happens to them after the weekend. Not with the Red Wings' drive for the Stanley Cup about to start. Not with the Pistons' generating more enthusiasm. Not with the Lions' holding the third pick in the NFL draft. The Tigers will drop from the public radar until June.

That is, unless a change in managers seizes everyone's attention.

You feel bad for Garner because he is a good baseball man who was basically doomed to fail when ownership shrank the budget. But the booing doesn't bode well for him.

"Yeah, I was a little surprised by it," he said of the crowd reaction. "But you've got to be a little thick-skinned if you want to manage in this business. Everyone's frustrated because they want to win now, but so do I."

Garner is taking hits — and deservedly so. He often speaks about the things he can't control, like an uncompetitive payroll.

Dombrowski's strategy for evaluating his employees apparently is giving Garner and general manager Randy Smith enough rope for self-hanging. They might already be in the noose.

Garner was fired two days later.

TIGERS, TAKE FIVE: OCT. 7, 2002

Give Ilitch credit for trying to fix team

Let's dispose of one myth right away. You know, the one that Mike Ilitch cares more about his gold-plated Red Wings than he does his sawdust-filled Tigers.

"I'm very proud of what the Wings have accomplished," Ilitch said. "But it would probably mean more to me personally if I can restore the confidence in the Tigers. That's what I want to do more than anything else. It would mean more to me from the standpoint of the city because I know, I know, how much baseball really means to the people in this city, and it breaks my heart to think that we haven't given them reason to care."

Ilitch is the caretaker of the worst stretch in the club's 102-year history — nine consecutive losing seasons. Public anger has morphed into apathy. He's in the market for his fourth manager in the last five years. His 3-year-old stadium has become a financial albatross, and its expansive dimensions a bone of contention with his players.

Is there another professional sports owner in America viewed in such wildly extreme contexts? Ilitch is revered in one breath for how he has kept the Wings among the NHL elite, but he's reviled in the next for the successive missteps taken with his Tigers.

In a rare exclusive interview, Ilitch offered his mea culpa. Contrition comes before redemption, and Ilitch is finally willing to concede his tactical errors. He often thought too much as a fan instead of a businessman, investing unwisely in bad contracts in an attempt to pacify his critics while artificially creating an appearance of competitiveness.

He insists he'll do it right next time, taking whatever time necessary to properly develop a young core. He's hoping for improvement in 2003 but understands it will take more time before the Tigers contend for the playoffs.

"Let's put it this way," Ilitch said. "We had better be competitive in two to three years."

If not, might he consider selling all or part of his interest in the franchise?

"No, that's not going to happen," he said. "I've invested too much personal emotion in this to give up on it before we've accomplished our goal. I have a lot of perseverance."

He also possesses a lot of pride and ego. He wouldn't want to leave this American League charter member in worse shape than when he bought it in 1992. But so far it is in worse shape. There has been no commitment to a single vision. Decisions have been impulsive. Each perceived move forward has pushed the organization two steps back.

"We've never been able to get that basic foundation in place," Ilitch said. "And I have to take responsibility for that. The Lions have more of that basic foundation in place right now than we do because of the young fella (Joey Harrington) they've got at quarterback now. He could be the cornerstone for the future.

"I was fortunate with the Wings that we got that foundation in place at the very beginning when I got Jimmy (Devellano) and then drafted Stevie (Yzerman). And it still took us 15 years to get the Stanley Cup. But we're still lacking that foundation with the Tigers, and nobody's more frustrated over that than me. I placed my faith in people, and it just didn't work out."

Do the Tigers lack that face, that personality with which people can identify?

"Absolutely," Ilitch said. "That's real important. I'm not saying that I need another Al Kaline, but we do need somebody that the community can embrace."

Might bringing back Alan Trammell as manager satisfy that criterion?

"The name Alan Trammell speaks for itself," Ilitch said. "He's been 20 years in this organization. I've spoken with him a number of times over the years. He knows the game, and he knows this city. He and Stevie are good golfing buddies. This is a storied franchise, and Alan Trammell symbolizes in many people's minds what being a Detroit Tiger is all about."

Sounds like an endorsement, doesn't it?

"I'm not getting directly involved in the interview process this time," Ilitch said. "I'm leaving it entirely up to Dave (Dombrowski). I was in the interview with (Phil) Garner. He was the only candidate we seriously talked with because it seemed like it was the right fit. But I've learned that it's best for me to remove myself from the process. Dave is well-connected in this game. He's going to talk with a number of candidates, and I have complete faith that he'll make the right move for all the right reasons. It's going to be Dave's call."

When assessing mistakes, Ilitch admitted the biggest was not working harder to develop the necessary contacts within baseball's inner circle from the beginning.

"We weren't exactly burning up the league prior to Sparky's departure" in 1995, Ilitch said. "When I came in, we didn't have a farm system, and when you step into baseball, with it being such a huge sport — much bigger than hockey — you've got to be well-connected. Maybe I could have been more aggressive in going around the country and introducing myself to more people so that I could have accelerated that process of getting yourself connected with people in the league. Perhaps I should have more aggressively promoted the jobs we were looking to fill around the league so that we would have made choices from a larger pool.

"I thought I had made the right choices, but they just didn't work out. And I have to take the blame for that."

There's no mistaking that Ilitch desperately wants the Tigers to win, but questions remain as to whether he knows how. And in that respect, he's on equal footing with the Fords and their Lions.

TIGERS, TAKE SIX: FEB. 19, 2003

Expect the cold hard truth from Alan Trammell

LAKELAND, Fla. — A con man's pitch is as much an attempt to sell himself as it is to sell others. It's not really snake oil in the bottle unless you believe it is, right?

Well, to the Tigers' credit, they aren't trying to sell us on the idea that a magic elixir can quickly cure this team's multitude of ills. And they aren't trying to convince us that there's a better alternative to the time-honored combination of hard work and unyielding patience.

"Sometimes you grow up," said second baseman Damion Easley, "and realize that you can't make something that it isn't, and you have to deal with what you have."

The Tigers have tried to con everyone in the last five years, nurturing false optimism with everything from signing washed-up free agents to preaching a more team-oriented family atmosphere. They always had a rationale for the previous season's disappointment, and they were ready to sell a quick fix.

They needed a professional hitter, so they signed the infamous Bip Roberts.

They needed a marquee name when they moved to Comerica Park, so they traded for Juan Gonzalez.

They needed more joviality in the clubhouse, so they traded for Dmitri Young.

Finally, the Tigers concede that the ones they conned the most were themselves.

"You can always trick yourself into believing whatever you want to believe," third baseman Dean Palmer said. "But there comes a time when you have to look at situations honestly. Who are we kidding? We're not going to out-talent anybody on the field. So that leaves one thing. We've got to work harder than the other guys. You don't talk about how many games you think you can win if this goes right or that goes right. You just take it a game at a time. That's all you can do."

The veterans are not worrying about what outsiders might think.

They already know what fans think about the Tigers:

They're not young and inexperienced; they're bad and lazy.

They're not an up-and-comer; they're at least three years from having a decent shot at playoff contention.

"We know it's not as easy as just saying that we've got to get everyone on the same page," Easley said. "Last year, I learned how many different pages there were. We had problems (in 2001), but we managed to outdo ourselves last season. You can't force chemistry or camaraderie. Either it happens or it doesn't. Let's just play and do the best that we can — whatever that may be."

Ditching the con job was Alan Trammell's first victory as manager.

But he can afford blunt honesty because there's no pressure on him this season. He can do no wrong in the public's eyes. He received a sizable ovation from the fans who waited outside the clubhouse for the team to take the field for spring training's first full workout. The players got only token applause when they passed by five minutes earlier.

Back in Detroit, season-ticket sales have increased modestly, and it's not because promising youngsters Omar Infante and Ramon Santiago are fighting for the starting shortstop's job. It's because a former shortstop — Trammell — has returned home along with coaches Kirk Gibson and Lance Parrish.

The pressure is on general manager Dave Dombrowski, who inherited the bulk of this disaster but also has contributed to the overall damage. He signed off on Young's four-year, $27-million contract in February 2002 and further contributed to the logjam of first basemen when he traded Jeff Weaver for prospective slugger Carlos Pena, eventual closer Franklyn German and pitching prospect Jeremy Bonderman.

Dombrowski can't fall to the same temptations of his predecessor, Randy Smith. He must stay loyal to the rebuilding plan — even if the Tigers surprise themselves with a few more victories than expected this season. There's only one way to right this wayward ship, and it will take a couple of years before you will even sense the Tigers are headed in the right direction.

Nobody wants to hear that. Everyone is in a rush. But we have seen the illusions created from the smoke and mirrors.

Trammell addressed his players for 30 minutes before the first workout. The message was fairly simple. They might lose plenty. They might get blown out with unnerving regularity. But a lack of professionalism won't be tolerated — even when it comes to rather innocuous irritants like leaving dirty clothes on the clubhouse floor for the equipment manager to clean up.

The Tigers' latest rebuilding project is at the rudimentary stage. Telling fans otherwise won't make them contenders any sooner.

AUG. 24, 1998

McGwire gets a boost in pursuit of Maris

At what price does competitive excellence come? And is the potentially heavy long-term cost worth the short-term benefits?

Apparently it is for Mark McGwire.

McGwire's acknowledgement that he has used a legal anabolic steroid called androstenedoine combined with an increasingly popular amino acid muscle-producing compound called creatine has added another dimension to his flirtation with immortality.

Is his record home-run chase another example of better athletics through chemistry?

Aaron Gibson represents the other side of the pharmaceutical debate.

Gibson, an offensive tackle from Wisconsin, is considered the top senior offensive lineman in the country. He's also the biggest at 365 pounds. But his equally uncommon athleticism (a 31½-inch vertical jump) raises questions whether he's that rare physiological marvel or a laboratory creation.

Wisconsin and Iowa are reportedly the only Big Ten programs that fully embrace creatine, a non-steroid, and openly encourage their players to use the supplement to increase muscle mass and endurance. The Badgers had the biggest offensive line in the country in 1996 — averaging more than 300 pounds — and Gibson wasn't even starting.

Gibson maintains he has done nothing more than consume four to five eggs daily to provide the required protein to maintain his immense strength. What bothers him are the cynics. Opponents who lined up opposite him on the football field often branded him a cheater.

And as another high school football season approaches, participants eagerly await the results of their off-season conditioning efforts to add bulk, but not at the expense of agility and perhaps without regard to the potential physical problems that could develop 10 to 20 years down the road.

High school athletes get their motivation from the actions of those they idolize. So what message does McGwire send?

McGwire has long been a proven power-hitter, but breaking Roger Maris' record of 61 home runs is as much a test of endurance as it is power.

"Everything I've done is natural," McGwire told the Associated Press. "Everybody that I know in the game of baseball uses the same stuff that I use. It's legal."

But is it ethical?

If McGwire gets to 62 homers or beyond, it would be perfectly logical for anyone to question the legitimacy of his accomplishment based on his use of a steroid, regardless of its legality. And major league baseball, seemingly forever willing to let every great promotional opportunity dribble beneath its glove, will be the most culpable if such a perception diminishes one of its most compelling stories in years.

The use of androstenedoine is permitted by baseball, although it's outlawed by the NFL, the NCAA and the International Olympic Committee.

Ben Johnson was stripped of his 1988 Olympic 100-meter gold medal, and Irish swimmer Michelle Smith was banned for four years from international competition because their sports' governing bodies have long understood the unfair physical advantages that anabolic steroids provide ultimately cheapens the accomplishments of those using the substances.

McGwire's actions suggest to everyone watching his superhuman shots that the difference between a 60-homer and a 50-homer season may be a steroid-stimulated boost.

And if so, is there any virtue in such an achievement?

Creatine has become the flavor of the month in muscle development, the best alternative to steroids. It's something that the body naturally produces, which eases some concerns about the supplement's possible detriments. It's readily available over the counter at nutritional supplement outlets. And advocates point to research over the last decade that has yet to discover any long-term medical risk.

"I don't take (creatine) because I really don't need it," Gibson said. "I'd be 410 pounds if I was on that stuff. I'm just big. I was born big. And I grew big. I have a big family. My little brother, Adam, is 13 years old, and he's already 6-4 and 310 pounds.

"But people don't believe it when I tell them I don't take anything. I guess I would have a hard time believing it, too, if I had to play against me. There are some things that people just don't understand. They accuse me of breaking the rules and that I should be tested. I guess you just can't be big and a good athlete. People just don't believe that's possible."

Wisconsin coach Barry Alvarez doesn't apologize for making creatine available for his players. Why should he, considering the research? It's up to the discretion of each program to weigh the merits against potential disadvantages.

"If you can possibly attain a competitive edge over your opposition within the rules," Alvarez asked, "why wouldn't you?"

Why wouldn't McGwire?

Competition's all about finding the advantage necessary to exploit your opponent's weaknesses. But even if it's done within the boundaries of the rules, there's no assurance that the result justifies the means.

OCT. 6, 2001

Because of '98, Bonds nets little interest

When the moment came, most of America was sound asleep — symbolic of the indifference that pushed aside Barry Bonds' run toward immortality. And when he finally did it, sending home runs Nos. 71 and 72 into the night air, most yawned at the record that once was baseball's most revered benchmark.

It couldn't have been any better for San Francisco Giants fans, though. The blast came at home in the final days of a heated division race and against the hated Dodgers.

But there was no emblematic transition of home run power as happened in 1998 when Mark McGwire hit the then-magical No. 62 and shared tears with Roger Maris' survivors, who sat beside the St. Louis dugout. Instead, Bonds' own family joined him, perfect for the man who finds the most comfort in his own company.

This time, the celebration was more personal than national in nature.

This time, few really cared.

This chase lacked the magnetic pull of McGwire's duel with Sammy Sosa. It had nothing to do with Bonds' often-churlish deportment, the lack of a running partner or the absence of Eastern interest stemming from the time frame of most of Bonds' games.

History implies a passage of time, and three years isn't enough.

Home runs no longer are the symbol of superhuman might they once were. Not when anonymous guys of modest power, like Bonds' teammate Rich Aurilia, hit 36 homers. Not when the combination of juiced-up hitters, baseballs and ballparks has diminished the long ball's significance.

Bonds rewrote the record books before Big Mac's ink even dried, and that has devalued McGwire's and Sosa's theatrics. So what's so once-in-a-lifetime about single-season home run records now?

Try as the baseball romantics will, there's nothing Ruthian about Bonds' achievement. When the Babe became the first to hit 60 homers in 1927, the next closest was Lou Gehrig's 47 and Hack Wilson's 30. This likely will be the third consecutive season in which there will be 40 or more players with at least 30 homers.

We went 71 years with one 60-homer season — Maris' 61 in 1961 — which contributed to its awe-inspiring magnitude. But there now have been six 60-home run performances in the last four seasons.

Home runs simply aren't a big deal anymore. Certainly not worth losing sleep over.

America awakens to a new home run king. Take a bow, Barry, and pat yourself on the back. But understand that life on this throne is short-lived. The way balls are skyrocketing out of today's band-boxes, it's not unrealistic to envision a push toward 75 homers before long.

If you're looking for something truly jaw-dropping, consider the 241 hits of Seattle's Ichiro Suzuki, a rookie record that surpassed Shoeless Joe Jackson's 90-year mark of 233 with the Cleveland Indians. The fall of a nearly century-old record is worth trumpeting, but there's nothing memorable about breaking one set so recently.

There's no denying that Bonds is enjoying a fabulous season, regardless of the home runs. He's on pace to become the first player since Mickey Mantle and Ted Williams in 1957 to reach base more than half the time. But excellence stacked too close upon excellence loses its historical prominence.

Fans begin taking it for granted. That already has happened with the 60-home run season, and the lukewarm reaction to Bonds' feat makes you wonder if the 70-homer season is destined to follow that same trail.

MICHIGAN, TAKE ONE: JUNE 19, 1997

Fisher was finished before he knew it

Communicating publicly these days only through printed statements, Steve Fisher has more in common with Howard Hughes than Brandun Hughes. The embattled recluse's last public appearance — a charity golf outing one month ago — revealed a man still optimistic although having aged 10 years in 10 months.

The wear and tear of the NCAA investigation into the Michigan basketball team's alleged "Better Basketball Through Baked Goods" system is evident.

Fisher can't win. He dismissed Hughes, a junior college transfer he never should have taken in the first place, in a fainthearted attempt to prove he has control over the program.

He fought to keep private his letter of admonishment from the university, only to have that rather tame correspondence deemed public domain.

And you didn't see any parades, commemorative posters or books celebrating the Wolverines' run to the NIT championship, did you?

But the interior cracks in the program's foundation should be of greater concern. They are a sign that Fisher is perceived as an albatross around Michigan's neck.

The recruiting season kicks off July 1, when coaches can first talk to prospects. A week later, coaches can make personal contact. And here is Michigan limping into battle with an already battered image ripe for further pummeling.

"Michigan can't afford to bring in a second straight recruiting class without one of the country's top 100 players," national recruiting analyst Bob Gibbons said. "And they've already gone two straight years without landing one of the top two players in-state. That's unheard of for Michigan." Three of the nation's top projected seniors are considering Michigan. "But that all changes July 1, after the negative calls from opposing coaches start coming in," Gibbons said. "All it usually takes with an impressionable 17-year-old is to just plant a little seed of doubt. But these coaches are going to plant a full-grown tree in their heads. Michigan has left itself vulnerable to such tactics."

Fisher likely won't survive NCAA scrutiny of this magnitude.

Head coaches rarely do.

Eddie Sutton took the hit at Kentucky. Larry Brown bolted UCLA just steps ahead of the NCAA storm troopers in 1981. Neither coach was directly implicated in the numerous violations that precipitated humiliating sanctions against prestigious teams. But both were tagged by the NCAA for lacking sufficient control.

It's in Michigan's best interest to bury the arrogance, recognize this inevitability and act accordingly. It should sever its association with Fisher now and guarantee leniency from the NCAA. By waiting a year until the NCAA demands that the school cut him loose, U-M risks sanctions that could set back this team even further.

Changing head coaches sends the strongest message to the NCAA that the school is serious about tightening its institutional control. Michigan State jettisoned George Perles one month into its internal investigation in 1994 for that very reason. It didn't matter that the NCAA ultimately determined that Perles wasn't culpable for any cited transgression. New leadership earned the Spartans a slap on the wrist.

Michigan State cut away the cancer to save the body, a surgical procedure Michigan obviously finds offensive. Defiantly and egotistically, U-M refuses to acknowledge it's even sick, maintaining its innocence until proven guilty.

But this isn't a court of law. The NCAA isn't bound by the Bill of Rights. The only constitution it's loyal to is its own. In its eyes, you are guilty until proven innocent.

Michigan State didn't agree with the NCAA's charge of two specific football violations. The university argued it couldn't find enough evidence to reach a satisfactory conclusion. The NCAA's response? "Too bad. You're guilty."

There's enough hypocrisy to go around in these situations. Players are smart enough to know what they're doing, but their only penalty is sitting out a year if they transfer. Discarded coaches usually achieve a cushy landing through a contract buyout.

That's why it's impossible to sympathize with a coach who's ultimately stabbed by the same sword he took into battle. Fisher created the Fab Five, unleashing a monster that has fattened itself off steadily increasing expectations. Fisher himself may be the next course. The monster apparently is tired of devouring birthday cakes.

Fisher and the University of Michigan parted ways four months later.

MICHIGAN, TAKE TWO: MAY 21, 1998

School's reputation begins to unravel

Mounted on a wall in the NCAA compound outside Kansas City, placed alongside the other quarry sacrificed in the name of legislative compliance, rests Steve Fisher's head.

That's all the NCAA wanted. That's all the NCAA needed to rubber-stamp the superficial findings of Michigan's investigation into its men's basketball program.

The NCAA's not-surprising decision to forego further inquiry has many in Ann Arbor and Michigan fans everywhere thumping their chests in triumph, smugly spouting their righteous indignation over what they perceived as a premeditated media witch hunt.

"The entire university is extremely happy this is over," athletic director Tom Goss said in a statement. "It's been like a dark cloud hanging around the basketball program."

But the storm hasn't passed.

Despite the self-imposed penalties — limiting recruiting visits — it's impossible for Michigan to claim it has been exonerated in the court of public perception. Not proving major violations is one thing, but not believing they probably occurred is another.

But there are concerns the NCAA's punitive slap on the wrist establishes a dangerous precedent. The usual defensive philosophy in such investigations is to fall on the sword — strongly penalizing yourself through scholarship reductions or probation to pacify the NCAA's thirst for blood.

Michigan, in essence, dared the NCAA to pursue the matter even further, knowing there were sufficient grounds for continued scrutiny on possible claims of lack of institutional control.

Why, then, should other schools take a carving knife to themselves when U-M has proven that a butter knife can produce better results?

"Inasmuch as the institution's actions in this case were substantial and meaningful," NCAA enforcement representative Cynthia Gable wrote in a letter to U-M, "no further action should be taken in this case."

As pointed out in this column nearly one year ago — when the thought of firing Fisher was dismissed as folly — coaches rarely survive investigations of such magnitude. Why? Because the NCAA adheres to the practice of assuming a program's guilt until it proves its innocence.

Pushing your head coach and his top assistant out the door and coaxing your athletic director to retire earlier than desired aren't the actions of an institution that honestly believes it is innocent of serious transgressions.

"We now have this behind us, and we can now concentrate on the future," Goss said. "Now our basketball coaches can go out and recruit the type of player and talent we need here at Michigan and tell them what we're looking to do in the future."

A future in which Michigan will be under close watch. The program didn't come crashing down in flames, but Michigan's reputation did. And in Ann Arbor, that's of far greater value.

MICHIGAN, TAKE THREE: MARCH 22, 2002

Fab Five's legacy left in shreds on courtroom floor

Now isn't the time for the usual piety and self-righteousness from the University of Michigan. A federal grand jury has confirmed what had been known for five years: Some prominent U-M basketball players allegedly were on the take.

The indictment of Ed Martin on charges of money laundering and running an illegal gambling operation provided the appropriate backdrop for commemorating the 10-year anniversary of the Fab Five's historic run to the NCAA championship game. But it certainly wasn't the gift U-M hoped to unwrap.

For all its celebrity, the Fab Five took U-M basketball down a road of deception. Its most prominent member, Chris Webber, is one of four former Wolverines accused of accepting loans from Martin worth more than $600,000. Nearly half of that money allegedly went to Webber from 1988, when he was a freshman at Birmingham Detroit Country Day, to 1993, when he left U-M for the NBA draft after his sophomore season.

Robert Traylor, Maurice Taylor and Louis Bullock are accused of taking money after the university banned Martin from associating with the basketball team, after Steve Fisher was fired as coach and after an internal investigation discovered only minor NCAA infractions.

The in-house investigators, who were supposed to uphold the university's integrity, meekly ended the case when players and coaches were uncooperative. The school never took accountability for a program run amok. This makes U-M susceptible to charges of lack of institutional control, the most serious offense in the NCAA code of conduct.

It's time for Michigan to do the right thing.

The school has had numerous opportunities to confess but never opted to cleanse itself of sin. Instead, U-M hoped time would wear down the interest of outsiders, as well as the memories of those directly involved.

But if Michigan wants to maintain a shred of moral standing, it should levy serious sanctions against itself. U-M should forfeit every game Webber played in during his two seasons, both of which culminated in national championship game appearances. And although coach Tommy Amaker had nothing to do with the transgressions of his predecessors, he must suffer the consequences of the university's inaction — loss of future scholarships and banishment from the NCAA tournament for at least two years.

If Michigan can't do that, then it should forever quiet its indignation over the improprieties of other schools. If Michigan doesn't act now, it no longer will have any credibility as a supposed paragon of athletic decorum. It will become just another school that wallows in the sleaze and scum that have contaminated college sports.

Michigan is no longer the answer. It's the problem.

I've warbled this tune for five years now, ever since the Free Press reported charges that U-M players took money and gifts from Martin. All the while, Michigan apologists have confused silence and ignorance with innocence. There's a double standard at U-M, fueled by arrogance. Don't ask, don't tell. And everything will be fine.

Why? Because they're the high, holy Maize and Blue, impervious to what lesser-known schools struggle to achieve without Michigan's national reach. But if there's even the slightest semblance of backbone in the NCAA executive corridors, there needs to be a swift, decisive message in this case.

Failure to respond accordingly would mean the NCAA has, in effect, rubber-stamped the Michigan blueprint for clouding an investigation. How then could the NCAA sternly penalize other schools that hide the truth? Why should any school cooperate with NCAA investigators if Michigan is allowed to walk away with a scolding — the equivalent of going to bed with cookies but no milk?

Fisher was held accountable for what transpired under his watch, and he lost his job. But the athletic department never has been held accountable.

If the powers-that-be in Ann Arbor have any guts, the avoidance ends now.

Every time I've asked athletic director Bill Martin about the Ed Martin debacle, his reaction was that it happened before he got the job, so how could he possibly have an answer to a question left by those who left before him? But the grand jury allegations leave him squarely in the cross-hairs.

Bill Martin inherited the mess, but the cleanup is his responsibility. His response likely will shape his legacy. He has attempted to mend the fissures that distanced the Fab Five from the Michigan family, but it's disingenuous to applaud whatever positives Webber and his teammates brought to Michigan without accepting the negatives.

The Fab Five's enduring legacy has emerged in a federal courtroom. It's one of deceit and a blatant disregard for the laws that govern college athletics.

MICHIGAN, TAKE FOUR: SEPT. 10, 2002

Webber's indictment keeps U-M under a cloud

A dark, seemingly unending tunnel finally revealed a glimmer of light. The closer it came, the closer Michigan athletic director Bill Martin sensed the end of the darkest chapter in his university's storied sports history. Then he realized the light was an oncoming train, and it would knock the Wolverines' basketball program to its knees once more.

"When is this going to end?" Martin asked with a hint of desperation.

Chris Webber's federal indictment on charges of conspiracy to obstruct justice and lying to a grand jury likely has ensured another delay in the NCAA's investigation of U-M basketball.

Former Michigan booster Ed Martin has admitted he gave gifts and money to former Michigan players, including Webber. The government has charged Webber with lying about what he got, and the indictment means the case will drag on even longer. The payments were first reported in 1997 by the Free Press.

"Who controls time?" Bill Martin said. "When I first got here as AD (in 2000), they told me to get ready because the Ed Martin thing was close to being resolved. So I familiarized myself with the matter and then, at the last second, he stonewalls and drops that first plea agreement. So that pushed everything back. Now we finally get to a point where we can finally close the door on this and put it behind us, and then this."

Webber's indictment understandably unnerves the university because it had long since surrendered control of its fate in an NCAA investigation. Michigan is twisting in the wind, and its athletic director can only hope that the NCAA judges the university fairly if severe sanctions are assessed.

And the penalty should be severe.

Bill Martin said he considered the university under NCAA investigation even though he's unsure whether Michigan received a letter of inquiry from the athletic governing body. When the NCAA explores allegations of major violations, it sends a letter stating its intentions and then sets a date for the school to plead its case before the NCAA infractions committee.

"I expect that we will go before the infractions committee," Bill Martin said. "Nobody from the NCAA has told us that, but we've agreed to be fully cooperative with them in regards to this investigation. We've told them that we want to be treated like anyone else. Let's look at the facts and find the truth, and then make a fair judgment on what the next step should be."

But now Webber will determine the next step.

Don't forget that criminal indictments and NCAA inquiries are separate issues, with differing burdens of proof. Webber has constitutional protections from the criminal charges and is deemed innocent until proven guilty. He can fight the charges in court or arrange a guilty plea that could keep him out of jail.

If convicted of all charges, Webber could face as many as 10 years in prison.

Michigan would be interested — and no doubt fearful — if a suddenly contrite and forthright Webber told everyone everything he knows. U-M says it wants the truth, but can it handle the truth along with its consequences?

Bill Martin has freely used the term "de facto probation" in describing the effects of the Ed Martin scandal on the Wolverines' basketball team. It suggests that the team already has been penalized, with no NCAA tournament appearances for four straight years and a shifting of the state power base to East Lansing.

But it was Michigan's choice to hire the wrong coach in Brian Ellerbe after Steve Fisher was fired. It was Michigan's choice to bypass its own talent-rich backyard for a national recruiting strategy because the Wolverines thought they were the Duke Blue Devils.

Probation implies that you're under closer watch, and any ensuing infractions are met with even stricter penalties. If Michigan argues that it already has served a form of probation, it also must acknowledge that violations occurred after the university investigated initial charges in 1997. Players Louis Bullock and Robert Traylor told the federal grand jury that they accepted money and gifts from Ed Martin after the university banned him from any contact with the program.

In some respects, Michigan and Webber made a perfect marriage because of their mutual arrogance.

The U.S. attorneys are going after Webber, his father, Mayce Webber Jr., and an aunt, Charlene Johnson, because the former Fab Fiver couldn't keep his big mouth shut. He haughtily scoffed at the government's accusations that he and his family accepted more than $280,000 in cash, gifts and other benefits.

The underlying message is pretty simple: Don't mess with the feds.

Time and evidence will determine Webber's guilt or innocence in a criminal court of law, but he already has been tried and convicted for one offense: the damage done to Michigan's reputation in the court of NCAA law.

MICHIGAN, TAKE FIVE: NOV. 8, 2002

University's shame doesn't cut deeply enough

The biggest bruise was to the ego — and in Michigan's case, that's a sizable blemish. The self-appointed moral conscience of college athletics has finally acknowledged that it cheated.

There was no getting around it this time. No feckless confessions about a lack of cooperation in its investigations. No deft wordplay about how the school already had been punished for the Ed Martin scandal.

Michigan had to stand before the nation — and, even more important, stand before the mirror — and make a critical assessment about how its employees fostered an environment in which players felt entitled to take money.

"We have finally fallen on the sword, as some have suggested we should," athletic director Bill Martin said.

Actually, it's more like a pen knife.

The opportunity to show courage was there, but Michigan opted for the easy way out. The university's self-imposed sanctions might satisfy the basic requirements of NCAA policy, but they stop far short of the ideals Michigan so boastfully espouses. The school should have gone further. It should have punished itself in future years.

The two-year NCAA probation, the one-year ban from post-season tournament play and the forfeiture of games is a necessary starting point, but any sanctions that don't include the loss of scholarships are nothing more than faint-hearted symbolism. If the NCAA infractions committee approves Michigan's proposed sanctions, then it becomes a willing accomplice in the lack of accountability that's gradually poisoning college sports.

No one is innocent here. The current players knew what might be coming. When you agree to wear the Michigan name, you have to accept the consequences as well as the benefits.

Where's the initiative to stand out boldly from the pack? The university took the national lead in the legal fight for affirmative action in college admissions. It could have set the standard for NCAA self-discipline, but instead of writing the blueprint, it followed the one in which expediency is the highest priority.

Michigan's only concern was getting the NCAA off its back, and it might have succeeded, but it blew a chance at re-establishing its ethical compass.

It doesn't matter that those now in charge weren't around when the infractions occurred or when fruitless internal investigations uncovered smoke, which many naively thought wouldn't lead to fire. New university president Mary Sue Coleman and Bill Martin are responsible for ensuring that Michigan complies with NCAA expectations, and with the even higher demands of the school's reputation.

"We believe that these sanctions are severe and consistent with similar NCAA investigations," Coleman said. "We're not making excuses. This is a day of great shame for our university. We've brought dishonor to our students, our alumni and to everyone who looks upon the University of Michigan with such pride."

There's relief that the end is approaching. Martin said the self-report wasn't the last page but rather the beginning of the last chapter. He's confident the university has done all it could to pacify the NCAA.

"The loss of scholarships revolve around violations regarding recruiting," Martin said. "And the NCAA does not consider this a recruiting matter. This is an excessive benefits matter."

He's wrong. This is a recruiting matter.

The Fab Five, starring Chris Webber, remains Michigan's strongest recruiting tool. This year, the Wolverines received commitments from basketball players whose first recollection of the team was the baggy shorts, black socks, black shoes and flippant attitude that were the Fab Five's trademark. They have recruited football players whose initial attraction wasn't the winged helmets but rather the shaved heads. They have attracted students from all over the country largely because a stylish college basketball team caught their eye with consecutive runs to the NCAA championship game.

You can erase the names in record books, but you can't erase the impact of memories, and Michigan has gained far more dividends from the Webber era than the $442,000 in tainted tournament money it will return.

Sports remain the mistress of higher education, and Michigan officially has become one of the admitted cheaters. Five years of stonewalling and political spinning didn't make the problem go away. Michigan finally had to step up and hold itself accountable, but it fell a step shy.

MICHIGAN, TAKE SIX: FEB. 17, 2003

Legacy of deceit will live on after Ed Martin's death

In time, the University of Michigan will overcome the disciplinary actions doled out due to its association with former booster Ed Martin. Probations and postseason bans will pass, but the scars of a carefully cultivated reputation that was brazenly compromised will endure.

That's Martin's legacy — a blemish on Michigan that will never go away.

Martin died Friday night much as he lived the past seven years, ever since a seemingly innocuous rollover accident elevated his notoriety, albeit under a shroud of secrecy. His death wasn't officially confirmed until nearly 24 hours later.

Martin never wanted people to know too much about him, and now that he's gone, you can't help but doubt that we will ever know everything.

But those suspicions will not go to the grave with him. They will live on with those basketball players who traded their integrity for his ill-gotten generosity and at a university that must live with the indignity of being the home of one of the worst scandals in NCAA history.

Martin's name has become synonymous with the poisoning of college athletics. And the three words that appeared before his name in obituaries published Sunday were "former Michigan booster."

Not "convicted numbers runner" or "self-confessed felon" or even "neighborhood basketball groupie," but "former Michigan booster."

That's the title he takes into eternity.

Martin, who pleaded guilty in May 2002 to conspiracy to launder money, told federal prosecutors that he took gambling money, combined it with other funds, and lent $616,000 to four former Michigan players while they were in high school and college. He was awaiting sentencing at the time of his death. The players were Chris Webber, Robert Traylor, Maurice Taylor and Louis Bullock.

Martin's name surfaced after Taylor lost control of his car on Feb. 17, 1996. Taylor was returning from a party in Detroit with four teammates who were entertaining recruit Mateen Cleaves. When Michigan found out that the recruiting visit included a stop at Martin's house, the school began to investigate his links with the basketball program.

You're not likely to hear any heartfelt eulogies from Michigan officials. Try as they might to extricate themselves from association with Martin, a retired Ford Motor Co. electrician, U-M knows that the institution and Martin remain joined at the hip.

Just hours before Martin took his final breath, a contingent of eight U-M officials began writing the final chapter to this seamy affair, appearing in Coral Gables, Fla., before the NCAA infractions committee.

The NCAA investigation is in the penalty phase. Michigan acknowledged its guilt in November and imposed sanctions on itself: a one-year postseason tournament ban; removal of banners from Crisler Arena celebrating achievements during the scandal years; forfeiture of half of its games in the last decade; repayment of $442,000 in NCAA tournament revenue; and two years of probation for the athletic department. The university hopes the infractions committee will believe the punishment fits the crime and hand down no further sanctions.

The NCAA will render its final report by the end of next month, and then the Martin matter will be closed, as far as the university is concerned.

Now, however, there will be speculation on how Martin's death will affect Webber's pending federal perjury and conspiracy trial. Martin's plea bargain was predicated on his full cooperation with the federal government in any potential criminal trials, so he would have been a star witness against Webber, Webber's father, Mayce Webber Jr., and Webber's aunt, Charlene Johnson.

More than 600 pages of Martin's grand jury testimony most

likely cannot be admitted in court because the defense wouldn't have an opportunity for cross-examination. But it's believed the government could use Martin's son, Carlton, to corroborate his father's account of his dealings with the Michigan basketball program.

Martin's health had been failing in the past year, and each time his sentencing was postponed, the growing sentiment was that he might not live to see one day in prison.

He may be remembered by some as a compassionate man, offering small gestures to those lacking the financial means to provide for themselves.

It might have been a pair of shoes or a previously worn winter coat. He might have picked up the bill for a couple of Big Macs. And who can forget the birthday cakes? But Martin's downfall was that he wanted celebrity, and that came with a much higher price tag.

What were once gifts evolved into investments.

Martin hoped those deeds would be remembered — and returned in kind — when Webber and the other players cashed in with multimillion-dollar NBA contracts.

His actions will be remembered.

Much to the dismay of the University of Michigan, they will never be forgotten.

MAY 3, 2001

NASCAR hides safety concerns behind closed doors

An anniversary awaits NASCAR, but it's a somber occasion. On May 12, 2000, 19-year-old Adam Petty, the fourth generation of stock car racing's aristocracy, died after his car slammed headfirst into a concrete wall on a New Hampshire track.

As if youth extinguished prematurely wasn't tragedy enough, Petty's death was the first lap of a horrific nine-month period during which four NASCAR drivers lost their lives in similar fashion — basal skull fractures from blunt force trauma so severe that blood oozed out their ears.

Danger is more than accepted in this sport — it's embraced. But the secrecy and inconsistencies surrounding NASCAR's investigation of Dale Earnhardt's fatal Daytona 500 crash raise concerns that the governing body might not want too much scrutiny out of fear that even such high-speed hazards have their limits.

NASCAR's standard investigative procedure is to keep everything behind closed doors. But how is anyone to know whether it's looking at potential evidence behind closed eyes?

Five days after Earnhardt's death on Feb. 18, 2001, NASCAR floated the possibility of a broken seat belt — a conclusion apparently reached without talking with the seat belt's manufacturer or Tommy Propst, the first emergency rescue technician to reach Earnhardt's car.

Both vehemently deny NASCAR's assertion of a possible flaw in the five-point body harness. Propst finally spoke out, venting to the Orlando Sentinel that any investigation surrounding the crash scene should include the person who assisted in removing Earnhardt from the driver's side of the car.

"Are they suggesting I wasn't there?" Propst said. "I did lean into the car and pulled apart the buckle. They can say what they want to. But I know the truth."

But NASCAR isn't saying anything. Its response to queries regarding the ongoing investigation and these alleged inconsistencies is that the inquest remains an internal matter. And what's outrageous is that NASCAR is getting away with such concealment. Since when are the deaths of four people from similar causes within a year a private issue? Where's the public outcry for an independent inspection of NASCAR driver safety?

You'd better believe that if four NFL players suffered paralyzing injuries in a year due to possible equipment malfunction or faulty design, you couldn't authorize government intervention fast enough to quell the public torrent for safety changes.

But because NASCAR is a sport that symbolizes what many perceive as one of the last vestiges of individual freedom, politicians in such NASCAR hotbeds as Florida and North Carolina assume a hands-off approach. They don't risk ticking off a fan base that doubles as their voter base. Instead, they've directed their efforts at stifling the media's efforts to independently investigate the Earnhardt crash evidence.

NASCAR epitomizes an anti-regulatory sentiment. Specialized head restraints might have saved Earnhardt, Petty, Kenny Irwin and Tony Roper, but NASCAR steadfastly refuses to make the system mandatory, leaving it up to the driver's discretion. "In NASCAR We Trust" is the overriding message here. They're the experts. They should know exactly what they're doing.

This isn't to suggest that NASCAR is insensitive to the well-being of its most important commodity, its drivers. It has made significant safety upgrades over time and, up until Petty's death, had the finest safety record in all motor racing. But like any other multi-billion-dollar private enterprise, it is sensitive to possible product liability litigation.

Is NASCAR worried that a potentially too rigid front car chassis might have contributed to the four deaths? That the drivers absorbed more of the shock than necessary from the tremendous G forces at the point of contact with the wall?

Once again, NASCAR won't respond, maintaining its rules and how it polices them are a private matter. And anytime an organization suspiciously operates behind closed doors, there are bound to be concerns regarding the integrity of any in-house inquiry. Would you blindly believe a billion-dollar chemical company if it investigated itself on water contamination charges without any governmental or independent oversight? You'd have questions regarding its credibility, wouldn't you?

But NASCAR is about image. Its drivers and officials are the last cowboys riding across the prairie, and nobody's going to tell them what they can or cannot do. That's a large part of the sport's attraction, and it's why nobody is willing to look over NASCAR's shoulder regarding the death of its most popular figure.

It's as much politics as it is sports, and as long as NASCAR's die-hard devotees would rather direct their anger at the media doing their job, then there's no reason to expect any pressure on NASCAR during the investigation to ensure that this racing monolith is doing its job.

AUG. 22, 2001

Earnhardt investigation avoids tough questions

NASCAR got what it wanted — an independently determined scapegoat.

Dale Earnhardt's death on the final lap of the Daytona 500 six months ago demands justice in the eyes of his passionate fans. A fatal accident notwithstanding, they think their hero was wrongly taken from them, and they want somebody's head on a stick.

NASCAR's extensive investigation gave them seat belt manufacturer Bill Simpson. It certainly beats the alternative, which might have pointed the finger at the Intimidator himself.

NASCAR's presentation of its investigation results listed the separation of Earnhardt's restraint system as a possible trigger to a sequence of occurrences that led to the blunt-force head trauma that killed Earnhardt. The accident came just seconds before his son, Dale Jr., crossed the finish line in second place.

Simpson Performance Products made the seat belts that went into Earnhardt's No. 3 Chevrolet, and the broken seat belt shown certainly pointed blame at the North Carolina company.

NASCAR president Mike Helton contended that the investigation wasn't designed to assess blame but find answers. Neither he nor the primary investigators whom the racing body retained directly implicated Simpson, but the overriding tone of the findings was pretty clear: Had Earnhardt's left lap belt not severed upon impact, he might have survived the crash.

Helton thinks there's no room for further discussion. Nobody can question the credibility of the inquiry. NASCAR, a multi-billion-dollar, family-run monolith, went outside of the inner circle for this investigation, retaining a nationally prominent biophysicist and an engineer.

But the investigation produced as many questions as answers.

Why didn't NASCAR mention that the seat belt wasn't defective, or the possibility of improper installation?

"I don't think NASCAR is trying to blame anyone, like they said," said Simpson Performance Products attorney James Voyles. "But I also don't think they went far enough in this investigation, particularly in the area of the restraint system installed by manufacturer's specifications. Separation was the result of the installation, not the quality of the system."

If installation was the primary culprit, then isn't Earnhardt culpable for any diminished protection in the driver's cage?

Why didn't the chief investigators get access to the Earnhardt autopsy photos?

"There was a court order prohibiting that, as you well know," said Dr. James Raddin, director of Biodynamics Research Corp., a noted expert in injury causation. "We had a thorough and comprehensive record from the medical examiner report."

The investigators read a written account of Earnhardt's injuries. But had they seen the photos, would that have prevented discrepancies between the NASCAR findings and those of an independent pathologist who did see the pictures?

Raddin played down an earlier report that violent head-whipping was the primary cause of Earnhardt's fatal skull fracture.

But the most important question from the past six months remained unanswered. Is a stock car's frontal chassis design unsafe because of its inability to dissipate the high forces at impact?

"There are opportunities for improvement, and we've been researching those possibilities for at least the past year," Helton said. "But as mentioned in this extensive report, nobody could say it would have benefited in this case when you consider the other factors involved, such as the separation of the restraint system."

Although NASCAR's inquest focused exclusively on the Earnhardt crash, it was initially perceived as an examination into the causes of four NASCAR fatalities in a nine-month span. All four died from basal skull fractures, consistent with violent head movement with rapid change in velocity upon impact.

But it seems NASCAR doesn't want anybody to fixate on anything beyond the seat restraint. And the fact that Simpson's attorneys were ready to strike back immediately following the NASCAR news conference suggests they suspected precisely that.

"We understand that this was a tragedy of magnificent proportions," Voyles said. "There are plenty of emotions involved from all directions. But it's important that if you're looking for answers that everything gets addressed."

But this investigation was as much about moving forward as looking back. NASCAR has an image to protect and a legacy to maintain. Earnhardt personified the "man's man" mentality that's the backbone of the sport's spiraling popularity. But how would it look if this icon compromised his safety and paid with his life when all the factors in the report unfolded, such as hitting the wall at a most dangerous angle?

"Our attempt wasn't to find blame but to possibly find ways for a better system," said Dr. Dean Sicking, a University of Nebraska civil engineering professor and an expert in impact absorption.

They're taking steps in that direction. Forty-one of the 43 drivers in this week's race at Michigan International Speedway wore a head-

and-neck restraint system. But the most important safety upgrade should involve the design of the car. That would require NASCAR to look more seriously at itself, though. And that remains a course it would rather not take.

JAN. 5, 1998

Michigan: No. 1 with an asterisk

Please forgive me the occasional chuckle as I watch Michigan wrestle with its unceremonious place in college football history — one of the few top-ranked teams to win a bowl and lose its top seed in a poll.

The humor isn't in the outcome but in its many ironies.

Michigan entered the 1998 Rose Bowl ranked No. 1 in both the Associated Press and ESPN/USA Today coaches polls but slipped to second behind Nebraska in the latter, even though the Wolverines defeated Washington State, 21-16.

How does such a media-friendly institution like Michigan feel about being crowned the writers' champion in the AP poll? How do you think it makes Lloyd Carr feel to concede that writers might know more than his coaching brethren?

And how did Nebraska coach Tom Osborne, his soul forever consigned to football hell by peers for consistently running up scores through his 25 years, suddenly become the coaches' darling over Carr, who directed college football's winningest all-time program to its first unbeaten season in a half-century?

The snub of the Wolverines in the coaches poll takes the bloom off the Rose Bowl victory and some luster off a special season. The coaches poll has historically meant more to the victorious coach because it's an affirmation from fraternity brothers.

It has left the Wolverines wondering, "What exactly did we do wrong?"

The Wolverines paid the price for the rapid deterioration of the Big Ten's image over a 24-hour period. The conference suffered a New Year's Day hangover that no headache tablet could cure. And nobody felt the pain more than Michigan.

The statistic that ultimately defined the Wolverines' season was 0-6.

That was the record of the six bowl-worthy opponents — five from the Big Ten — that Michigan played during the regular season. Those teams lost their bowls by a combined score of 180-65. Not one of those games entered the fourth quarter with the outcome in doubt.

Viewers were frequently reminded of the Big Ten's collapse leading to Michigan's Rose Bowl meeting with Washington State. And you could sense the national skepticism percolating, especially with the Wolverines' penchant for spontaneous combustion in bowls.

The Big Ten's failure placed the Wolverines in a position where they had to steamroll the Pac-10's Cougars. But Michigan was always more about substance during the season. And the Wolverines again displayed the same boring but successful efficiency that got them into this position.

The five-point victory didn't adequately reflect the Wolverines' domination in the second half, when they kept Washington State quarterback Ryan Leaf on the sideline. But coming on the heels of New Year's embarrassments by Wisconsin, Penn State and Ohio State, all it did was cast greater doubt over the Big Ten's competitiveness.

When Leaf casually marched through Michigan's vaunted defense for a 99-yard touchdown drive, the excellent defensive numbers the Wolverines produced against Big Ten quarterbacks such as Todd Schultz, Mike McQueary, Matt Sherman and Stanley Jackson lost some luster.

Suddenly, a schedule that appeared the toughest in the land in September looked as if it could have barely stimulated a sweat gland in January. The self-described climb up Mt. Everest seemed more like a stroll through a rolling countryside.

Michigan's schedule didn't help in the computer rankings. The Wolverines finished third in the New York Times poll, which puts a heavy emphasis on degree of schedule difficulty. Nebraska and Florida State were 1-2.

"Michigan's argument is that it played the toughest opponents at the time," outspoken Nebraska quarterback Scott Frost said. "But what if time proves that the opponent clearly wasn't as good as their ranking then?

"We beat a No. 2 (Washington) on the road early. They beat a No. 2 (Penn State) on the road later. Which of those two teams do you think today is the far better team? I think most would agree that it's Washington. So what does that say about us?"

You can't blame Michigan for its opponents' incompetence, just as you can't blame the Cornhuskers because officials earlier in the season blew a call in the Missouri end zone that led to a Nebraska victory. The only thing both teams could do was keep winning — and both did.

But the fact that Michigan lost 25 percent of its Associated Press support and about 40 percent of its first-place backing in the coaches poll meant that even perfection can be debated and diminished when you don't have a real national championship forum.

And this is another area where you can point the finger at the Big Ten.

The Rose Bowl's arrogance in 1995 opened the door for politics and perception to play a role in determining the national champion, as they did this season.

The bowl, abetted by its Big Ten and Pac-10 accomplices, had an opportunity to join the Bowl Alliance and create a format that, though far from perfect, would have brought Michigan and Nebraska together at the Orange Bowl.

Many coaches privately condemned the Big Ten and Pac-10 for thumbing their noses at the alliance. And don't think for a second that there weren't a few voters who saw the final poll as the perfect opportunity to make the Big Ten pay for contributing to the postseason quagmire.

After all, why reward Michigan and its conference when it wanted nothing to do with creating the only objective method of determining a champion?

The startling ESPN/USA Today poll exodus wasn't the result of sympathetic coaches giving one of their own a nice retirement gift. Osborne had very few friends within the coaching circle. Voters decided the Huskers were the more deserving team. And without a championship game, who's to say they weren't?

There are hundreds of personal memories surrounding the Wolverines' run to the co-national championship, coming in the form of letters, voice mail, phone conversations, angry stares at restaurants, public challenges to my sanity, threats of finding an anatomically challenging home for my columns, etc.

But the fact is the Southeastern Conference and Pac-10 played at a higher level of competition, and the bowls exposed the Big Ten for the generally slow-footed, weak-armed, offensively challenged fraud that it was.

And as the Big Ten lost respect, Michigan lost its invincibility.

Maybe now you'll understand that Big Ten football isn't as great as its television ratings and top 25 rankings make you believe. After all, we writers obviously know more about football than those coaches.

Right, Lloyd?

HOOPLA, TAKE ONE: FEB. 20, 1998

Players' indiscretions reflect on Izzo

The real victim in Mateen Cleaves' arrest and brief stint behind bars had been sound asleep at 4:45 a.m., when East Lansing police stopped Andre Hutson's 1982 Oldsmobile. Officers discovered an open can of beer, which precipitated a chain of events that skewered the spirits of Michigan State basketball just as it was on the brink of a Big Ten championship.

And nobody felt the repercussions more than coach Tom Izzo. His delightful dream of where his team had been and where it was headed was shattered when he received an early-morning telephone call. At that point, Izzo became a modern-day college basketball coach, an occupation in which off-court headaches are far greater than on-court concerns.

Izzo now must determine what disciplinary action he will take against Cleaves and Hutson for their alleged alcohol-related transgressions.

And the answer will come in the mirror.

Those who have talked to him have never known Izzo to anguish more over a decision. But they also know he will do what's appropriate because he couldn't look himself in the mirror if he did anything less.

Izzo really has no choice. Even if it means jeopardizing the Spartans' chances of winning the Big Ten regular-season championship, Cleaves and Hutson should miss Saturday's game at Wisconsin.

Izzo not only has to send a message to Cleaves and Hutson. He needs to send a message to the rest of his team, the university administration, potential recruits and skeptical onlookers who understand all too well the double standard of inflicting punishment in today's athletically obsessed climate.

Too often, athletes get a slap on the wrist. This is a case in which Izzo should deliver a club to the head.

A victory at Wisconsin would assure the Spartans a share of the Big Ten regular-season title, a distinction nobody — including Izzo — thought his young team could achieve when the season started.

You may not think it fair to penalize an entire team — and possibly to sacrifice a cherished goal — over a civil infraction, but if Izzo plays Cleaves and Hutson and the Spartans win at Madison, you'll need a dam to contain the surging tide of charges that Izzo is guilty of hypocrisy.

The underlying factor in this case is underage drinking, something most college students have done at some point. But it's a problem that has gained increased public awareness because of recent deaths at other campuses stemming from binge drinking.

Michigan State president Peter McPherson made curtailing underage drinking one of his primary objectives during his recent State of the University address.

There isn't a better opportunity to send a stronger statement — even if the punishment doesn't necessarily fit the crime.

Coaches don't have textbook guidelines when their players misbehave. Each case is different. Most often, the reaction depends on the person passing judgment.

Former Michigan State All-America Scott Skiles was convicted once of marijuana possession and twice for drunken driving, yet the only game he missed during that time was an exhibition in 1985. Some contend that coach Jud Heathcote acted as he did to spite a voracious media, hungry to chew up and spit out his best player. Nobody was going to tell Heathcote how to run his team.

Others contend Heathcote just wanted to win, and he wasn't going to slit his own throat to pacify potential critics.

But Izzo isn't six years removed from a national championship, as Heathcote was. Nor is he yet an established member of the coaching fraternity. He joked a week ago that only now is he getting comfortable enough to offer an opinion at the annual coaches meetings.

His reputation remains in its formative stages, when perception can mold an image as much as reality. The worst thing that can happen to Izzo is to provide ammunition that his tough disciplinarian talk is nothing more than rhetoric.

He will do the right thing. The only judge Izzo answers to is the reflection he sees in that mirror every morning. And that always has been his harshest critic.

Three days later, under the headline "Spartans rally to beat Wisconsin, clinch share of Big Ten title," the Free Press reported the following:

Mateen Cleaves went to Michigan State with dreams of winning a Big Ten championship. But when the 14th-ranked Spartans took the floor Saturday with a chance to clinch at least a share of the conference title, Cleaves found himself on the bench.

The sophomore guard and freshman forward Andre Hutson sat out the first half as part of their punishment for alcohol-related arrests Wednesday at East Lansing. In their absence, the Spartans sputtered, falling behind Wisconsin by as many as 11 points in the first half. But Cleaves scored 14 points to lead the Spartans to a 56-47 victory.

HOOPLA, TAKE TWO: MARCH 30, 1998

Tournament brings out the best and worst

SAN ANTONIO — Try as he could to push such thoughts into the deep recesses of his mind, Tubby Smith knew the possibility existed when he accepted Kentucky athletic director C. M. Newton's offer to replace Rick Pitino and become only the fifth Wildcats basketball coach since 1930.

And their first African-American coach.

There would be those who — fervently loyal to the segregationist ideals of the revered Adolph Rupp — would refuse to accept a black coach as caretaker of the Baron's legacy.

"But you know what he told us when we asked him about that?" said his son, freshman point guard Saul Smith. " 'So what?'

"He's always believed, and he's taught us that you can't allow your life to be dictated by what others say or do. I think he may have always dreamed of Kentucky as his dream job, and you can't allow any possible concerns to stand in the way of that dream."

How ironic it would be if Smith could mold a collection of role players into the seventh national championship team from Kentucky — an institution he couldn't even have played for before the 1970s.

"I'm not even thinking about it along those terms," Smith said. "We all know of the history of Kentucky basketball and Adolph Rupp, but it's just that —history. I haven't had one racial comment, not one racial slant to any letter that I've received. The criticism that I've received just comes with the territory of being Kentucky head coach."

But Smith also knows that such discussions are unavoidable.

Try as you might not to look at situations through racially tinted filters, it was inescapable here as the NCAA prepared to crown its national basketball champion. This Final Four has in some ways become a microcosm of the national sentiment of race and athletics.

We don't want race to be an issue, but it's easy to imagine Rupp spinning in his grave at the prospect of Smith winning a national championship in his first year.

We don't want race to be an issue, but the fact that Utah starts four white players was a natural story angle for many national writers because of its historical significance. Don't think for a second that there aren't those — tired of the perception that basketball has turned too urban for its own good — who would love to see Utah win for no other reason than its complexion.

We don't want race to be an issue, but it often is.

Utah needed to call a news conference so freshman forward Britton Johnsen could respond to Makhtar Ndaiye's postgame accusations that Johnsen peppered him with racial epithets, so, in turn, North Carolina's Ndaiye showered Johnsen with a little expectorant.

Ndaiye's charges, which Johnsen vehemently denied, so outraged Utah coach Rick Majerus that he said he would submit his resignation if it were ever proven that Johnsen so coarsely offended Ndaiye.

"It's unfair, and it's unfortunate that this has got to come up and possibly take away from what we've accomplished," said point guard Andre Miller, the Utes' only black starter. "I think Makhtar was just getting frustrated because things weren't going well for him because he stayed in foul trouble. For him to take it out on Britton that way was wrong."

Miller believes basketball, like life, should be color-blind. But we all know it isn't.

HOOPLA, TAKE THREE: SEPT. 11, 2000

Bob Knight, a fine teacher, didn't learn from his mistakes

The outcome was inevitable. Bob Knight was doomed to fail in the new atmosphere of zero tolerance at Indiana University because he was, well, Bob Knight. He was his own worst enemy during an impressive coaching career marked as much by his transgressions as by his accomplishments.

Knight was the only person capable of throwing his coaching career a life preserver. Instead, he tossed himself an anchor.

The once unthinkable is now reality. Knight is gone, fired. The school at which he had become an icon did to him what Knight once did to a fan: It tossed him and his 763 career victories, 11 Big Ten championships and three national titles into a trash can.

Indiana finally grew tired of all the garbage, belligerence and nastiness.

If there was any surprise to the news, it was the timing. Most thought Knight would at least get into the season before detonating that quick temper one last embarrassing time.

But Knight couldn't last 17 weeks after the university, which had previously looked the other way regarding his often boorish behavior, imposed what it promoted as a stringent code of conduct. Just one more false step, university officials warned Knight, and his days in Bloomington were done.

After about another half-dozen false steps, the university finally had no choice but to sever its ties with the man.

Pride has its limits, and Knight crossed that line numerous times after the school's high-profile public warning May 15.

Knight wasn't going to play the university's game. It was his way or the highway. And university president Myles Brand gave him the road map during a telephone conversation.

"We gave Coach Knight every opportunity to maintain his position as the head basketball coach at Indiana University," said Brand, "but he decided against taking full advantage of that opportunity. Instead, he continued a pattern of unacceptable behavior that we believed violated the language and the spirit of the code of conduct."

The president branded Knight as "hostile and defiant," citing numerous examples of Knight's repeated unwillingness to work within the framework of the athletic department's chain of command.

It wasn't even the most recent incident — his alleged grabbing of 19-year-old Kent Harvey — that triggered his coaching demise. It was his reaction. The slightest hint of contrition might have spared the 59-year-old coach.

When Brand asked Knight to delay a Canadian fishing trip until this issue could be resolved, the two reportedly engaged in a heated exchange in which Knight, in essence, told Brand what he could do with his investigation.

"He did not fulfill the promises he gave me," Brand said.

But the university remains as much at fault for the climax of this tragicomedy as Knight does. That's why it was such a joke to hear Brand espousing the conceit of the day — that the interests of a single individual can never supersede the interests of the community at large.

The university was 10 years too late implementing a code of conduct. Where was this impetus to put Knight on a leash when he was embarrassing the university while still winning Big Ten championships?

Indiana created the 800-pound gorilla that was Robert Montgomery Knight.

"The actions we've taken this year should not be interpreted as an indictment of the past," said Brand, "but rather an indication of what's to be expected in the present and in the future in regards to those who coach at Indiana University."

But despite his many flaws, Knight was often a solitary sane voice amid the undisciplined wilderness that college basketball has become. And his departure means the game has lost part of its moral compass. Disagree with his occasional antics, but let there be no dispute that Knight always sought the higher ground in terms of graduating his players. That made him an anomaly in college athletics.

It's hard to feel sorry for the man because the wounds that finally ended his career were self-inflicted. But neither is this a time for gloating that a man seemingly hell-bent on self-destruction proved unwilling, or perhaps unable, to save himself.

On Feb. 10, 2001, Drew Sharp wrote again about Bob Knight, who had recently been interviewed in Playboy magazine. Here's what he concluded about Knight, who would be named head coach at Texas Tech later that year:

Knight remains an enigma, someone you loathe one minute and laud the next. The Playboy Q&A, conducted by writer Lawrence Grobel, ably delves into complexities. It peels away the crude layers, revealing Knight's insight and passion for college athletics.

There were the customary volcanic eruptions, like trying to seize and destroy Grobel's tape recorder and threatening to throw him out of a car while heading down the interstate. But there was also the boldness that is sorely lacking in college basketball today, like Knight's suggestion for academic reform: Every player who doesn't graduate within five years would cost his team a scholarship.

Despite the justifiably adversarial relationship between Knight and the media through his Indiana career, this is one writer who dearly wants to see him return to a school with the ability to win national championships.

There's a head-coaching seat awaiting Knight, but it's probably at a smaller school where expectations and interest are equally low. It may not encompass bright lights and big money, but it will provide a flawed yet principled man a final opportunity to do what he does best — teach and mold young men.

HOOPLA, TAKE FOUR: MARCH 9, 2001

Protecting coach's job wrong battle for NAACP

CHICAGO — Fairness has little in common with the coaching profession. In this business, opportunity is measured with a sliding scale. Time was once its friend, until the influence of big money suddenly placed a premium on expediency.

The Detroit chapter of the NAACP apparently doesn't comprehend this changing dynamic of college basketball. If so, it wouldn't fight the right battle carrying the wrong banner.

The Rev. Wendell Anthony, president of the chapter, has aired grievances about Brian Ellerbe's tenuous position as Michigan coach in a letter to university president Lee Bollinger. The NAACP raised legitimate concerns about a perception of discrimination at the school, but branding Ellerbe as a martyr is without merit.

Ellerbe's job is in jeopardy because he can't effectively run a major-college basketball team. He likely will be fired in the wake of Michigan's gut-wrenching exit from the Big Ten tournament because his own actions have contributed to the erosion of a once-proud program.

Anthony's complaint shouldn't be that Michigan hasn't given Ellerbe a fair chance, but rather why the administration didn't commit the financial backing three years ago to bring in a black coach capable of succeeding, despite limitations imposed by U-M itself.

"I think the University of Michigan has been fair," Ellerbe said. "When we earned this opportunity four years ago, I was given a six-year contract because it was understood that it would require time, particularly considering our special circumstances. We weren't interested in quick fixes. And I think the guys we were able to bring in here despite the cloud overhead has been amazing."

But Ellerbe has had sufficient time to lessen the cloud, and the team's blight was only deepened when some of his recruits didn't stay. Three years is enough time to offer a blueprint of a coach's vision. Instead, the Wolverines resemble a team in need of a road map, looking rudderless and lacking direction.

A lack of fundamentals, one of the strongest indictments against Ellerbe's coaching, ended the Wolverines' season. A failure to box out underneath the basket enabled the Nittany Lions' Gyasi Cline-Heard to grab an offensive rebound and put back the winning basket with less than a second remaining.

Forgotten is that the Wolverines fought back from a nine-point deficit. What's remembered are the inopportune lapses at inopportune times, making this potentially lethal final chapter no less forgiving than the other blown opportunities that signify the Ellerbe era.

U-M athletic director Bill Martin remained noncommittal about Ellerbe's future, and he appeared downright defensive when approached about the NAACP letter. He said he knew nothing of the correspondence, admitting that he had never heard of Anthony. But some of those who work for Martin attest to his commitment to heightening minority involvement in the athletic department.

"These are very serious charges, and I'm not going to comment on them until I see the letter," Martin said. "I'm not going to comment on something that I'm getting second-hand."

The NAACP addressed the departure of some highly prominent African Americans in the athletic department in the past year as a cause for concern. But whereas Martin's predecessor, Tom Goss, resigned under pressure from Bollinger, the others apparently left on their own volition for better opportunities.

Alluding to discrimination always is risky for someone who's trying to heighten awareness of injustices. Repeated frivolous fights lessen the public impact when the shouts aren't justified. It's quite possible that in a moment of overzealousness, the NAACP lost sight of this objective when rushing to Ellerbe's defense.

The never-ending fight for fairness and improved opportunities is valid, but Ellerbe's predicament isn't necessarily the proper example in this case.

HOOPLA, TAKE FIVE: FEB. 28, 2002

Arkansas coach blazed trail, then lost his way

We don't live in a color-blind world, and we never will. The concept is illogical. Our cultural and racial differences are in plain view, but that doesn't mean we can't gain a better understanding of each other.

Some people continue to view the complexities of life through a narrow prism, and that's unavoidable. Nolan Richardson understands that better than most.

Richardson, the Arkansas basketball coach, was one of his profession's trailblazers. He helped pave the path for today's generation of black college coaches, including Tommy Amaker and Stan Heath. Richardson didn't have the luxury of quietly turning the knob and walking through the door as Amaker did at Michigan and former Michigan State assistant Heath did at Kent State. Richardson had to kick the door open, knowing full well that there were many on the other side trying to keep it shut.

Richardson became the first prominent black head coach in the Southeastern Conference when Arkansas merged into the league in 1992. Yet for all the strides made, the SEC is still waiting for its first black football coach, which might take a lot longer for the Old South to accept.

That sort of attitude was the origin of Richardson's recent outburst to reporters. His allegations weren't even thinly veiled. He said the team's fans and the all-white media that regularly cover Arkansas basketball were unfairly out to get him because he's enduring what could be his second losing season in 17 years with the Razorbacks.

There can be only one reason, right? Everyone's jumping on the brother!

A proud man, a principled man, Richardson is nonetheless a misguided one. He condemned the media and Arkansas fans with a blanket indictment without realizing that he's more likely a victim of his own standard of excellence.

"I know for a fact that I do not play on the same level as the other coaches around this school play on," Richardson barked. "I know that. You know that. And people of my color know that. And that angers me."

The university wisely won't discipline Richardson for his statements. He shouldn't be treated like a child for speaking his mind. But that shouldn't prevent Richardson from publicly apologizing for equating his perceived mistreatment with slavery.

"My great-great-grandfather came over on the ship, I didn't," Richardson said. "I didn't come over on that ship, so I expect to be treated a little bit different."

It's more than a little unsettling to listen to a millionaire liken his difficulties to those of people once shackled. Richardson helped change the archaic perceptions about the ability of black coaches. But wasn't the battle for equal opportunity based on giving everyone the chance to rise or fall based on his or her own competence?

Richardson, who won the national championship at Arkansas in 1994, has set a high standard, so it's rather disingenuous for him to complain about criticism of an atypical mediocre season. Maybe Richardson has spoiled everyone in Arkansas, taking the Hogs to three Final Four berths in 12 years and 13 NCAA tournament appearances in 14 years.

"Being black and being in a place where they expect you to win every game, I probably understand his frustration better than most," Kentucky coach Tubby Smith said. "If you don't win every game, there has to be a reason. You have to have a reason."

But unfortunately, when Richardson gave his reasons, it exposed his thin skin. And that contradicts the sturdiness of heart and commitment necessary to be considered among the elite coaches in college basketball.

Richardson left Arkansas at the end of the season. Heath replaced Richardson the following season.

MICHIGAN STATE, TAKE ONE: DEC. 1, 1999

Saban: Good-bye, Green... hello, green

The ever-blurred priorities of high-stakes college athletics came into sharper focus as Nick Saban departed the Duffy Daugherty Football Building.

Walking a few paces ahead of a pack of photographers, cameramen and reporters, Saban hopped into his Cadillac sport-utility vehicle and, before he had backed out of his reserved parking space, was on his cell phone taking care of business. Saban was heading to the airport and multimillion-dollar opportunities in Louisiana.

No tears. No waving good-bye. No looking back.

Business today is often devoid of emotion, even when it involves an occupation that many naively think is bound by loyalty.

College athletics is motivated by self-interest, whether it's a football coach or 19-year-old sophomore basketball player who abruptly bolts for riches in the NBA.

The Saban episode is another chapter.

"The opportunity at LSU was one I had to seriously consider as far as my family and professional future were concerned," Saban said minutes after telling assistants of his decision. "This was a very difficult and tough decision because of the time and energy I've invested here to develop this program from a football, people and academic standpoint. It's very hard to leave."

A final decision didn't come until 5 a.m. and, according to those around Saban and his wife, Terry, Saban weighed the pros and cons all night.

Taking into consideration the thin skin of Michigan State supporters, Saban worried about the reaction to a sudden departure. Some suggested he didn't owe anyone an explanation and advised him to leave for Baton Rouge under a cloak of darkness.

He vetoed that idea, but the discussion underscored Saban's opinion that he was unappreciated at Michigan State. If so, he has only himself to blame. He couldn't handle the mildest questions skeptical of his expertise.

Saban succeeded in creating something from next-to-nothing at MSU, which makes Louisiana State attractive. But his occasionally brusque manner prevented the MSU community from fully embracing him and his ambitions.

Like any other personal business decision, this was ego-driven.

Who doesn't want to feel wanted? Who could turn down becoming the third-highest-paid coach in college football?

Those who criticize Saban's submission to LSU's big dollars and question his allegiance to Michigan State expose themselves to hypocrisy. They were probably the same ones out for his scalp earlier in the year, when the formerly fifth-ranked Spartans were coming off two straight losses.

"I'm really sad that Nick's not going to be here," basketball coach Tom Izzo said. "But you know what? I understand where he's coming from. Getting criticism is part of the job, but that doesn't mean it doesn't hurt to hear or read others questioning your ability, especially when you know it's not deserved."

So why not take the money and run?

"There's a lot of money involved in college sports now," said freshman running back T. J. Duckett, Saban's top recruit last winter. "And I don't think many people are naive enough to think that when you sign with a school, the coach is obligated to stay there for four years. Players leave early. Coaches leave, too."

And you move on.

There's little sadness in East Lansing because Saban didn't leave the rubble he inherited when he drove up five years ago. His legacy is a burgeoning program, but his departure also reflects the skewed landscape of sports today.

Just follow the dollar and leave your loyalties behind.

MICHIGAN STATE, TAKE TWO: DEC. 6, 1999

Stand by your man: MSU hires Bobby Williams

EAST LANSING — Normally fragmented, Michigan State University stood together as one — one team, one university, one family.

Bobby Williams' introduction as the Spartans' 21st football coach was as much a spiritual awakening as a historical benchmark. A university whose athletic judgments are often burdened by insecurity discovered the virtues of looking within.

And Michigan State may never feel better about itself than it did during a news conference that turned into a 30-minute emotional cleansing that left few green-and-white eyes dry.

This day was about gratitude. Williams thanked his players and assistant coaches for fighting for him. He thanked the administration for having the courage to give him the opportunity to "carry the banner" as the first African-American head football coach at a public Big Ten institution. (When Williams was hired, there were only four other black head coaches at major colleges.)

But Williams was most thankful that Michigan State went with a Michigan State man. After all, isn't that what solid programs do?

"What we have at this university is special," said Williams, MSU's running backs coach for 10 seasons. "And you understand that and appreciate that when you've been here 10 years like I have. I've been blessed with everything that's happened to me in the last week."

Williams, 41, brought up his assistants to stand with him. Nick Saban — the departing coach — had offered seats on his flight to Baton Rouge, La., for any assistant who wanted to come. But Saban left alone.

The 10 assistants got the head coach they wanted.

Williams' wife, Sheila, gave each coach a heartfelt hug. Ever the stoic, emotionless businessman, MSU president Peter McPherson wiped an eye. Men whose jobs are to teach the infliction of physical punishment surrendered to the emotional sincerity of the moment. There was no feeling sorry for themselves, no lamenting life in another guy's shadow. Rarely has MSU stood together so tall and so single-minded.

"I've never been through anything like that in my 39 years of coaching," said offensive coordinator Morris Watts, who played an integral part in selling McPherson on the merits of hiring Williams. "And it's all coming from the heart. There's nothing scripted about this. We've come to understand the true meaning of the word 'team.' "

It was Watts who united the assistants behind Williams just hours after Saban left for Louisiana State. It was Watts who orchestrated the assistants' meeting with McPherson at the president's office. But perhaps more important, it was Watts whose opinion McPherson trusted most in the hours leading up to the decision.

McPherson considers himself a pretty sharp political operative, but he underestimated the assistants' resolve. He figured that Saban's abrupt departure would trigger the in-fighting that too often has been synonymous with Michigan State athletics. Williams, Watts and offensive line coach Pat Ruel each would stake a claim to the head coaching job, dividing the staff and ensuring that some assistants would leave with Saban for the bayou. That would open the door for McPherson to recruit the "name" coach he initially wanted.

But Watts called McPherson and told the president he was confident that most, if not all, the assistants would remain at MSU.

Keeping the assistants would negate McPherson's concerns about Williams' ability to assemble a quality staff quickly.

"I was prepared to say no to Nick even if I didn't have a job," Ruel said. "It was always easy for me to bet on myself. But I'm betting on that man up there that he's going to take this program even further than where we got with Nick. There's something about this that just feels right, and we all knew that pretty early."

The assistants were quick to say their decision to remain was more a credit to Michigan State than a dig at Saban. But conciliatory words aside, Saban's departure for Louisiana empty-handed was a backhanded slap.

Saban had been the right man at the right time for the program, instilling much-needed toughness and discipline after the George Perles years. But Saban went through assistants like disposable diapers. Some former assistants privately complained that Saban was a thankless taskmaster who didn't fully appreciate their efforts.

Now Williams has become the right man at the right time. He understands he's nothing without his team, whether it's the 50 or so players who wildly cheered him at the Clara Bell Smith Center or the nine men who stood behind him on the podium.

"These guys rallied behind me," Williams said, stopping short as tears welled. "They rallied behind me because there was a plane leaving this morning. They had to make a choice. And every one of them stayed. That should tell everyone exactly what we have here."

What they have is a university that's breeding a culture of athletic success and is finally understanding that looking within may provide the rosiest peek at the future.

Williams was fired during his third season, having compiled a 16-17 record.

MICHIGAN STATE, TAKE THREE: NOV. 4, 2002

Coach must take blame when players let down teammates

Rumor and innuendo have been replaced with cold, cruel reality. Michigan State football has hit rock bottom.

Its former quarterback's parents have acknowledged that he's seeking treatment for substance abuse. Its starting tailback has been kicked off the team after he resisted arrest while allegedly driving under the influence of alcohol.

And tomorrow is another day, which probably scares Michigan State more than anything else because it doesn't know where the next ticking time bomb sits, waiting for detonation.

A football coach can't watch his players 24/7. All he can do is create an environment in which they understand that there are rules and there are consequences when those rules are breached. All he can do is impress upon them the importance of team and how their individual actions carry collective ramifications.

And this is where Bobby Williams has failed.

And this is where he's accountable and why he should lose his job.

Team leaders are supposed to set the standard for the entire team. It's their footsteps that the younger players follow. But Williams' "leaders" are the biggest reasons that a once-promising season has collapsed into the abyss.

You never want to see a young, vibrant soul demonized through substance abuse, and you pray for Jeff Smoker's recovery. It's sad. It's unfortunate. But it's also the height of selfishness that someone who seemingly had the life most 21-year-olds would envy could so recklessly throw it away.

Smoker was a co-captain, as was tailback Dawan Moss.

Moss earned the respect of his coaches and teammates for losing 30 pounds in the off-season so he could switch from fullback to tailback. He struggled with the transition but was considered a positive influence in the locker room.

But then Lansing police pulled him over and smelled alcohol on his breath. He tried to get away and drove into another police car.

And to a lesser extent, Charles Rogers questioned his team's commitment and heart following a 46-point loss to Michigan, doubting the Spartans could win another game. But where was Rogers' commitment when he went to his coaches earlier this season and asked not to be used on special teams because of the risk of injury that could jeopardize his NFL draft value.

This is leadership? This is team-first?

Williams can't know what his players are doing when they leave the Duffy Daugherty Football Building, but he's nonetheless accountable for facilitating a climate of self-centered egotism. What are these guys thinking? Don't they know that college players don't live in a vacuum these days? Don't they realize that they have a responsibility to the university they represent?

According to the Smoker family's statement, Smoker battled his torment in private. But the parents expressed their gratitude to Williams and his staff for quickly getting Smoker help when he finally approached Williams about his problem.

"Substance abuse, a serious issue in our society, must be met head-on by those of us in leadership roles," athletic director Ron Mason said. "Jeff's situation, we hope, is an isolated one — both in its nature and degree."

The family's statement implies that Williams and his staff apparently had no prior knowledge of Smoker's problem, despite the fact that he had struggled all season. But it's difficult to imagine that nobody connected to the team had the slightest inkling that one of their own was suffering.

Then again, considering the self-absorption that's engulfed the program, we shouldn't be surprised that someone missed the signs.

And that might be the most telling sign that a coaching change is inevitable.

MICHIGAN STATE, TAKE FOUR: NOV. 15, 2002

QB sacked by substance abuse — who's next?

EAST LANSING — Temptation isn't limited to the convenient stereotypes. Its victims aren't always the socially or financially neglected. Sometimes, temptation finds weakness in the freckle-faced, athletically blessed boy next door who seemingly has it all, only to discover even that isn't enough.

Jeff Smoker, who was suspended from Michigan State's football team for unspecified reasons in October, confessed to his temptation — cleansing his soul but not erasing his sins — at a news conference. He was vague about specific substances he abused and occasionally contradicted himself when he attempted to answer the one overriding question:

Why?

"I ask myself that same thing," he said.

If Smoker knew the answer, he might not be a recovering abuser.

The reasons for how a life recklessly spiraled out of control are irrelevant. Smoker's selfishness reduced the MSU football program to titillating Internet innuendo, ripped apart a potential championship contender and ultimately cost coach Bobby Williams his job.

That chapter is closed, and the first page of the rest of Smoker's life has begun with what everyone hopes will be the first of endless clean and sober days. He has a tough haul ahead of him, a challenge that will require far more fortitude than staring down a 250-pound blitzing linebacker.

Smoker deserves our support, but not our sympathy. He's not a victim. He made a conscious choice to place his body and career in peril, and he must face the consequences. It's called accountability. Pitying Smoker is an insult to those teammates who adhered to team rules and busted their humps all summer with the hope of contending for the Big Ten championship, confident that Smoker could lead them there.

Smoker can't apologize enough to them.

"What I did not only affected myself but others, as well," he said. "I do realize that I'm a public figure, and I need to carry myself in a certain manner. But I feel comfortable where I'm at now in my life and where I'm headed."

Smoker sounded as much like a quarterback trying to save a football career as he did a troubled young man trying to save his life.

And that was the most distressing aspect of this public cleansing.

Maybe Smoker doesn't want to hear this, but it doesn't matter if he ever takes another snap from center or ever hears the roar of inspiration from 70,000 fans. His main priority is to control the temptations that brought him to this unfortunate moment. That's the only victory that will matter for the rest of his life.

But Smoker wants to play football again, and if that's the goal that keeps him focused, that's fine. Smoker, a junior, wants to make amends for letting down his teammates and contributing to his coach's dismissal, but he also wants personal redemption. It would be counterproductive, though, for him to judge his attempts at winning over a new coach and getting his starting job back next season in terms of success and failure.

Success for him is each clean and sober breath he takes.

"I'm a football player," he said. "It's what I love to do, and I'll do whatever is asked of me to have the privilege of playing Michigan State football once again. I was very privileged to play for the Michigan State Spartans. It's not a right. I may have taken advantage of that. But I very much plan on returning."

Rumors about Smoker's problems had floated around for weeks, but he insisted there was no basis for many of them. He said he wasn't involved in any federal or local criminal investigations about drug trafficking or gambling. And he said he never flunked a university-administered drug test.

"I wish that I could do whatever is necessary to take away what I've done to myself and how I've hurt others," he said, "but that's not possible. I realize that. This has been a turning point in my life. All I can do now with my life is move forward and hold my head high."

But that life is now one of short 24-hour steps. One hopes the 21-year-old has matured more in the past 21 days than at any other point in his life. The strongest lessons usually inflict the most pain, and clearly this young man is hurting. Indulgences come at a price, but fortunately Smoker sought help before he paid the ultimate price.

Smoker hopes to serve as an example to others who risk bowing to similar demons. He has become the latest symbol of a pox that isn't going away. Smoker already has put a more realistic face on a substance-abuse problem that permeates every segment of our nation.

Nobody is immune. Nobody is insulated.

JAN. 2, 2002

Notre Dame hides its red face behind black coach

The symbolism, possessing all the subtlety of a champagne hangover, wasn't lost on anyone. The new year, with its fresh hope and opportunity, has been christened with the hiring of a black football coach at Notre Dame, the most storied program in the college game.

Tyrone Willingham was quietly happy at Stanford. He never had to win big, only enough to appease the deep-pocketed donors. A lavish university endowment already made him a millionaire. A reluctant trailblazer, Willingham was nonetheless presented an opportunity he couldn't refuse. The former Michigan State running back will follow the footsteps of Rockne, Leahy and Parseghian.

Notre Dame is hoping that a black man can conceal its red face.

The embarrassment surrounding the hiring of George O'Leary and his subsequent resignation gave athletic director Kevin White no option but to make a dynamic statement with the next hire. Naming Willingham certainly wakes up the echoes, but one wonders if it were done as much to quell criticism of the university administration as to hire a coach with a resume nobody could impeach.

Notre Dame's president, the Rev. Edward Malloy, sounded like someone looking for pats on the back, thinking that Willingham's hiring brought absolution for his athletic administration's bungling. But why wasn't Willingham approached initially?

He was mentioned on numerous short lists, and Stanford reportedly granted Notre Dame permission to interview Willingham. But the Irish never did.

Strange, isn't it? Here was a man who satisfied every criterion that Notre Dame wanted in a coach. He won on the field — a Pac-10 championship and four bowl appearances in seven years — and in the classroom — graduating nearly all of his players without the academic shortcuts prevalent in practically all other major programs. Yet he didn't even get a courtesy phone call.

All Notre Dame wanted then was window dressing. It was sweet justice to watch the school's hypocrisy blow up in its face when O'Leary's lies about his past became public. If Notre Dame were true to its ideals, O'Leary would have been removed from consideration with his appalling 33 percent graduation rate at Georgia Tech.

Instead, Notre Dame comes across as visionary, striking public relations gold, by hiring Willingham.

"This opens up doors for a lot of people," said Floyd Keith, executive director of the Black Coaches Association. "There are a lot of Tyrone Willinghams out there."

Let's hope Willingham's rise to the Golden Dome is a sign that a new year brings us closer to the end of lip service.

JUNE 21, 2000

L.A. can learn from Detroit's winning ways

LOS ANGELES — A hint of tear gas wafted through the late-evening air, along with fumes of burning debris. Helicopters whirred overhead as dozens of police cruisers sped down streets. Officers draped in riot gear marched into position, forming a human barricade and threatening retaliation if challenged.

If this scene were 10 miles north, you would think it was a Hollywood movie set and they were filming the sequel to "Escape from L.A."

Instead, this was outside the Staples Center, about three hours after the Los Angeles Lakers won the NBA championship. The Game 6 victory over the Indiana Pacers gave the Lakers their first title in 12 years, and it ignited a celebration that quickly turned into violence and destruction.

This sort of exhibition has become all too familiar around the country. A few liquored-up malcontents think winning a championship gives them license to loot and vandalize.

Unfortunately, many people still equate such behavior with Detroit.

I had to straighten out a couple of local writers who suggested that watching police cars burn must have made me homesick.

"Feel like you're back in D-town, don't you?" said former Piston and current Laker John Salley when he saw me. "It's not Devil's Night, is it?"

Try working on some fresh material, Sal-Sal.

Los Angeles has become the city identified with wanton lawlessness.

Detroit happily passed the baton.

Amazingly, we're still taking a hit for the photograph of Bubba Helms waving a championship banner in front of a burning vehicle outside Tiger Stadium the night the Tigers clinched the 1984 World Series.

I was working that night, reporting the story. Things got a little crazy, but I didn't fear for my safety as I did trying to get to my car while mob mentality ruled around the Staples Center.

Dozens of vehicles were burned or ravaged. A crowd converged around comic Jamie Foxx's limousine, rocking it back and forth. The driver got out of the limo and was attacked.

Foxx got the news via cell phone as he waited like everyone else for police to permit us to leave the arena once the situation outside cooled.

"I told him before the game that he probably shouldn't stick around because it could get wild afterwards," Foxx said of the driver. "Those fools put him in the hospital. Don't they realize that all they're doing is taking away from what the Lakers did?"

A few even jumped onto Shaquille O'Neal's sport-utility vehicle as he tried to leave. Just as he did to any Indiana Pacer who got in his way during the NBA Finals, he plowed right through.

"Let's keep last night's vandalism in perspective," Los Angeles Mayor Richard Riordan said. "This was the act of a few hundred hooligans, losers who were more interested in trashing the city. And unlike other cities that were celebrating winning athletic events and the destruction spread citywide, that wasn't the case around Los Angeles."

Police said they made 11 arrests. Two police cars were set afire, two television news vans were damaged or destroyed, and at least 74 vehicles were damaged at auto dealerships. Glass storefronts were broken, and police fired rubber bullets to disperse the crowd.

Damage was estimated in millions of dollars. Fortunately, the human toll was relatively minor — three were hospitalized with burns, bruises and other injuries. But that shouldn't diminish the outrage. Nor does it absolve the city and the Lakers from poor preparation and bad execution.

As I explained to those looking to use us as another punch line, Detroit has become the example of how to celebrate respectfully. We learned from our mistakes.

The dignified way we celebrated the Red Wings' Stanley Cup title in 1997 — their first in 42 years — exorcised our demons. Police steered revelers away from Joe Louis Arena and closed off downtown.

The Lakers erred in showing the game on a giant television screen outside the Staples Center. As many as 10,000 congregated, and they grew rowdier as the evening progressed. It was trouble waiting to happen. And fearing a repeat of the 1992 Rodney King riots, the police immediately backed off when some threw bottles at them.

"Our plan was one of restraint," police chief Bernard Parks said. "We felt that if we were too aggressive, the situation could have exploded into something far more serious."

Unlike its basketball team, the city dropped the ball. When a TV reporter asked a drunken reveler why anyone would want to cast a blight on the occasion, he said they wanted a warm-up now so they'll know how to really raise hell next year, should the Lakers win again.

If that was intended to be funny, the joke's on Los Angeles. Instead of Detroit, the City of Angels has become the punch line.

CHAPTER THREE

Two Lions walk into a bar ...

NOV. 7, 2000

Ford to blame for our lackluster Lions

It has become an all-too-familiar routine for William Clay Ford — another new coach, another assurance that this time the Lions have found the man capable of finding the right path for this hopelessly lost football team.

Gary Moeller became Ford's 11th "right man," assuming the job that Bobby Ross willingly surrendered because he no longer could motivate his team. And Ford is so sure of Moeller's ability that he opted against an extensive search following the season and gave the former University of Michigan coach a three-year contract.

Poor Mo. Doesn't he realize that a Ford vote of confidence is akin to a kiss of death?

The man is fortunate that a referendum on his ownership isn't on the ballot this Election Day.

"What do you want me to do? Fire myself?" said Ford, responding to my hammering at his accountability for his team's traditionally poor performance. "I'm not going to do it."

Then why should anyone think anything will change? The Lions need a fresh start similar to what Bill Ford Jr. proposed after the 1998 season: Bring in a well-connected football man like Matt Millen to run the operation and finally bring full accountability to the front office and scouting departments. But that requires an ownership philosophy grounded more in logic than loyalty.

And that requires the big man to broom himself out of office.

Ross threatened to quit if Millen usurped any of his authority, and Ford Sr. scuttled his son's plans out of allegiance to Ross. That drove Bill Jr. away from the team and silenced any further discussion of an immediate transition of power.

Ross didn't know it then, but he was doomed the day the elder Ford made that decision. History has shown that if Ford thinks it's the right move, it isn't.

"I'm not saying that they should or shouldn't have any trust in me," Ford said, responding to my question about why anyone in this city should think he's capable of selecting the right coach. "I don't really worry about what others think. I have to do what I feel is best for my team. And this is my team, and it's my decision."

That thought underscores why few fans have faith in Ford. It's not that he isn't a decent, likable man. Nor is it that he doesn't want to win. But it's a question of his competence to hire football coaches and management. At some point, you'd think, something would register upstairs. If he hasn't found the championship formula in nearly 40 years, then perhaps it's time to pass the baton to someone who might.

But Ford either doesn't get it or doesn't care. And if it's the latter, then the fans who blindly support this team through rise and ruin have only themselves to blame for more than a generation of mediocrity.

"Have we been successful during my years?" Ford said. "Well, if you judge it on Super Bowls, we haven't been to one. And we've only won one playoff game during that time. Looking at it from that point of view, no, you can't say that we've been successful."

Then where is Ford's epiphany? Where is his pause for introspection? If another meaningless turn of the coaching carousel isn't deserving of self-evaluation of his ownership, then what is?

Two vital components of his team raised their hands in surrender and abruptly left in a 16-month span — Ross and Barry Sanders. Some of Ford's players publicly adore him in a kind, grandfatherly way, but privately they wish he would step aside for a more contemporary approach.

"No, I don't see the need for self-reflection," he said.

Ross left the Lions' offices for the last time just minutes before Ford, Moeller and chief operating officer Chuck Schmidt approached the podium to announce the switch. Team security chief Jocko Hughes escorted Ross to his car. When approached by reporters, Ross declined to comment on his decision.

But in a statement, he thanked Ford for the opportunity and apologized "for not giving you the championship trophy you so richly deserved. Your strong support was my constant motivation throughout my time here."

Ford twice tried to talk Ross out of quitting, to no avail. Although Ross never blamed health reasons for his decision, Ford wondered if Ross had physically and emotionally worn down from the 16-hour days in the office and the pressures from Ross' own high expectations.

But Ross lost control of his team. Players feared making mistakes and drawing Ross' wrath. The hope was that Moeller could create a more relaxed climate, resulting in improved performance. And if he does, everyone will step on that all-too-familiar land mine, gullibly thinking that the right man is finally in place at the right time.

But until the right man resides in the penthouse, it's just another dance to the same old discouraging tune.

The Lions were 4-3 under Moeller, and he was dismissed at the end of the season.

JULY 29, 1999

Barry bolts for Europe — Ross opts for denial

The damage assessment of Barry Sanders' retirement bombshell pointed more to a psychological than physical toll. It was measured in the dashed illusions and crushed expectations strewn throughout the Lions' practice field and executive offices, and a still-disbelieving community. If emotional decimation were Sanders' intent, then he must have been vacationing in Europe with a satisfied smile.

"It would have been nice if we would have gotten the chance to say good-bye," wide receiver Johnnie Morton said. "Unless our paths cross, we may never see him again. I'm still shaking my head in disbelief that this is actually happening."

Shock begat anger before settling into composed disappointment.

Coach Bobby Ross chose his words carefully, determined to conceal feelings of betrayal that rested beneath the surface. This was no time for outrage or outbursts. It was another occasion in which we try to make some sense out of another nonsensical chapter of Lions football in the William Clay Ford era.

"Barry expresses himself in his own way," Ross rationalized. "I can't speculate on what might be going on inside Barry's head. I'm sure he wanted to take the time to determine exactly how he felt about playing. But understand that I'm not angry with Barry. I highly respect him as a person, a player and a father. But, yes, I was still disappointed by his decision."

Had Ross exercised this sort of restraint during some of his caustic postgame tirades last season, perhaps we wouldn't be prematurely waving good-bye to the game's most exciting player. No heroes emerged from this latest spectacle, only tarnished reputations stemming primarily from self-inflicted wounds.

Sanders lost whatever honor comes with sacrificing monetary and historical gain for personal serenity. He's perceived more now as a quitter than a competitor, content to run away rather than confront the front office with his differences.

But Ross created the chasm in the locker room by an apparent lack of public accountability, openly chastising his players for wanting paychecks more than victories while absolving himself and his coaching staff from the players' incessant mistakes. And the gulf has widened with Sanders' announcement.

"This is about Barry," Ross said. "This isn't about me."

Oh, yes, it is. It's about whether he can bring together a divided team without the assistance of its most valuable component. It's about a legacy forever stained as the coach who helped push Sanders into retirement. It's about the greatest coaching challenge Ross has faced in 34 years in the business.

"I've gone through much worse than this in my life," he said defiantly. "This certainly isn't something that I wanted to have happen, but what we have to do as a team and an organization is move on. We intend to be competitive even with this loss. We're not going to back down. The challenge now falls on all of us to make that big difference between a contribution and a commitment. We need a bunch of guys that are going to make that commitment."

But how can Ross make a convincing argument for commitment from his players when management's commitment is questioned once again? Although Sanders' actions are indefensible, his motives were justifiable. He was fed up with the team's futility.

There's plenty of blame to spread and, as usual, a sizable share falls on ownership. Why wasn't Ford more assertive in trying to find a resolution to Sanders' discontent? Morton stopped far short of wagging an accusatory finger at Ford for this latest embarrassment, but he thought the owner's intervention much earlier might have prevented this unfortunate outcome.

"I think it would have helped," Morton said, "because, as a businessman, he does have ultimate control over who's here. And if it meant that much to have Barry here, and he has the opportunity to do something, then something should have been done because if you want to put people in the seats, compete for a championship and have everybody happy, you need to have Barry here."

And with him gone, the onus falls on Ross. There's no deflecting accountability any longer, and let's hope Ross will use this disappointment as cause for introspection. What did he do wrong? What could he do better?

"Do I feel that Barry left because of me?" Ross said. "No, not at all."

Apparently, Ross is in denial. Ross thinks he did all he could. He wrote or phoned Sanders 15 times during the off-season. And not once did Sanders respond. But obviously Ross didn't understand the severity of Sanders' discontent or he would have arranged a face-to-face meeting.

Perhaps Ross thought chasing Sanders around the country would be a demeaning exercise, resembling all those missed tackles in Sanders' 10 seasons in the NFL. But now he's faced with an equally futile task — trying to pump life and excitement into an organization left in the dark again as its greatest player runs for daylight one final time.

AUG. 28, 2000

Roller-coaster Lions season easy to envision

A new season symbolizes hope. Well, it does in most places, anyway.

If you believe your heart, this could be the year the Lions get to the Super Bowl without needing tickets. But if you trust your head, you know you'll be banging it against a wall by November.

So having safely locked away all the sharp instruments, let's take a game-by-game glimpse at Lions 2000, otherwise referred to as Y2Kick.

Game 1 at New Orleans: Sporting News reporter Dan Pompei, only recently released from psychiatric evaluation, gives the Lions a pregame speech on why he picked them to win the Super Bowl. And then he slaps Charlie Batch on the back, separating Batch's shoulder.

Lions 15, Saints 10 — 1-0

Game 2 vs. Washington: Coach Bobby Ross boasts that any nobody from the Silverdome crowd could temporarily replace Batch, and, proving his point, actually finds someone. But before Ross could persuade the guy to quarterback the Lions, Joe Dumars promised him the job as the Pistons' center.

Lions 18, Redskins 17 — 2-0

Game 3 vs. Tampa Bay: In his first matchup with new Bucs threat Keyshawn Johnson, Bryant Westbrook makes league history, drawing the fastest pass-interference penalty ever — during the national anthem. Ross simplifies the offense in Batch's absence, sending out kicker Jason Hanson on every second down.

Lions 12, Bucs 7 — 3-0

Game 4 at Chicago: The NFL asks Attorney General Janet Reno to appoint an independent counsel to investigate the Lions' first 3-0 start in 20 years. Batch is healthy for the first time in four weeks but suffers three cracked ribs when Aaron Gibson stampedes over him on his way to the training table.

Bears 23, Lions 12 — 3-1

Game 5 vs. Minnesota: Concerns regarding Ross' suspected

senility arise when he suggests the Lions will work out Bobby Layne as their newest backup quarterback. When told Layne is dead, Ross intimates that should make it easier to fit him under the salary cap. Hanson establishes an NFL record with his 27th field goal in five games.

Lions 24, Vikings 20 — 4-1

Game 6 vs. Green Bay: A parade for Detroit mayoral candidate Pompei is planned after the Lions sack Brett Favre six times, compensating for the six interceptions new backup Milt Plum threw. Foolhardy fans and media dare to use the dreaded "Super" phrase, signaling a fast fall back to reality.

Lions 27, Packers 23 — 5-1

Game 7 at Tampa Bay: Hanson doubles as offensive coordinator. Attempting to ensure a high playoff seed, the Lions petition NFL commissioner Paul Tagliabue to cancel the second half of the season.

Bucs 15, Lions 12 — 5-2

Game 8 at Indianapolis: The Lions drive for a late score, cutting the Colts' lead to two with eight seconds remaining. Ross bypasses the two-point conversion, opting instead for the point-after attempt. "You can't fool an old codger like me a second time," he says afterward. Management promptly schedules Ross an appointment with Pompei's doctor.

Colts 24, Lions 23 — 5-3

Game 9 vs. Miami: It's Charlie Batch Rosary Beads Day at the Silverdome as the unlucky quarterback professes full health once again. But the microphone to quarterback coach Jim Zorn's headset accidentally pokes Batch in the eye during a sideline meeting. Ross wonders why he didn't buy that chicken ranch when he had the chance.

Lions 17, Dolphins 13 — 6-3

Game 10 vs. Atlanta: Errant Tiger Woods drive from a tournament 2,000 miles away rips through the Silverdome roof, striking Batch on the head, rendering him unconscious. Concerns over Ross' mental state heighten when he's seen in his office afterward, flipping through his Rolodex for Y.A. Tittle's phone number.

Lions 16, Falcons 7 — 7-3

Game 11 at N.Y. Giants: When told he was playing against a team from Michigan, Heisman Trophy winner Ron Dayne hyperventilates before kickoff. Dayne calms down when assured he's playing the Lions instead of the Wolverines. But when running out of bounds, he inadvertently steps on Batch's foot,

breaking the QB's baby toe.
Giants 31, Lions 20 — 7-4

Game 12 vs. New England: Turkey Day is synonymous with Lions football. Though hobbled, Batch looks brilliant, throwing for two touchdowns and running for another two scores. But the postgame euphoria is muted when Gibson mistakes Batch's right hand for a turkey leg at the team Thanksgiving dinner.
Lions 38, Patriots 14 — 8-4

Game 13 at Minnesota: Ross wonders why nobody has signed Sammy Baugh. Doctors double his medication. Batch assures the media he will be ready for the playoffs, whereupon one wise-guy columnist insists that Batch must be expecting a late-season trade to Tampa Bay.
Vikings 26, Lions 10 — 8-5

Game 14 at Green Bay: Hanson develops cramp in his right leg, decimating the offense. Juan Gonzalez offers to step in, provided the goalposts are moved in 20 feet. A delusional Ross calls up to the Fox football booth to inquire about Pat Summerall's availability. Ross orders 52 one-way bus tickets out of town after the Lions are penalized a league-record 39 times.
Packers 31, Lions 0 — 8-6

Game 15 at N.Y. Jets: Ross can't understand why he's all alone in the locker room 30 minutes before kickoff until his assistants remind him that he fired his entire team the previous week, except for Hanson. Doctors finally wrestle the coach to the floor, sedating him. Ross is strapped down and carried away, screaming, "Abandon ship! Womp! Womp! Womp!"
Jets 6, Lions 0 (forfeit) — 8-7

Game 16 vs. Chicago: Defensive coordinator Larry Peccatiello is named interim coach and spends half of his introductory news conference profusely thanking his owner. Oh, no! Not again! So impressed that the Lions finished the season in an eight-way tie for the last NFC playoff spot, William Clay Ford signs Peccatiello to a five-year contract. And further signaling a continuation of Lions tradition, Ford also names Pompei his new general manager.
Bears 23, Lions 14 — 8-8

NOV. 6, 2000

Devastating loss leaves Bobby Ross a beaten man

An already ugly season has turned disgusting, leaving everyone connected with the Lions — coaches, players and fans — in desperate need of self-reflection. Just when you thought new lows of humiliation were unattainable, the Lions' 23-8 loss to the Dolphins revealed far deeper depths. The frustration of a season quickly unraveling crudely revealed itself, and most unflatteringly.

This is a lousy team with classless fans. Misery that deserves each other's company. And the most miserable disposition belonged to the coach.

Bobby Ross officially joined the exclusive Lions coaching fraternity after the game, succumbing to futility and suggesting for the first time in his four years in Detroit that changing the course of this backwardly mobile team is beyond reach.

This wasn't the bloodied-but-unbowed fighter who often challenged media skepticism following similar exhibitions. Instead, this was an emotionally beaten man standing before his executioners, lacking blindfold and cigarette.

"Obviously, you don't have a good coach," Ross said in response to my question about why the Lions have become such a poorly coached team, particularly the past three weeks.

Where was the resistance, the combativeness? And when Ross rambled about legacies and his future with his wife, Alice, you had standing before you a coach with every instinct of self-preservation sapped from him.

Ross arrived in Detroit with a reputation for demanding discipline and preaching preparedness, but the Lions started abysmally for the third straight game. They've been outscored, 40-0, in their past two first halves. And despite a 5-4 record, the Lions have played progressively worse the past three weeks.

How can a team look so unprepared in every facet of the game? It's as much a question of readiness as it is ability. Ross has failed. And he knows it.

"You want your team to be a model of who you are and what you are," Ross said. "I expect us to fight. I expect us to compete. But we never fought back. We never competed. We need to ask ourselves some questions this week. Are we going to fight or are we going to sit there and take it?"

In the locker room, the usual post-calamity outrage was replaced by quiet resignation.

"Nothing ever surprises me about this game," said Johnnie Morton, who symbolized the day's frustration, drawing a personal foul for giving an official a few choice words. "I never thought Barry (Sanders) would quit. Hopefully, he (Ross) is just reacting to the emotion of the moment. After thinking about it a night, things might look a little clearer the next day. But we as players have to be ready for anything."

Ross is bearing the cracks that ultimately eat away at every Lions coach. He seemed at the brink of tears when describing the annoying repetition of mindless penalties, poor tackling and bad execution. But perhaps nothing hurt more than when the sold-out Silverdome crowd derisively cheered when injured quarterback Charlie Batch fell to the carpet with a concussion.

What were these people thinking? Maybe they're too young to remember Lions receiver Chuck Hughes' death from a heart attack on the Tiger Stadium grass during a Bears game in 1971. Or maybe they were too inebriated to remember three years ago, when linebacker Reggie Brown sustained a neck injury, an accident that claimed a career and almost another life.

"That was as sickening a scene as I've ever been a part of," Herman Moore said. "Charlie's still down on the field, and I got people in the stands right behind the bench screaming at me and cheering and saying, 'Hey, Herman, maybe you can get the ball more.' What's with that crap? I saw a side of our fans that I thought I'd never see. It was an all-around embarrassing day."

And an oh-so-typical Lions day, from which nothing redeeming emerged. They lost a game, a quarterback, possibly a coach and every semblance of sportsmanship and decency.

Ross resigned the next day.

DEC. 25, 2000

Lions fall flat with playoff berth on the line

It's a Lions Christmas, an occasion worthy of spreading holiday jeer. A time for frustrated loved ones to huddle around the fireplace, cursing themselves for foolishly believing that these Lions would somehow reverse the course that history has bestowed upon them. A time for singing carols that symbolically capture the spirit of new faces keeping alive an old tradition.

"Stoney Case roasting on an open fire. Charlie Batch lunging for his lungs."

Or how about an appropriate yuletide poem.

" 'Twas the choke before Christmas. And all through the town. Not a pass was completed. Nor could they get a first down."

And the Lions — who lost the season finale on Christmas Eve — wonder why they breed cynicism.

A town's leap of faith once again has come to a crashing thud along with the Lions' playoff hopes. They lost a game they shouldn't have, against a team whose only motivation was getting the game over quickly enough so they could get home to their families.

File this 23-20 collapse to the Chicago Bears alongside the 51-7 first-half deficit against Philadelphia in the 1995 playoffs and Sterling Sharpe's last-second touchdown for Green Bay in another first-round slap to the face in 1993.

As Paul Edinger's 54-yard field goal sailed over the crossbar with two seconds remaining, Luther Elliss dropped to his knees and shouted to the heavens, "Not again! Not again!" Ron Rice swore, kicked the carpet and disgustingly slammed his helmet against the turf. Johnnie Morton merely shook his head in disillusionment.

No, this shouldn't have happened. Not at home. Not against a 10-point underdog. Not against a pathetic opponent that hovered at the brink of insurrection over a quarterback controversy earlier in the week.

"It's going to take awhile for all this to sink in," Morton said. "We try not to think about what our history has been here, but it's impossible to completely forget it. But I really thought that this was going to be different. We were going to have 10 wins. We were going to finally slam the door on that history."

But once again the door slammed the Lions in the face. They're like that one holiday fruitcake passed around in perpetuity. The packaging changes, looking more inviting each time. But when you look inside the box, it's the same old, stale, unsatisfying product.

That they've gotten this far is a testament to parity-induced mediocrity throughout the league. The Lions aren't going to the playoffs because they didn't deserve an invitation. Their 9-7 final record is misleading because only an opportunistic defense kept it from becoming 5-11.

"Dammit," Gary Moeller muttered as he left the podium following his postgame news conference. The pain was evident on his face, but he wasn't deluding himself. Moeller must have realized that even if they had stumbled into the playoffs, another first-round embarrassment was inevitable with an offense incapable of putting the ball in the end zone after driving within the opponent's 10-yard line.

"And what kills me is that we started out strong on our first possessions," he said. "That's the best that we've looked offensively early in quite some time. But then, for whatever reason, we just lost our intensity. We lost our focus. And the opportunities we had near the end, we just couldn't do it."

The game was theirs. A playoff trip to Philadelphia was theirs. Allen Aldridge gave it to them when the linebacker stripped the Bears' James Allen of the ball and recovered it at the 10 with 2:22 remaining in the game. But as was often the case this season, the Lions settled for a Jason Hanson field goal.

"It's hard to explain," said wide receiver Herman Moore, part of the offensive problem, dropping what could have been a momentum-turning touchdown pass early in the game. "It's always something with us."

That should be the Lions' marketing slogan.

"It doesn't make any sense," Morton said. "We were a 10-point favorite playing against a team that already had their stuff packed. And we still couldn't get it done. The NFC playoffs are more wide-open than at any time since I've been here. And we still couldn't get it done. We could have gone into the playoffs with confidence with road wins at Tampa, New York and New Orleans. And we still couldn't get it done."

What's so hard to figure out? These are the Lions!

AUG. 29, 2001

Lions coaches sometimes die, others fade away

The residents of the William Clay Ford Clinic for Coaching Rehabilitation are largely forgotten. Visitors do not often frequent this home for recovering Lions head coaches because who else would want to relive the coaches' horrors?

But a curious Marty Mornhinweg arrives at the doorstep, choosing not to run away from the Lions' rather morbid coaching history. He seeks the coaches' counsel.

"Coach, this is a surprise," the clinic's doctor says. "What are you doing here? Your eyes aren't glazed, your speech isn't slurred. You're able to distinguish good football from Lions football. We weren't expecting to see you here for at least another two weeks."

"This is a new era," Mornhinweg says as though he's reading cue cards. "A new regime. A new attitude. The days of believing that the coaches of this franchise are cursed are over. That's why I'm here."

"Let me explain some of the rules here, Coach," the doctor says. "No questions about quarterbacking. Sharp objects are never permitted within six feet of our patients. And cell phones are strictly prohibited."

"I like this place already," Mornhinweg says.

Mornhinweg understands the Lions' coaching heritage. There's no avoiding it. Mornhinweg is Ford's 12th head coach in his 38 years of sole ownership, and not one of his predecessors was a head coach in the NFL again after leaving the organization. They're football's version of Hester Prynne, consigned to live their remaining days with a scarlet letter "L" attached to their breasts.

One — Don McCafferty — barely got through the opening days of his second training camp before he dropped dead of a heart attack.

"Why is the roof leaking in this place?" Mornhinweg asks.

"We wanted to re-create the atmosphere of the Silverdome as much as possible," the doctor says. "It's reassuring to our patients."

Mornhinweg enters the Monte Clark wing, where he sees a solitary figure in a rocking chair, staring out the window.

"Coach Ross," the doctor sings, "there's somebody here to see you."

"Coach, I'm Marty Mornhinweg. I just want you to know that

you were one of my mentors as a young assistant, and it's my intention to show you that all this nonsense about this football organization turning minds into mush is just a bunch of — "

"Marty," the doctor interrupts, "Bobby hasn't spoken in nine months."

"How does he communicate?"

"He keeps a card in his back pocket that we use to identify his reaction to certain situations."

"But Coach Ross is just an isolated case, right?" Mornhinweg asks.

"Absolutely," the doctor responds. "Most of our patients are happily delusional. See those two out there on the practice putting green? That's Coach Fontes and Coach Rogers. Coach Fontes is the one in the golf cart that's stuck in reverse."

"They look fantastic, although maybe the one guy could lose the mouse ears," Mornhinweg says. "They seem content. And that's precisely my point about this supposed curse. Coaching the Lions hasn't emotionally devastated them. They didn't need the validation of coaching somewhere else. Look at them. They're all smiles."

"You'd smile, too, if you stole paychecks while masquerading as an NFL head coach. You still want to talk with them?"

"Well, maybe not."

The Lions aren't known for their coaching resurrections. Mike Shanahan bombed during his brief stay with the Raiders, but he became a deity in Denver. Marv Levy failed in Kansas City, but he became a Hall of Famer in Buffalo. As a first-time head coach, Mornhinweg understands that success sometimes doesn't come until the second or third try.

But the Lions' history is staunchly unforgiving. Whether it's fate or coincidence, the Lions' head coaching position is one in which careers die. Mornhinweg soon will realize that merely fighting the past doesn't make it go away. But just like his predecessors, Mornhinweg arrives confident that he's a good coach and certain that the NFL always has room for good coaches.

"I plan on winning here," Mornhinweg tells Joe Schmidt and Tommy Hudspeth before leaving. "But if it doesn't work out, I'm not too worried. Unlike some of the other first-time head coaches in this team's history, I'm a pretty young guy. I'm not even 40. I'll have plenty of opportunities because people won't forget about me."

"You haven't been to the Rick Forzano wing yet, have you?" Schmidt asks.

"Rick who?"

"That's precisely the point, Marty."

SEPT. 4, 2001

QB or not QB? With Lions, that is always the question

The best day for a new Lions quarterback is always his first. The poison hasn't had enough time to seep through his pores.

Approaching his 34th birthday and playing for his fifth NFL team, Ty Detmer has become the latest savior from the reclamation scrap heap. Rest assured, his stature in the eyes of forlorn fans will grow with each Charlie Batch misread or mis-thrown pass.

The Lions acquired the Heisman Trophy winner from Cleveland for a fourth-round draft choice because of his familiarity with Marty Mornhinweg at Green Bay and San Francisco. Detmer knows Mornhinweg's system, and it's important to have at least one experienced player around during Batch's adaptation to the West Coast offense, a process that could take a few years.

Detmer will be loved here — until he spoils it all by playing.

That's the staple of this franchise — the best Lions quarterback in fans' minds is always the one on the sideline. He's incapable of wrongdoing, until he drops back in the pocket.

"Charlie's the No. 1 guy here," Detmer said after his first practice with the Lions. "There's no question about that. Matt (Millen) and Marty brought me in here because of my experience in the system. There's some familiarity, and that's why I'm really excited about reuniting with Marty."

"He's spent seven years in the system," Batch said. "It didn't take him long before the terminology came right back to him. That's an invaluable tool for me to have and learn from. He already gave me a couple of tips when I first saw him at the start of practice."

Batch could educate Detmer, as well, schooling the veteran on the pitfalls of this occupation. As a rookie, Batch quickly moved up the depth chart and into the infatuated hearts of long-suffering fans thirsting for somebody — anybody — who could satisfy their quarterbacking desires. He initially attracted adoring sighs, but, three years later, bearing the sins of the past, Batch drew sneers.

"The quarterback position is the most high-profile, so it gets most of the attention," Batch said. "That comes with the territory. But you (media) guys make the job more difficult because you're always bringing up the past. You're always getting compared to the problems of the previous quarterbacks. A guy should be judged solely on what he has done."

Despite his vast West Coast offense experience, Detmer is more insurance policy than competitive threat. He's here in case Batch breaks something again, like in his back (1998), thumb (1999), leg and ribs (2000).

"This is going to be a good offense for the Lions," Detmer said. "You've got plenty of big-play capability guys like Germane (Crowell), Johnnie (Morton) and Herman (Moore). It takes time for everyone to get comfortable in a new system, so that's where having some experience helps. But I'm really excited about the possibilities here."

A refrain we've heard from other newcomers, unaware of the torment awaiting them. The world is perfect for a new quarterback on his first day. He has yet to take a bad sack or throw an ill-timed interception.

And by our standards in this town, that makes him a Hall of Famer.

Batch lasted one week as the starting quarterback. When the change was made Drew Sharp was there:

Mornhinweg didn't like what developed in the season opener at Green Bay and moved decisively, sacking Batch after just one game. The Lions' starting-quarterback carousel came full circle for the embattled Batch, who lost the job with the same stunning suddenness as when it was presented to him.

Detmer, the latest Lions quarterback du jour, isn't the same novice Batch was two games into the 1998 season, when Bobby Ross unceremoniously dumped Scott Mitchell to third string. Detmer has nine years' experience in the NFL and has played in Mornhinweg's offensive system, so the new Lions coach isn't bailing on the new season with this decision.

"I have been evaluating Charlie ever since I got here, No. 1," Mornhinweg said. "No. 2, as you know, the standard for quarterback play is high, and it will always be high here. I was unsatisfied with the level that Charlie played at."

But the move should not instill confidence that the Lions have averted impending disaster.

SEPT. 10, 2001

It's Marty's first game, but we've seen it all before

GREEN BAY, Wis. — Actually, the Lions lived up to their latest slogan. A new attitude has indeed swept through town. As another abysmal afternoon in Green Bay dragged on, many in Detroit believed the declawed Tigers packed more offensive power than the Lions.

The anticipated start of a new season brought with it the demoralizing stench of nightmares past — offensive linemen posing as statues and wild-armed incompetents masquerading as quarterbacks. So exactly what's new about kicker Jason Hanson being the lone scoring option?

It was only the first step in a 16-game test of endurance, but the Lions wanted this opening game to establish the initial strides in the right direction. Instead, the 28-6 loss to the Packers was a comedy of errors, from the West Coast offense to the West Curse defense (as in, "Damn, can't these guys tackle anybody?").

The new coach reflected old frustrations. Marty Mornhinweg angrily stomped his foot outside the locker room when recalling the shoddy execution on both sides of the ball, shaking his head in bewilderment.

"You cannot let that happen in this league!" he seethed. "When plays had to be made, we couldn't make them. The game's barely started and we're down three touchdowns. But this is just the beginning. What matters most is the finish. Things are going to change."

The first change came in the voice of a veteran. Herman Moore has never been a particularly vocal locker-room presence. But he took it upon himself to speak with his teammates immediately after the loss. He had been around long enough to see the signs of dejection even one game into the season. He's well versed in how disappointment snowballs into disaster with this franchise.

"If we think the season's over after just one game, then we're definitely in for some disappointment," Moore said. "I wanted to avert that before it even had a chance to start. I reminded everyone that this was just the first game. It's over. We move on. This was not the time for anybody to start pointing fingers at each other. We can't have the offense blaming anyone in particular like the quarterback or the offensive line, or pointing the finger at the defense."

And you can't have the players fuming over management's decision to cut veteran defensive tackle James Jones on the eve of the opener in a salary-cap move. Jones struggled during the exhibition season, but more than a few players thought he would have been an upgrade in production over what the Lions got from rookie Shaun Rogers and Travis Kirschke.

The Packers sliced through the Lions' front seven for 179 yards on the ground.

That the Lions lost wasn't a surprise. Their last win in Wisconsin was in 1991. And a healthy Brett Favre combined with an injury-riddled Lions secondary was a formula for calamity. But the missed tackles on Ahman Green's two long touchdown gallops were inexcusable. Injuries or not, first unit or not, a defense has got to make tackles.

And it appears the new era has an old problem — the makings of a quarterback controversy. Mornhinweg stayed with Charlie Batch despite his difficulties. Batch was intercepted twice and sacked seven times, finishing with a woefully low 52.9 passer rating. But the only way he's going to master the new system, if ever, is through learning from his mistakes. Batch missed reads as often as receivers, holding onto the ball too long too often, causing sacks that shouldn't have occurred.

Mornhinweg said he never glanced over to his new No. 2 quarterback, Ty Detmer, and Batch insisted afterward that he never feared getting the hook. But the coach clearly wasn't pleased with his quarterback.

"How do I assess my quarterback?" Mornhinweg said. "We didn't score a touchdown. That's the first thing you look at. There were some times when it appeared that Charlie didn't have a chance, but there were other times when he simply has got to get rid of the ball."

Remind me again. What exactly was different about this?

JAN. 5, 2002

As Silverdome closes, Panthers remembered fondly

It's not difficult to say farewell to a tease. You embrace the parting. You know you're better off for its leaving.

For 27 NFL seasons, the Silverdome stood in cold, sterile isolation, pretty much in the middle of nowhere. That's precisely where it has left fans who blindly and loyally ventured there in anticipation of watching something memorable.

Let's rephrase that, shall we? Something happily memorable.

There have been a few trinkets worth saving. Remember Trevor Francis? For a brief while, Britain's gift from the soccer gods made watching the Express an enjoyable experience.

But it shouldn't be surprising that perhaps the most cherished memory of the Dome doesn't pertain to its primary occupant, the Lions.

On a Sunday afternoon in July 1983, conditions were perfect for spending a day outside at the ballpark. Instead, close to 62,000 — the largest crowd in the first year of the United States Football League — weathered the sweltering humidity inside to witness what many long thought impossible. A Detroit professional football team was one victory from playing for the league championship.

"What made it great," said Panthers left tackle Chris Godfrey, "was that it was so unexpected. Nothing much was expected from us, but we clicked around the middle of the season, and we just captured the imagination of the city."

The champagne-and-plum-clad Michigan Panthers beat the Oakland Invaders, 37-21, to earn a trip to the USFL championship game. It made a strong statement for the league's contention that it could find a niche in the NFL's off-season.

When the game was over, many fans stormed the field in celebration, actually tearing down the goalposts, which hadn't happened much in Detroit.

I was there, marveling. I had long since vowed never to spend a dime from my own pocket to watch the Lions. But there was something intriguing about how the Panthers suddenly breathed purpose into the lifeless soul of the Detroit football fan.

Godfrey remembered driving home after the victory over Oakland and seeing congratulatory banners draped over freeway overpasses.

"We won the league championship the following week," Godfrey said, "but the Oakland game was the most special moment because it happened in front of our fans. It was just a spontaneous expression of everyone's enthusiasm."

The Panthers were a source of irritation to the Lions. In one year they became everything the Lions weren't. Their owner, Alfred Taubman, was financially aggressive. Lions owner William Clay Ford was frugal. The Panthers were bold, convincing Anthony Carter to sign with an untested league as a rookie coming out of Michigan.

They drafted a lanky quarterback out of the Cajun swamps of Louisiana who had eluded the NFL radar. Bobby Hebert provided this city with something it fervently craved — a championship-winning, big-play-making quarterback.

Godfrey remembers an incident on the Silverdome turf during the Lions' 1983 season. He and other Panthers were filming a commercial just as the Lions were leaving practice, and Lions general manager Russ Thomas tried to get the Panthers removed from the building.

"They were a little envious of what we had with the city," said Godfrey, an attorney in South Bend, Ind.

It was a definite sore point for the Lions that the crowd that July afternoon outdrew some of their home games in the fall.

"What still stands out to me about that day was the enthusiasm of the fans," said Tim Pendell, the Lions' community affairs senior director and a former Panthers assistant public relations director. "It was incredibly high. Anytime I run into guys from then, we immediately think about that season because it was so much fun. You never forget that."

The ride was short. The Panthers played in Pontiac for only one more season, eventually merging with the Invaders, and the franchise remained in the Bay Area. The USFL failed to force the NFL into a merger during a much-publicized antitrust lawsuit. A court awarded the USFL $3 in damages.

The little league that couldn't quietly expired after the 1985 season. Many of its stars later prospered in the NFL. Carter went on to have a splendid career with the Minnesota Vikings. Hebert fulfilled his dream of quarterbacking his home-state New Orleans Saints but never again enjoyed the rapture of that special season at the Silverdome.

He'll always have that summer day in Pontiac. And so will the rest of us.

JAN. 7, 2002

Good-bye and good riddance to 2001

The woman held onto her quarry, refusing to let go until she had achieved her objective.

"You've got to give me something," she pleaded to Robert Porcher, clutching his arm.

Prying free from her grasp, he took off one of his shoes and gave it to her. Apparently, the agony of one of the worst seasons in Lions history is worth it when, in the end, you get a sweaty, smelly shoe as a reward.

It was hard to tell which was the more eagerly anticipated farewell — that of the Silverdome or the Lions' 2001 season. Both drew to a merciful conclusion with a 15-10 victory over Dallas. It was one final twist of the knife as the Lions finally put together those necessary elements of winning football — no turnovers, no sacks and one penalty — with no games to follow.

There were no tears shed. The drips falling from the Silverdome roof weren't sentiment, just another leak. Afterward, Porcher spoke for the players in an impromptu ceremony at the 50, expressing their gratitude for the fans — an average of about 75,000 per home game — and their support despite a season in which the Lions morphed into a circus sideshow, providing material for comedians and columnists alike.

Perhaps he should have first offered an apology.

"I've been apologizing all season for what's happened," Porcher said. "But our fans stuck by us. Our fans are the best. I'm not a betting man, but I'd wager there aren't other fans who would turn out in the numbers that ours did despite all the problems and frustrations of this season."

He's right. It wouldn't happen anywhere else. Proof once again that Lions fans are suckers. All hail the greatest 2-14 football team that ever jumped before the snap.

Sympathy is wasted on these people. You can't feel sorry for those who continue to throw good money at bad football only to later curse their misfortune and vent their outrage when their hearts are trampled once again. Detroit, you get what you deserve.

The Lions know how good they have it. They know that regardless of the pitiful product they provide, the fans will frantically lean over the railings as they did in the season finale just so they could touch one of their boys.

Scott Dreisbach had been with the team only three weeks, yet he raced around the stadium a second time to exchange high-fives. It didn't matter to the fans that he was a newcomer to the asylum. He was still one of their 2-14 heroes.

Luther Elliss gave up his shoes, socks, practically everything but his pants. His celebratory turn through the stadium ranked as one of his career highlights.

"It just tells you how much the fans here are hungry for a championship," he said. "And that makes you, as a player, even more determined because you realize that you're not just doing this for yourself. You're playing for the people who call the Detroit Lions their team."

This isn't to suggest that Lions management doesn't want to win. That's ludicrous. But the organization's arrogance comes from knowing it risks no penalty from the public despite failure after failure. Masochists that they are, Lions fans always come back for more.

"They're starving for a championship," Porcher said. "This team hasn't won a championship since it left Detroit, so maybe we need to go back there and change our luck."

Porcher didn't want to delve into any purported demons, but the Silverdome has symbolized this team's futility. Known more for drunken fights in the stands than fighting spirit on the field, the stadium never became home. It was just a place to go to work.

"I've never had any real emotional attachment to it," kicker Jason Hanson said, "and this is the only place I've known in all my years in the league."

It's not the building but who's playing inside that matters most.

In 2001, the Lions' new president, new coach and new attitude reached new lows. Yet fans loved them as much as ever. So much so that they even raised a stinking shoe in tribute.

AUG. 10, 2002

Harrington joins ranks of quarterback saviors

BALTIMORE — The newest incarnation of the long-awaited quarterbacking savior took the field for the first time a little after 10 p.m. And a city's interest in a normally meaningless second half of an exhibition game piqued, everyone looking for the tiniest clues that the possible answer to a gray-whiskered question had arrived.

He got his teammates out of his first huddle smoothly. So far, so good.

But on his second snap, he took a quick drop and tried to dump the ball to his fullback over the middle. The ball ricocheted off the intended receiver's hands and into the diving reach of a Baltimore linebacker.

Welcome to your nightmare, Joey Harrington. You've officially become a Detroit Lion.

You can't say "quarterback" in Detroit without instinctively following it with "controversy." Debating the virtues of who best can stumble the Lions' offense backward up the field is sacred tradition passed down through the generations.

Bobby Layne or Tobin Rote. Milt Plum or Karl Sweetan. Greg Landry or Bill Munson. Scott Mitchell or Anybody with a Pulse.

Whether it's Harrington or Mike McMahon in 2002, the offense will struggle from a lack of experience taking snaps and a lack of surrounding play-making capability.

"It was about what I expected for my first game," said Harrington of his 12-for-21, two-interception night. "I knew that I would be comfortable, but it would take me some time to gain control over what I'm doing. I'm finding my way, but it's something that you can't push. I'm a rookie, and that means I'm going to make rookie mistakes. There are some things that I'm going to have to learn."

It was impossible to draw any conclusions about how good Harrington could become from his initial taste of action, but you could sense that he might be good enough to assume the starting responsibilities earlier than originally projected. And that's a bad sign.

"I thought that Joey showed some good things," coach Marty Mornhinweg said. "There were also some things that were horrendous. But we expected that. There are some things that we're going to have to get straightened out on offense, and we'll have to do it quickly."

The Lions, 2-14 last season, aren't a good team, but that doesn't preclude them from exceeding expectations.

"I'd like to see what we can do if we just get a fair amount of good luck," defensive end Robert Porcher said. "That's all. Last year, it seemed like we just didn't get our rightful share of injuries but we got everybody else's, as well. Yet despite all that and all the losses, we stayed together. The coaches never gave up, and the players never gave up. That says a lot. So why shouldn't we be optimistic about this season?"

Dare I say it? It's because they're the Lions!

SEPT. 5, 2002

Matt-cam reveals another dismal Lions season

Time for our final Lions season-opening checklist: Rose-colored glasses? Check.

Three-month supply of Tums? Check.

ESPN will introduce Skycam in the NFL season opener between San Francisco and the New York Giants, but the true network innovation will come when Fox introduces Matt-cam to chronicle the game-day contortions of Lions president Matt Millen.

Game 1 at Miami: Air-traffic controllers at neighboring airports restrict flight patterns over Pro Player Stadium in the second half after getting a hint of Mike McMahon's accuracy in the first half. Matt-cam catches Millen in his suite wearing a precautionary hard hat.

Dolphins 24, Lions 9 — 0-1

Game 2 at Carolina: The most important game in Marty Mornhinweg's short coaching career concludes in familiar fashion, a breakdown in the secondary on the Panthers' final drive when aging cornerback Eric Davis gets tangled up in his walker.

Panthers 16, Lions 10 — 0-2

Game 3 vs. Green Bay: McMahon is knocked unconscious when one of his first-quarter passes finally comes back to Earth and strikes him in the head. Portable oxygen sales soar locally after Joey Harrington completes successive passes to a teammate. Matt-cam cops a peek of Millen demonstrating the proper way of fighting off a blocker to his suitemates.

Packers 28, Lions 24 — 0-3

Game 4 vs. New Orleans: It's five minutes to kickoff and the Saints haven't come marching in. They're in Pontiac. It took 10 minutes of avoiding stationary monster trucks before they realized that they weren't the Lions.

Detroit 6, New Orleans 0 (forfeit) — 1-3

Game 5 at Minnesota: Harrington throws a touchdown pass. Unimpressed, Mornhinweg names Ty Detmer the starter. Matt-cam finds Millen on the phone with Fox to see if the network might be in the market for another color analyst.

Randy Moss 24, Lions 16 — 1-4

Game 6 vs. Chicago: Detmer throws eight interceptions against the Bears, but Mornhinweg hails his execution, saying that Detmer hit those defenders in stride, the mark of a veteran quarterback. Matt-cam catches Millen looking for the combination to unlock the utensil drawer.

Bears 20, Lions 6 — 1-5

Game 7 at Buffalo: Harrington's long-awaited debut as the starting quarterback saves Mornhinweg's job — for at least one week. Harrington throws three touchdown passes, giving him four for the season, placing him seventh on the Lions' career TD pass list. Matt-cam monitors medical technicians attempting to revive Millen in his suite.

Lions 30, Bills 17 — 2-5

Game 8 vs. Dallas: Feeling strangely cocky after matching his career high for victories, Mornhinweg reinserts McMahon as starter, maintaining that injury can't cost somebody his job. But a mysterious hair-moussing accident temporarily blinds McMahon. Harrington starts, impresses once again and two days later is elected governor of Michigan.

Lions 27, Cowboys 23 — 3-5

Game 9 at Green Bay: After demanding that McMahon shave his head, Mornhinweg returns him to the starting lineup. He still doesn't think much of Harrington's success, saying that "when you keep throwing accurately at your receivers, people are naturally going to think that you're good. But where's the challenge?" Where's the team president? Matt-cam can't find him.

Packers 33, Lions 16 — 3-6

Game 10 vs. New York Jets: Second-year reserve linebacker Jason Glenn, a Lions draftee, wasn't good enough to warrant a spot with Mornhinweg. But he picks off a McMahon pass that was initially intended for the radio broadcast booth and returns it for the game-winning touchdown.

Jets 20, Lions 17 — 3-7

Game 11 at Chicago: Adamant that there is no quarterback controversy, Mornhinweg insists that he makes his decision on who gives the team the best chance to win. Funny thing is, he never identifies which team. Matt-cam spies Millen asking one of his associates to find the correct spelling of Mariucci.

Bears 28, Lions 16 — 3-8

Game 12 vs. New England: Sensing that Harrington is finally ready, Mornhinweg names him starter, much to the fans' delirium. Harrington promptly goes out and proves worthy of the title of official Lions starting quarterback. He throws four interceptions. Millen takes a bat to Matt-cam.

Patriots 19, Lions 12 — 3-9

Game 13 at Arizona: Hopes for a less penalty-prone team are dashed when the Lions are flagged for three Brenden Stai false starts — and he's now an offensive lineman for the Washington Redskins.

Cardinals 38, Lions 34 — 3-10

Game 14 vs. Tampa Bay: Responding to public outcry, vice chairman William Clay Ford Jr. extends his front office a vote of confidence during a halftime interview. Matt-cam II catches a glimpse of Millen on the phone speaking with former Ford president Jacques Nasser.

Bucs 23, Lions 14 — 3-11

Game 15 at Atlanta: The Recall Gov. Harrington movement gains steam as the rookie's interception-to-touchdown ratio approaches 2-to-1. Local media outlets rate the Lions' odds in the Rex Grossman draft lottery.

Falcons 9, Lions 6 — 3-12

Game 16 vs. Minnesota: The Lions win a thriller in the final seconds on a well-engineered scoring drive. The wildly enthused fans leave Ford Field confident that — this time — they've got a quarterback: the newly re-signed Scott Dreisbach.

Lions 34, Vikings 30 — 4-12

SEPT. 9, 2002

After bungling opener, it's open season on Lions

MIAMI — Robert Porcher removed his helmet and took a knee on the Pro Player Stadium turf. His expression was equal parts exhaustion and exasperation. It was the look of a man grown tired of the same old mess. And this was barely midway through the second quarter of the season's first game.

In all fairness, nobody expected much from the Lions against Miami. The Dolphins are Super Bowl contenders and the Lions are merely contentious. And when James Stewart was a last-minute scratch because of a temperamental knee, even less was anticipated.

Hope, if any at all, would be measured by the number of self-inflicted powder burns on the Lions' feet afterward. If they're not executing any better, then at least are they playing a tad smarter? Are they cutting back on penalties? Are they learning how to curtail their turnovers?

But nothing remotely uplifting emerged from the Dolphins' 49-21 victory. Not one granule of optimism came from the players or those directing them. No one has the tiniest clue how to turn around a franchise that remains a laughingstock.

"We were awful," lamented a disgusted Matt Millen. "It pisses me off."

When asked to think of one positive — just one teeny-weeny positive — the Lions' president resembled his team. He came up blank.

The Dolphins "didn't do anything that surprised us," Millen said. "We knew that they were going to try to run the ball. And that was supposed to be one of our strengths, stopping the run."

Outside linebacker Brian Williams, a newcomer in the Lions' three-down circus, expressed shock that anybody could run wide on this team as easily as Miami did. Luther Elliss shook his head in dismay, sincerely stunned that the Lions couldn't contain the Dolphins' ground game.

It doesn't matter who's quarterbacking this team, folks. Arguing about whether Mike McMahon or Joey Harrington provides the best opportunity to win is wasted breath. As long as the defense remains soft in the middle, slow along the perimeter and old at the corners, the Lions will stare at sizable deficits all season.

Chris Claiborne couldn't hide his discontent. He's the middle linebacker and has become the face of a defense that must stop the run. But he was pulled in third-down situations, and he didn't like it.

"There's nothing I can do if Ricky Williams makes a big gain on third down and I'm not out there," Claiborne said. "All I can do is stay pissed on the sidelines if we're defending against the pass and they decide to run on third down and get big yardage, because it reflects upon me."

But there's a flaw in Claiborne's reasoning. Only one yard of Williams' 111 for the day came on third down. The other 110 came on first or second down, when Claiborne was on the field.

A dejected Porcher declined to talk as he left the locker room. Before he left, he ran into former teammate Tracy Scroggins.

"How ya hangin'?" Scroggins asked.

"Surviving," Porcher responded.

One game into the season and the Lions are already gasping for air.

But one positive emerged from another lifeless Lions season opener: Only 60 more quarters remain.

SEPT. 16, 2002

Even by Lions' standards, this loss is embarrassing

CHARLOTTE, N.C. — The smoky clouds hovering over Ericsson Stadium were attributed to the remnants of a tropical depression, but they also were reminders of the stench rising from the football depression on the field.

It was the familiar aroma of another Lions season spontaneously combusting. And the fumes from tempers burning and false hope collapsing into ashes are suffocating the franchise.

This is the lowest the organization has ever fallen. The Lions are without question the worst team in the NFL, an indignity wrested away from Carolina in an embarrassing 31-7 loss.

The steady rain added to the funereal mood. The players and coaches stood mummified on the sidelines as the second half unfolded, reflecting a quiet resignation that nothing's getting better. They resembled a team that's gradually giving up on its coach.

Afterward, Marty Mornhinweg had the look of a man in the

crosshairs, dodging reporters' questions so as not to provide a target for what will be the most-asked question in Detroit: How much longer does Marty have?

"I'm fine with Marty," team president Matt Millen said. "I'm not fine with how we're playing. We've got to re-examine everything from the top on down, and you better know that that also includes me. This was ugly. It was pathetic. We need to take a step back and take an assessment of where we are."

Only two games old, and already the season is beyond salvaging. And Mornhinweg's job is beyond saving.

Millen professed no lack of confidence in his coach, but he has been around the game long enough to understand the inevitability of the snowball rolling down the hill. It doesn't stop. It doesn't reverse course. It just gains size, strength and speed as it approaches its destination, steamrolling all in its path. It's just a matter of time before Millen pushes Mornhinweg in its path. He will have no alternative.

But Millen must be equally accountable for this clown act masquerading as a professional football team.

"I understand everyone's frustrations, and I know that it's going to be pointed in my direction," Millen said. "I'm OK with that. But I still believe that we're going to start playing better. We're going to look into everything and see how it goes, but it's not pretty right now."

In successive weeks, the Lions have attained a new level of dazed-and-confused. People want answers, and soon they will demand heads.

"I'm past disgusted," Millen said. "I don't know what it is that comes after that. I believe that we have the talent on this team to do better than what we have, but we haven't done anything right in these first two games. We've given up 80 points, haven't forced one sack or caused one turnover. And today we couldn't complete a pass.

"The best thing about this team right now," Millen said, "is the new stadium."

What's sad is, he wasn't joking.

SEPT. 19, 2002

Ford Jr. makes the call: Harrington gets early start

So now it's Mike McMahon's fault. When all else fails, change the quarterback. That has been the Lions' strategy for 40 years in their perennial attempt to mine a tiny grain of hope from an otherwise hopeless predicament. Change the quarterback and, miraculously, a slow-footed defense gains speed and the aged turn youthful. Change the quarterback and, magically, all the other ailments are cured.

That's what the Lions want you to think with Joey Harrington's coronation. Marty Mornhinweg now has had twice as many starting quarterbacks (four) as career victories (two). But this is nothing more than a diversionary tactic, a smoke screen designed to divert your attention from what's really troubling this franchise.

There could be only one benefit in starting the third pick in the draft three games into his NFL career, and that would be avoiding the national humiliation of a sold-out crowd in Ford Field's debut booing the home team before the national anthem.

This was the equivalent of waving the white flag. The winless Lions have conceded the season after just two games, acknowledging positional deficiencies so great that matching last season's two-victory total might prove challenging. This franchise possesses only two viable assets — a new stadium and a new quarterback — both too fresh to be tarnished by an inglorious past, so they will showcase them simultaneously against Green Bay in the home opener.

This was a panicked move, and nobody's sweating the fallout more than William Clay Ford Jr. There are suspicions that the vice chairman's fingerprints are all over this decision. Some players suggested that Harrington's promotion was an edict from upstairs. Perhaps Mornhinweg had no alternative.

"This is obviously a decision that came from the top," said offensive lineman Tony Semple, who has endured numerous quarterbacking changes during his days in Detroit. "And it's something that has to be respected. As players, we don't ask why or judge. It's our job to play. Who it came from or why it came doesn't matter from the players' standpoint. We know that it's just a part of the business."

Starting Harrington temporarily cools the public heat on Ford because, as pathetic as the team as a whole looks, everyone will fixate on Harrington. And in the gullible fans' minds, he will do no wrong, even if he occasionally throws to the wrong receiver.

It is believed that it was the younger Ford's decision to draft Harrington, much to president Matt Millen's dismay, as was plainly evident when an agitated Millen addressed reporters soon after the selection. There are whispers that Ford did an end-around behind Millen's back and went directly to the team's scouts to get their input on whom they thought was the third-best player available in the draft. And when the scouts told Ford it was the Oregon quarterback, he apparently overruled Millen, who wanted more immediate help from the third pick, either a cornerback like Quentin Jammer or a trade down for additional choices.

But nobody wants to think about potential front-office fissures now. Nor do they want to be bothered with the harsh realities of a team that has won only twice in its last 18 tries. All they want is to dream. They want to fantasize. They want to pretend things are better than they actually are.

Rather than feeling sorry for McMahon, perhaps we should reserve our sympathy for Harrington. His nightmare is just beginning.

NOV. 11, 2002

Sure, they lost again, but look on the bright side

GREEN BAY, Wis. — Nobody said it would be easy, but a promise is a promise.

I vowed to find something positive to say about the Lions' annual pilgrimage to the high cheese holy land. After all, the game's outcome wouldn't matter because expectations were minimal. What's another road loss when the tally's up to 13 straight?

It would be about looking at the bigger picture, not dwelling on insignificant minutiae like first downs. First downs are overrated.

And how can you not respect how the Lions receivers strive for perfection? Either the quarterback delicately places the ball precisely into their hands without the need to break stride, or they're not going to bother catching passes. What's wrong with demanding a higher standard?

And how about the offense awakening from its six-game, second-half slumber with a hard-earned, fourth-quarter touchdown, turning this into a four-possession game with 10 minutes left. That's pride. That's professionalism. That's . . . that's . . . that's about as far as I can go until I get a couple of aspirin.

"How many other teams, if they were in that kind of situation, would have packed it in and let the score get to 60-7?" Lions quarterback Joey Harrington asked. "We're not going to do that. I'm proud of the way we kept fighting. That tells you something about a team."

It tells you that this team is full of cra— . . . excuse me, full of creativity in finding ways to learn from adversity. The Lions' 40-14 loss to Green Bay was an opportunity for growth, a measuring stick of how much work remains before this team becomes playoff-worthy. But it shouldn't detract from the strides already taken.

This is a franchise on the way up and I . . . I . . . I CAN'T KEEP UP THIS CHARADE ANY LONGER! I TRIED! I REALLY TRIED! BUT IT'S IMPOSSIBLE TO TURN THIS REFUSE INTO CHICKEN SALAD! DROPPED PASSES! POOR DECISIONS! POOR EXECUTION! CAN YOU IMAGINE WHAT BRETT FAVRE WOULD HAVE DONE WITH TWO GOOD KNEES?

YOU'VE GOT COACHES AND PLAYERS LOOKING FOR WAYS TO JUMP-START A STALLED OFFENSE! HERE'S A SUGGESTION: TRY INVESTING IN FREE-AGENT RECEIVERS WHO ARE PRONE TO CATCHING THE BALL!

Ah, that felt better.

NOV. 25, 2002

Marty's lesson: 'Tis better to receive than kick off

CHAMPAIGN, Ill. — The only breeze stronger than the one the Lions had at their backs in overtime against the Bears will be the growing gale of discontent that just might blow Marty Mornhinweg out of town.

We already knew the Lions lacked talent. But this comical chapter confirmed that their head coach lacked a clue.

What was Mornhinweg thinking when the Lions won the overtime coin toss and elected to kick off? Even if there is a monsoon blowing through Memorial Stadium, you shouldn't voluntarily surrender the ball. Not when your defense relinquished 10 points in the last 2½ minutes of regulation. Not when your team is looking for new and creative ways of losing a 14th straight road game. And not when a suddenly revitalized opposing quarterback believes he can leap tall buildings in a single bound.

"I couldn't believe that they didn't take the ball," said Chicago middle linebacker Brian Urlacher.

He wasn't alone. There were plenty of stunned and confused faces on the Detroit sideline when the Lions opted to take the wind at their backs.

In fact, Mornhinweg probably kicked the wind out of his chances of getting a third year. How can ownership's confidence in the coach — and the team president who hand-picked him — not erode after a 20-17 loss that solidified this franchise's claim as the league laughingstock?

This was the Lions' best chance for a victory for the remainder of the season. The Bears were already two months into hibernation, one defeat shy of a franchise-worst ninth straight loss. The Lions had a 10-point lead with less than three minutes remaining in regulation. And they blew it.

All the chatter about needing to work harder and maintaining poise is falling on deaf ears. You start wondering if even the Lions believe their recycled spin. How can a team exhibit poise if its coach freezes in the clutch?

Mornhinweg contradicted his rationale for taking the wind when he didn't decline a Chicago holding penalty that would have given the Bears a fourth-and-eight decision at the Lions' 35.

"I thought it was reasonable to expect them to try a 52-yard field goal, even with that wind," he said.

THEN WHY NOT LET THEM TAKE THAT CRAZY GAMBLE? WHY LET THEM OFF THE HOOK?

Apparently nobody on the Lions' sideline noticed Chicago's Paul Edinger practicing 40-yard kicks into the wind as the team captains met at the 50 for the overtime coin toss. Edinger barely cleared the crossbar then, so how was it "reasonable" to expect him to nail one from 52?

"Paul is very frank about what he can and can't do on the field," Chicago coach Dick Jauron said. "He didn't feel like anything beyond the 26-yard line into that wind was reasonable. The 26 was his outer limit."

Jauron hinted that he probably would have gone for it on fourth-and-eight had the Lions declined the holding penalty, but he had punter Brad Maynard on the field. And Mornhinweg eventually conceded that he probably erred in taking the penalty and giving the Bears another crack at a porous Lions secondary.

But, Marty, didn't you say you took the wind because you had faith in your defense? And wasn't this the same defense that was on the field for 8½ of the last 10 minutes of the fourth quarter because it couldn't make a stop, even on fourth-and-20?

"I really had confidence in our players at that point," he said. "It's a controversial call, it really is, but again, the wind did play a big, big factor in that game. If I had to make that call again, I'd do it again."

And the result would be the same.

A day later, Drew Sharp visited the Lions' training facility in Allen Park. Here's a portion of what he found there:

Owner William Clay Ford, making a rare appearance at practice, sat with president Matt Millen and observed the workout from a second-level balcony, insulated from the fire that was once again directed at the franchise. They avoided questions from reporters, leaving Mornhinweg alone to twist in the wind.

How appropriate.

It wasn't a comfortable sight watching Mornhinweg squirm, and finally he cracked from the third degree with the rubber hose and gave reporters the mea culpa they wanted.

"It didn't work, OK," he said, exasperated. "It didn't work. It was a mistake. Put it on me. Put that one on me. I'll take it."

It was his only alternative.

JAN. 28, 2003

Millen sticks his neck out, fires Mornhinweg

The bar is . . . closed. But the graveyard remains open. The latest casualty in a five-year plan that has taken five minutes of thought was interred in the sacred Lions burial ground.

Here lies the career of Marty Mornhinweg.

Who now passes through the pearly gates of Lions heaven.

He thought he would take Detroit to the Super Bowl.

Instead, he took the wind and went 5-27.

The tombstones are multiplying with cryptic regularity. First came the Tobin du jour. Then vice president Kevin Warren was axed, and now comes Mornhinweg's mercifully quick sacrifice, not even a month after his job was declared safe. All along, though, he was set up for a slow demise that seemed bound to drag through next season.

But the biggest grave remains unfilled.

And Matt Millen knows that, as the Lions' chief executive, he is just one more misstep away from stumbling into the pit.

Has there ever been a more transparent performance from a local sports figure than what Millen delivered when asked to explain how Mornhinweg fell out of favor in four weeks? Nothing but an empty suit stood behind the podium. No substance. No accountability. No reason to think that the novice who screwed up his first key hiring has somehow gained the experience to fulfill his championship mission.

"I have a plan in place," Millen pleaded at his news conference, "and you're going to have to trust me."

During a one-on-one conversation afterward, I asked Millen why any football fan in Detroit should have the slightest confidence that he has the tiniest clue about what he's doing.

"That's a difficult question to answer," he said, "because people are going to understandably look at the record. But I think I've learned. I think I'm much better at handling the various aspects of this job now than I was when I first started. And I'm determined to get this thing right."

Millen knows he will get to hire only one more coach, and common sense would tell him to cast his fate with a proven winner.

The job is Steve Mariucci's if he wants it. It's that simple.

Mornhinweg was still the Lions' coach on New Year's morning because Mariucci didn't want the job after being approached near the end of the regular season. Mariucci thought he would receive a contract extension from the San Francisco 49ers or, at the very least, finish his current deal at $2.2 million a year.

You don't jettison a coach 27 days after you tell him he's safe unless you clearly have identified his successor. Millen understood that the only thing worse than paralyzing his franchise with a lame-duck head coach for another season was to permit his No. 1 coaching choice to play the free-agent market while the Lions weren't shopping.

For a change, the Lions took the initiative. They saw something they wanted, and they will go after it hard — even if that means making a sham of the NFL's initiative to hire more minority coaches.

The Lions say former Minnesota coach Dennis Green is on the short list, but Green has been available all season, and he had expressed interest in the job weeks earlier to close associates. Millen already could have had Green in place as his head coach if he really wanted him.

The league's intentions are sincere, but the NFL isn't helping the cause of black coaches like Green by threatening sanctions against teams that snap up established Super Bowl champions, as Dallas did with Bill Parcells without looking at other candidates.

A lesser example is Mariucci, who never took the 49ers to a

Super Bowl but would give Millen and the Lions something they lack — credibility.

"We respect and support the league initiative," Millen said, "and we intend to go through the process."

But you can see through Millen's words just as you can see through his actions during his two years at the Lions' helm. His reign has been more lip service than results and substance. He will play along with the NFL minority name game and pacify Johnnie Cochran by giving longtime assistant coach Sherman Lewis a token interview. Whatever it takes.

And that's fine, as long as he gets Mariucci to sign on the dotted line.

Millen knows that failure is no longer an option. He has lopped off the heads of those around him, leaving only one for the guillotine — his own. The graveyard is growing, and unless he makes the right move this time, Millen will be in it.

JAN. 29, 2003

The last laugh belongs to Marty

They arrive confident, only to leave confused. But through his shock over no longer coaching the Lions, Marty Mornhinweg can find solace in that he's free. He's liberated. He has been emancipated from the never-ending circus act in which offensive linemen draped in yellow flags spring out of the trunk of a Volkswagen to the dancing cadence of a calliope.

Mornhinweg was warned when he arrived in 2001 that he was working for a bizarre franchise in which bizarre things occurred for bizarre reasons.

"And we're in the middle of one right now," Mornhinweg said on his front door step, the day after being fired.

Always classy if not competent, Mornhinweg refused to get into a spitting match with his former employers. But there were some subtle digs, as if to suggest that though his many critics might not think he's a good head coach, he knows how a good organization operates, and the Lions' don't qualify.

He stroked his chin, making sure everyone present noticed the

Super Bowl ring he earned as Green Bay's quarterbacks coach six years ago. He has seen the difference between consistently successful NFL franchises and those that hold victory parades for 8-8 seasons.

"I really hope that one day I'll see the Detroit Lions on that platform holding up the Super Bowl trophy," Mornhinweg said. "Maybe it'll happen before I'm done coaching."

Translation: maybe in another 30 years.

A man of leisure now, Mornhinweg couldn't recall the last time he could sit at the dinner table in the middle of the afternoon with a cup of coffee. Instead of preparing for the college draft, he was preparing his youngest son for a tonsillectomy.

"I'm disappointed that I couldn't finish what I started," he said. "That bothers me more than anything else."

But this is the nature of the beast, so the man shouldn't be pitied. Mornhinweg deserves to be searching the coaching classifieds because this is a result-oriented business. The legacy of his brief tenure is a winless road record, symbolized by the infamous overtime against the Chicago Bears in Champaign, Ill.

At least Mornhinweg said he had learned from that mistake.

"Well," he said, "when you're going to take the wind in overtime, you'd better have a damned good defense."

Mornhinweg laughed along with everyone assembled. It's easier finding humor when you're no longer wearing the clown suit.

He was disappointed. Deep down, he was probably steaming mad that promises were broken and assurances conveniently forgotten when the availability of his former boss, deposed San Francisco coach Steve Mariucci, suddenly made him expendable.

The Lions' owners gave Mornhinweg their word that he wouldn't lose his job if the team faltered after they demanded that rookie quarterback Joey Harrington be promoted to the starting lineup before the third week of the season.

There were fissures in his relationship with team president Matt Millen that widened in the days leading up to his dismissal. There were doubts about the manpower in the personnel department and questions about the organization's structure. Millen still has a seat at the poker table because he had something Mornhinweg lacked — an ace up his sleeve, the Mariucci card. Millen's saving grace in the eyes of owner William Clay Ford has always been that, if the opportunity arose, he could deliver Mariucci with a phone call.

And now Millen is forced to play that Mooch card.

"Disappointment is a part of this game," Mornhinweg said. "It's about the highs and lows, and I've been to both. But it's also about picking yourself up and looking for the next challenge. We don't know right now what that next challenge is going to be."

He's young. He's optimistic. And unlike other former Lions coaches, he has his sanity. But he might not get another opportunity as an NFL head coach, continuing an inglorious history started when Ford became the Lions' sole owner in 1964. Once you have coached the Lions, you never get another head-coaching opportunity in the NFL.

But it could be worse. Don McCafferty dropped dead of a heart attack just days into training camp in 1974.

"I'm not going into hiding," Mornhinweg said. "I'm going to be around. I'm going to resurface. I'm thankful that I got the chance at this unique opportunity, and my family and I are grateful for everything."

He should be particularly grateful that he now can laugh along with everyone else about his former team.

FEB. 5, 2003

Gulp! By hiring Mariucci, Lions did something . . . smart

You will have to forgive any disjointed prose because I'm still a little woozy, still susceptible to blacking out at the mere suggestion that the Lions have done . . . the Lions have done . . . (You can do it, Drew. Just think about baseball) . . . the Lions have done . . . the right thing.

Ouch!

Do you have any idea how much it hurts to concede that?

Anyone who has grown up with the legacies of Tommy Hudspeth and Jeff Komlo, among the many symbols of Lions futility, understands that questioning this organization's judgment is a natural reflex. Initiative has long been a foreign impulse with these guys. Always reactionary, ever willing to lag two steps behind the rest of the pack, this franchise's unflinching philosophy through four decades of mediocrity has been to reach the bare minimum. Strive just enough to whet appetites and stir hopes.

But busting the bank to land Steve Mariucci revealed a never-before-seen aggressiveness and, dare I say, foresight.

The Lions knew all along whom they wanted, much to the disappointment of political correctness, and they refused to hedge when the dollar figures skyrocketed. The boldest statement owner William Clay Ford ever delivered in his 40 years of competitive stagnation was to green-light Mariucci's five-year, $25-million contract.

That translates into a million dollars for each victory he can expect next season.

The deal puts Mariucci atop the NFL coaches' salary scale with Steve Spurrier of Washington. But the real significance is that it places the Lions in a strange new light. It's the first time in my 42 years that I can recall the Lions' doggedly pursuing and successfully securing someone the rest of the NFL wanted.

Give them credit for not letting the price scare them away from what they wanted at the top of the menu, instead of settling for the more affordable special of the day.

Mariucci is the flavor of the week. He's the hot candidate. He could have relaxed and rejuvenated himself for another year, with the San Francisco 49ers picking up the tab. Absence makes football hearts grow fonder, and Mooch could have played the field until other suitors, possibly Chicago, Miami or Arizona, entered the bidding next winter.

The Lions' preemptive strike avoided that. And in the process, the Lions pretty much made this Mariucci's team.

You don't commit $5 million annually for five years for just a coach. You're paying for a presence, an identity you think fills a vacuum.

Saying hello to Mariucci is the equivalent of saying good-bye to Matt Millen.

Contrary to Millen's insistence when he dismissed Marty Mornhinweg, Mariucci is now the lead dog. He had the leverage. The Lions couldn't afford to let him slip through the cracks at the last second over a hazy interpretation of his power. They gave him what he wanted. Mariucci will have considerable influence over personnel. Even more important, he will have vice chairman William Clay Ford Jr.'s ear — a privilege Millen lost barely a year into his tenure.

The Lions had no choice but to acquiesce to Mariucci's demands. They couldn't get anyone of a comparable pedigree to interview with them because those prospective candidates knew Mooch was the Lions' first and only choice, creating some customary nervousness because, after all, these are the Lions.

And had they blown this deal, it would have been the darkest moment yet for a franchise perpetually lost in a black hole. But Mooch is coming, and that unusual sensation coursing through your veins is the realization that maybe — just maybe — the Lions are ready to lead rather than follow.

History remains a formidable foe for this franchise. Knowledgeable people have come here only to see their careers and reputations disintegrate. And who's to say Mariucci won't meet a similar fate? He might prove to be nothing more than an average coach propped up for six years by a great organization in San Francisco.

But verdicts are reached only on what we know. And what we know is that this is the most eagerly anticipated coaching arrival since the Red Wings lured Scotty Bowman out of retirement in 1993. Perhaps this more closely resembles 1979, when the Tigers aborted the Les Moss experiment weeks into his first season after Sparky Anderson expressed interest in becoming their manager.

Unlike Bowman and Anderson, Mooch comes to town without world championship credentials. But he's taking over an organization with no playoff credentials — just one victory since 1957.

Even so, his arrival has earned something perhaps even more miraculous than a second playoff victory in five decades would be.

And that's a pat on the back from me.

CHAPTER FOUR

There must be a painless way to turn this heart back to stone

OCT. 19, 1998

Marathon man goes the distance, inspiring others

Beverly Knight knew she needed a miracle. The 46-year-old from Haslett, Mich., was the last of the 2,358 entrants in the Detroit Free Press/Flagstar Bank International Marathon to enter the Detroit-Windsor tunnel, seven miles into the race. A police officer, trailing in his cruiser, offered to give her a ride up to the finish at Hart Plaza.

"I was close to taking him up on it, too," she said. "This was my first marathon, and I just didn't think that I had it in me."

The miracle Knight needed was just ahead in the tunnel, a solitary figure with a determined gait.

"I came up to him and asked him if I could walk with him, and he said that would be fine," Knight said. "And then when he told me he was Jim Ramsey, I couldn't believe it. I had heard and read so much about him. And he told me he was going to make sure that we finished together."

And they did. Hand-in-hand they approached Hart Plaza just before 3:30 p.m., nearly eight hours after they started, about six hours after the men's and women's winners. But the final two finishers of the Free Press marathon might have been the proudest, as well.

Ramsey is indeed a miracle. At 90, he was the oldest to participate in a Free Press marathon. Ramsey was a veteran of more than 20 marathons. And as a tribute to his recently deceased wife, he wanted to run just one more. And run he did — for the first mile.

But the early morning rain and wind in his face quickly reduced Ramsey to a slow, sustained walk. And even that became a struggle at times. There were several occasions along the final five miles when it seemed neither Ramsey nor Knight could go any farther. Then they would grab each other's arms, one seemingly trying to keep the other moving forward.

A friend of Ramsey's, Dave Mitchell, followed the two in his vehicle as they inched down Mack Avenue. Protecting them from oncoming traffic, he watched and waited in case the additional physical toll that came with each mile became too much for them to endure.

"I was so glad to have Beverly with me and to keep me company," Ramsey said. "It was going to be tough for me to try and do this alone."

It would have been impossible for Ramsey to be alone. There

isn't a soul among running circles in this city who doesn't know — and doesn't adore — Jim Ramsey. Well-wishers cheered him on during the 26.2-mile course. Some walked part of the race with him. Four of his six children and several of his grandchildren and great-grandchildren greeted him with cheers and signs when he approached the 21-mile marker on East Grand Boulevard.

And you can only wonder how often runners asked race volunteers about Ramsey's whereabouts on the course.

"There aren't many people associated with this race who don't know me," Ramsey said. "I've been a very lucky man. I have plenty of good friends and family who look out for me. That's what keeps me thinking young and acting like a 70-year-old."

But his greatest impact on this day was on his newest friend.

"He's my inspiration," Knight said. "I always thought it would be an honor to just meet Mr. Ramsey, but to have the chance to walk with him is more than I could ever hope for. I really didn't think I was going to have the strength to just finish. But we're going to do it. We're going to finish, aren't we, Mr. Ramsey?"

"And we're going to catch up and pass the next walkers up ahead," replied Ramsey, with his customary wry wit.

There was no laughter two months earlier when Julia, Ramsey's wife of nearly 70 years, died. Ramsey thought his long-distance days were over. It had been three years since his last marathon. But he decided to try once more. And one more marathon became one final tribute.

"My wife and my family have always been the inspirations for what I've done in my life," Ramsey said. "I worked for 40 years in the auto parts supplies business. I paid for all six of my kids to go to college. But after I got tired of working, I needed something to do, so my wife thought I should start running. She was probably joking, but I took it seriously."

Ramsey's children had reservations about their father taking up such a taxing activity at an advanced age. But after seeing the benefits, especially in Ramsey's forever-positive outlook on life, they also became involved in the sport. Two of Ramsey's daughters, 54-year-old Brenda Njiwaji and 52-year-old Jeannette Browner, ran in the marathon and were waiting at Hart Plaza, along with about a dozen other family members, when Ramsey and Knight arrived.

At 73, Ramsey ran a marathon in the amazing time of 4½ hours. The garage of his Detroit home is filled with 20 years worth of trophies, awards and commendations. But perhaps the greatest honor Ramsey ever received was when one of his great-granddaughters draped a medal around his neck after he crossed the finish line Sunday.

"I've been blessed with a great family and great friends," Ramsey said. "It's been a beautiful life."

JULY 26, 2002

History lesson hits home for Lloyd Carr

CHICAGO — Who vacations at Omaha Beach? A former American history teacher hoping to widen his perspective while lessening his insecurities, Lloyd Carr walked the shores of Normandy, visiting the site of the Allies' D-Day invasion on June 6, 1944, considered the turning point of World War II.

"I knew that it would be a growing experience for me," Carr said. "I just didn't know that it would be as emotionally profound an occurrence as it was for me. I mean, when you stand before those 9,000 American crosses at the cemetery, your definition of what pressure is shrinks to nothing."

Carr, beginning his eighth season as Michigan football coach, is still picking splinters from his hindquarters from the New Year's Day 2002 pounding Tennessee gave his team. He has gotten a few too many early-morning telephone calls from police questioning his players' off-field conduct, and his crowning achievement — the 1997 national title — gets pushed further into the recesses of history with each Citrus Bowl appearance.

But Carr appears more at ease than at any other time since he succeeded Gary Moeller in the spring of 1995. He thinks retracing the steps of D-Day better crystallized his appreciation for opportunities in life. Time is too short to waste on needless worry, waging battle with those perceived to be working against him.

"What's the worst thing that can happen to me as a coach?" he asked.

"Getting fired?" I replied.

"That's all," he said. "Losing a job is not losing your life."

This isn't your customary, introspective, post-9/11 reflex. Carr is well-versed on the details of the Allied assault. He had planned his trip well before the 9/11 terrorist attacks, but those events reaffirmed its purpose.

A British tour guide took him to a crumbled estate where Allied Supreme Commander Dwight Eisenhower held strategic meetings. He walked along the sands at Omaha, stunned at the extent the Germans fortified the beach. After grasping the immensity of the mission awaiting the Allied forces, Carr ventured to the cemetery and saw the enormity of its cost. It left him trembling.

"Those men died then so that we can stand here today and

quibble about football games," Carr said. "Think about that for a second, and you realize that something doesn't make much sense. We complain. We don't get along. We allow ourselves to get upset over things that are said or written that — when looking at the larger picture — are pretty trivial."

Carr, 57, becomes a little surer of foot with each passing year, more comfortable at lobbing a little levity during normally dry news briefings. He boasted that one of his players, Joe Sgroi, will attend Michigan Law School, saying that he turned down a chance to go to Harvard because he wanted a better education.

But Carr's Omaha Beach visit hasn't tempered his competitiveness. It bothered him that the 2001 Wolverines had the school's worst season-ending stretch since 1984, when Bo Schembechler went 6-6. Michigan badly lost its last two games and was a fluky, last-minute bounce at Wisconsin from its first three-game losing streak since 1979. The Wolverines finished 8-4.

Carr recalled a climactic moment from what is naturally one of his favorite movies, "Saving Private Ryan," which begins with vivid images of the guts and gore at Omaha Beach. Before he takes his last breath, the Army captain who rescued Ryan tells him to live up to the sacrifices made in his name.

Standing before those 9,000 sacrifices along the French coast emboldened Carr's resolve to make sure the young men in his charge fully appreciate the boundless possibilities ahead of them. Life was once confined almost entirely to football, but it took an enlightening trip to remind a history buff of the relative insignificance of a game.

9/11, TAKE ONE: SEPT. 12, 2001

Best response to terrorism is to bring back the games

It's somewhat disrespectful of the breadth of the horror even to think about the triviality of kids' games played by grown men. But sports, normally a nice diversion, was a small part of the American lifestyle that crumbled into dust along with the World Trade Center towers.

The lights went dark on the sports world as a stunned nation gradually came to grips with the coordinated terrorist attacks that would claim thousands.

Who really cares right now that Barry Bonds rests seven homers away from No. 70? So what that the Lions are embarking on another new quarterback experiment, that Michigan is recovering from a harsh loss or that Michigan State's punt coverage can't block anybody?

Context, sadly often missing in sports, struck with blunt force at the sight of a city's signature skyline falling, and of frightened people jumping 80 stories to their deaths.

"How can you possibly talk sports on a day like this?" said WXYT-AM's Kevin Wall, host of "Wall to Wall Sports." "Taking calls on whether Marty Mornhinweg did the right thing in benching Charlie Batch is certainly pointless in light of all that's happened."

Sports assumed its proper place in a national emergency. It took a back seat, with players, coaches and fans watching in stunned silence like everyone else. Sports-talk radio stations dumped regular programming, simulcasting network TV coverage of events in New York and Washington. Major league baseball postponed its schedule, marking the first time since the D-Day invasion of Normandy on June 6, 1944, that outside developments precipitated a shutdown.

The PGA Tour canceled first rounds of its events. Tiger Woods called the tragedy a "sad, sad day in America" upon completing a practice round for the World Golf Championship in St. Louis.

"In the intent of security and out of a sense of deep mourning for the national tragedy that has occurred today, all major league baseball games for today have been canceled," commissioner Bud Selig said. "I will continue to monitor the situation from a baseball perspective on a daily basis and make ongoing decisions accordingly."

But it's important the games resume as quickly as possible. Terrorism promotes fear. That's its central objective. Terrorists want to see us sweat, to see us suspiciously watch those around us every time we board a plane or enter a building. These cowardly murderers attacked our sense of security. Nothing can be done to reverse the enormous human price paid, but they seek an equally huge emotional levy, as well. They want to see Americans dread participating in the simple pleasures that come so naturally for us. Like going to a ballgame on a late-summer evening.

The longer our normal lifestyles are interrupted, the sweeter the perceived victory in the sick minds of those who spearheaded these acts.

Selig's response takes you back to a similar numbing of the national soul — the assassination of President John F. Kennedy in 1963. The NFL's young commissioner, Pete Rozelle, didn't shut down the league, and games were played two days later.

The NFL played to small crowds and much criticism. But Rozelle thought the nation needed a momentary distraction from the shock and sadness. He often acknowledged later that his lone regret as commissioner was playing that weekend. Life can't immediately go on as if nothing happened with a tragedy of this magnitude.

When baseball resumes, stadium security will increase in the short term because cataclysmic events like this one leave scars. For a while, sports has been removed from its fantasy world and has collided with the reality that unfolded before our shocked eyes.

9/11, TAKE TWO: **SEPT. 15, 2001**

In Dearborn, life and football go on

Where were the little American flags? Wasn't there supposed to be a group hug during the national anthem? There was little to distinguish the Dearborn Fordson-Romulus football game played three days after the terrorist attacks from any game played last week.

And that was the idea. All anyone wanted to do was watch a game and take one tiny step toward returning to a regular way of life — if that's possible in the aftermath of 9/11.

Still, as Fordson — made up almost exclusively of Arab-American players — warmed up, a cowardly voice in the bleachers behind the Romulus bench at Carl Ross Memorial Field shouted:

"Why don't they go back where they came from?"

The attacks have spawned a different form of racial profiling.

"I was born in America, but my parents were Lebanese," said a Wayne County sheriff's deputy who requested anonymity. "I'm from here. I proudly served my country in the military. I became a law enforcement officer. But none of that matters. We're no longer Americans after what happened in New York. We're now Arabs first, and people just have these crazy ideas about us that the media perpetuates."

Despite the taunts of a few, the game was happily uneventful as Fordson won, 28-13.

A Romulus game usually employs two to three security guards, but the number was doubled as a precaution. Normally, the gate under the visitors' bleachers is unlocked so children can run under the bleachers during the game. But these aren't normal times, and the gate stayed locked.

There were no demonstrations or confrontations. If you didn't know the political and cultural dynamics entering the game, you wouldn't think this was any different from any other game between division rivals.

"Actually, we just did a few things differently than what we would do for an average game," security guard Tony McKinnie said. "We just want to make sure these people can watch a football game and these kids can play a football game in peace without anyone bothering them. They're hardworking Americans just like everyone else, but they're getting grouped together. It's stereotyping, plain and simple."

The masses bear the sins of the few. We're depressed. We're angry. And worse, we're helpless. We want vengeance for this horrific crime. But generic venting isn't the answer.

It was galling to witness a black man hurling epithets at the Fordson players and their families. We, of all people, should be the most sensitive to racial profiling, people singling out and scrutinizing others simply because they're suspicious of the way others look. The Fordson kids and their families are Americans like everyone else. They're hurting like everyone else.

"I was attacked by all this like every other American," said Hassan Makled, whose cousin is Fordson quarterback Ali Alammar. "And it's not right that people take it out on us and harass us. People are making quick judgments, but we had nothing to do with it. We understand that people are hurt and mad, but so are we. We want to see the people who did this terrible thing get the punishment they deserve."

It was important that the high schools assumed some veneer of normalcy — and football Fridays are a big part of that familiarity. We have witnessed courage at the highest level this week with those making the ultimate sacrifice. And in the context of not buckling to community fear and apprehension, Fordson displayed some measure of bravery in showing up and playing as scheduled. The easiest remedy would have been canceling the game, sparing players the unwanted attention.

The school day ended prematurely at Fordson. Someone called in a bomb threat in the morning. Officials didn't initially react. But the caller phoned two hours later, wondering why the school hadn't been evacuated.

"That was it," the deputy sheriff said. "At that point, we didn't want to take any chances. But you know what the sad thing is? The kids are starting to get used to the threats. And I'm just afraid that it's going to get worse as this thing escalates."

Football offered a momentary escape, but it's not going to get easier for these kids and their families. Their country is laying the foundation for war against those elsewhere who share their cultural heritage. But as the players banded together on the field, they wanted everyone to know that at this time of mourning, they walk shoulder-to-shoulder on another level.

First and foremost, they are Americans. And they're suffering like everyone else.

9/11, TAKE THREE: SEPT. 18, 2001

Same old song stirs brand new feelings

One nation, one voice — albeit off-key. But holding a tune wasn't as relevant as keeping the faith. Rarely have mere words resonated with such force of conviction.

"Gave proof through the night that our flag was still there," Hockeytown diva Karen Newman sang.

And the half-filled Joe Louis Arena roared. Those who brought flags waved them, and Newman enjoyed accompaniment through the remainder of her rendition of the national anthem. So what if the voices behind her were flat? The message was strong. A nation spiritually knocked down to its foundation seven days ago lifted itself to one knee, striving to regain some normalcy.

And a song we often take for granted gained renewed significance.

A little boy stood along the stairs, just a few rows from the ice.

He couldn't have been older than 6. A man, possibly his father, stood behind him. The boy placed his hand over his heart when the national anthem began. And before it was over, the little boy raised his hand and saluted.

The immediate image that came to mind was another national nightmare and another little boy saluting. And just as 3-year-old John Kennedy Jr. was too young to grasp the substance of his actions then, it's doubtful this little fella understood his motives now. But it tugged at the heart nonetheless.

Newman was initially approached about performing "God Bless America," which has become the unofficial battle cry of the last week. But she wanted to deliver "The Star-Spangled Banner" because it's emblematic of our most cherished symbol — our flag.

"I've never been more nervous before singing the anthem as I was tonight," Newman said. "I knew that the words were going to mean something much more this time than they normally do, and I wanted to make sure that I conveyed the emotion that everyone's been feeling the last week."

The Red Wings' exhibition opener against the New York Rangers was the city's first professional sports gathering since the terrorist attacks. The first opportunity to check the pulse. Were some a little jittery about assembling en masse? Or were we ready to bust loose after a solemn six-day vigil in front of our televisions?

Patriotism aside, exhibition hockey remains exhibition hockey. It didn't matter that the game marked Dominik Hasek's debut between the pipes in Detroit. There was no Steve Yzerman or Brett Hull or Mark Messier or Eric Lindros. But the players dropped the gloves a few times, eliciting some of the most spirited crowd reactions.

Sounds like things are getting back to normal.

"But what impressed me was that those who did come stayed for the anthem," Newman said. "Usually, they're making their first stop to the concessions at that time, but they knew it was important that we show that we're together."

It was good to finally cheer again at goals scored and punches thrown, and good to rekindle the celebration of those aspects of the American sports experience that should never be ignored.

9/11, TAKE FOUR: APRIL 24, 2002

Don't let gamesmanship undercut sportsmanship

A 33-year-old French citizen sat in a Virginia federal courtroom, calmly and coldly telling a U.S. district judge that he prayed for the destruction of the United States and, in effect, the free world. Where's the outrage? Where are the angry e-mails?

There's no question Zacarias Moussaoui, indicted for his suspected role in the Sept. 11 terrorist attacks, plays for the most evil team of all. Yet it was the booing of national anthems at two sporting events — games that remain basically meaningless and insignificant — that brought the most rancor this week.

Fans at the Palace booed during "O Canada" at a Pistons-Toronto Raptors playoff game. Later in the evening, fans in Vancouver booed during "The Star-Spangled Banner" before the Canucks played the Red Wings in their playoff series. And once again, perspective is lost as Detroit finds itself engulfed in a mindless border skirmish.

The playoff series are no longer the Wings versus Vancouver or the Pistons versus Toronto. They're the USA vs. Canada. Good friends and neighbors become heated rivals on the athletic stage one more time. Apparently, the Canadians believe the Americans hold a grudge for losing in the Olympic gold-medal hockey game earlier in the year at Salt Lake City.

There was as much interest in what happened before Game 4 at Vancouver's GM Place as in the game itself. Would a few more Canadians boo "The Star-Spangled Banner" in retaliation for the booing at the Palace?

There was a smattering of boos — and a good deal of cheers — at the beginning of Mark Donnelly's American rendition. All who were on their feet waved their white towels and the occasional Canadian flag when he went into the Canadian anthem. Clearly, the crowd knew that many would be watching.

Let's keep our eyes on the bigger puck, shall we, folks? It's ridiculous for any Canadian or American to suggest that the actions of a misguided few in Auburn Hills or Vancouver are indicative of two nations no longer willing to fight each other's battles or share each other's pain. But sports are often the repository for our collective irrationalities.

The national anthems remained a hot topic of conversation for the lunch crowd across the river in Windsor.

"That was real classy, what Detroit did," said Arthur Fournier of Windsor. "How dare they treat us in that way? But it shouldn't surprise anyone, should it? They were the ones who set the city on fire after they won the World Series, so there's a history of unsportsmanlike conduct."

Mary Williamson of Amherstburg, Ontario, can't understand why Detroiters would spit on her country when most of their beloved Red Wings are Canadian-born. "What bothers me the most are those people who choose to use a sporting game as a political forum," she said.

Pardon me while I chuckle over that last comment. Booing another country's national anthem is tacky and childish. But it's no less juvenile than the nationalistic venting that emerged from the Olympic figure skating scandal.

You remember Jamie Sele and David Pelletier, don't you? Weren't they just elected Canadian prime ministers? That incident epitomized the fusion between sports and politics. Americans and Canadians banded together to fight those evil Russians whose moral vacuum precipitated the supposed coercion of a French skating judge. What a heinous conspiracy!

Based on the media attention, so blown out of proportion, you would have thought a contested gold medal was more of a threat to the free world than what's unfolding in that Virginia courtroom.

"It's just sports, so why should anyone get too bent out of shape?" asked a Windsor resident named Marcel. "I spend a lot of time in Detroit. I'm a big fan. And if the Wings were playing Toronto, I'd probably boo, too, just because I'm a fan. There's too much other important stuff going on to worry about whether someone's cheering someone's national anthem."

Finally, a voice of reason escaping from the shrill. Sports remain nothing more than a diversion from the tumultuous world. Let's not lose sight of that as Detroit takes on Canada in hockey and basketball. Sadly, our world has become one in which sides must be chosen. It is us versus them on the only battlefield that really matters.

Try to remember the banner that drapes the duty-free building on the Detroit side of the border. It reads, "United we stand," with the U.S. and Canadian flags. Regardless of the shortsightedness of some, it stands for an ideal unaffected by the outcome of an inconsequential hockey or basketball game.

AUG. 29, 1997

Football takes backseat to brotherly love

Every time his telephone rings, Travis Reece's heart freezes for a split second — fearful that this might be the call. It might be the word from his family that his older brother, Chip, desperately needs something that perhaps only Travis can give him.

Chip might need one of Travis' kidneys.

If that becomes necessary, Travis wouldn't hesitate to undergo the delicate transplant procedure. Travis, a Michigan State senior fullback, volunteered as a donor in 1994 even though it could've meant sacrificing his football career and possibly a full college scholarship. It didn't matter because he thought his best friend's survival depended on him.

"There was no need for discussion," Travis said. "I'd give him my kidney in a second without thinking. He'd do the same thing for me."

In 1994, Chip fell ill. A victim of severe high-blood pressure, Chip's kidneys ceased functioning when he was 22. Three times a day, Chip is hooked to a dialysis machine, which does what his kidneys no longer can — remove wastes from his system. Yet courageously, Chip goes about his life as normally as possible. He doesn't like talking about his condition. He doesn't want anyone looking at him any differently. His family says his health remains good. But there's no avoiding the obvious. He needs a transplant. And a blood relative usually provides the best chance of organ compatibility.

"We've been waiting and praying for another donor," Travis said. "But if I got a call right before the biggest game of the year that he needed it, I'd be gone in a second. I love football, but . . ."

At that point, this 6-foot-3, 245-pounder, whose job is punishing defenders, collapses in his seat. His head falls into his hands and he softly sobs. There's no punishment more devastating than watching a loved one suffer.

For Travis, coming to Chip's aid could hardly be considered a sacrifice. As the younger brother, Travis was regularly in need of Chip's assistance while growing up in Detroit. Despite the age difference, the two were extremely close as children, virtually inseparable. That's why it doesn't surprise the Reece family that Travis could so easily say good-bye to a football future that could involve, at the least, a free-agent tryout at an NFL camp.

It's somewhat surprising that Travis is even preparing for his senior season. He was prepared to quit football after his freshman season so Chip could have the transplant. He eventually was talked out of it when doctors and his family assured him that Chip's condition wasn't immediately life-threatening.

That's when life became a game of wait-and-see. Chip's name was placed on a nationwide donor list. But since his life wasn't in immediate danger, he wasn't given top priority. In 1996, Chip was among the top 500 kidney transplant candidates. Now he's among the top 100. But doctors have set no timetable for when a donor must be found.

"His strength has kept me strong," said Travis, who attended Detroit Denby. "He doesn't let it get him down, and he's determined to live his life the best that he can. He's been an inspiration to me, and I just want to help anyway I can. There's nothing more important than family — and that includes football. If my family needs me, I'm there."

Travis' role on the football field is to create holes for MSU's bevy of tailbacks. Sedrick Irvin, Leroy McFadden and Marc Renaud dominate the ground game, leaving little recognition for the fullbacks. But Reece doesn't fret that he hasn't carried the ball much. He's just pleased that he can play.

"I understand that this might be my last year of playing football," Travis said, "and not just because of my brother. Everyone dreams about playing in the NFL, but that's no guarantee. You can't help but think about it, and it makes you appreciate this senior year because this might be it."

Travis' role has changed through the years. When Nick Saban arrived as coach, he briefly moved Travis to linebacker because the Spartans were lean at that position. Saban later moved him back to fullback, but Travis never lost sight of his most important role.

Football fans don't see Travis as an impact player, but they're not looking in the right direction. Reece may not be a star on the field, but his aura off it has never been brighter.

Travis Reece played for Georgia of the Arena football league during the 2003 season, and Chip remained in reasonably good health.

OCT. 9, 1998

George Webster walking tall despite hardships

The voice, weakened by a battle with throat cancer, resonates with a renewed vigor. The body, once a spectacular combination of power and grace, is a little more forgiving of the maladies that have plagued it in never-ending succession. The mere act of walking is better tolerated, in minute doses. But the greatest symbol of George Webster's resiliency is his spirit.

A year ago, Webster lay in a Houston hospital, occasionally falling prey to the fear that his health was irreversibly declining.

"I had gone through so much that you start to wonder if you were going to leave that hospital alive," said Webster, 52, who lives in Houston. "I had been there so long that the depression was almost as bad as actually being sick. It just seemed like it was just one thing after another. But, thankfully, I'm still here. And, even more thankfully, I'm overall feeling a little better."

Webster finally got out of the hospital, and this weekend he will return to his true home. Back to Michigan State. Back to where he remains a revered emblem of national football excellence. Back to where many still consider him the greatest ever to wear the green and white.

This will be a special homecoming weekend in East Lansing because Webster will be a focal point of the celebration. He will be the grand marshal of the homecoming parade down Grand River Avenue. He will address guests at the weekly Downtown Coaches luncheon. During the game against Indiana, Webster will be introduced at Spartan Stadium, and afterward he will be the featured guest at a reception at coach Nick Saban's home.

The theme of the homecoming parade is "Family and Friends Forever," a sentiment that bears more meaning with Webster's return.

"You have no idea how much I'm looking forward to getting back there and seeing my Michigan State family," said Webster, an All-America linebacker in 1965 and 1966. "And it is my family. I'm closer to the guys I played with at Michigan State than to a lot of the guys I played with in the NFL. It's always special to say hello to people you haven't seen in a while."

Even more important, Webster wants to say thank you.

Former Michigan State assistant coach Hank Bullough

spearheaded a drive that has raised more than $150,000 to help Webster since his physical and financial ills attracted public attention one year ago. A third of the money went toward repairing Webster's home, which was run down. The roof and floors were replaced, and central air conditioning was installed, helping make 100-degree summer days a little more bearable. Much of the rest of the money has gone toward reducing an eight-year medical bill that exceeded $250,000.

Unable to work for the past three years, Webster has no health insurance. Contributions as large as $1,000 from businesses to as small as $2.25 from grade-school students filtered in to Bullough throughout the year. Though Webster wreaked havoc with their team, many Michigan fans made sizable donations.

Webster's life has been one medical crisis after another since he was diagnosed with throat cancer in 1990. Chemotherapy damaged his vocal cords to the point that he was reduced to a raspy whisper for years. In July 1997, Webster was diagnosed with prostate cancer. While he went through radiation treatment, doctors noticed a number of open sores on his right foot, which refused to heal because of circulation problems in his legs.

A month after the prostate cancer diagnosis, doctors performed a double bypass on both of Webster's legs to alleviate the symptoms of hereditary circulatory disorder. Doctors told Webster the ulcerated sores would never heal completely, but they have improved enough in the last few months that walking isn't as painful as before.

"I'm getting a little bit of fight back in me," Webster said, triumphantly.

Mention the NFL to Webster and you can sense the ferocity that made running backs quake in their cleats. He remains angry that he fell short of qualifying for a pension because the league refused to recognize the time he played in the old American Football League. Earlier this year, the U.S. Supreme Court rejected Webster's suit against the NFL. The league provides Webster with a modest disability check, but he said he didn't receive his September check because he was unable to get to a doctor for the mandatory monthly physical.

"The NFL wants me to take a physical every month to prove that I'm still very sick," he said. "I'm going to be 53 years old soon. I've had cancer twice. I've got heart problems and circulatory problems. And they think that I'm suddenly going to get better so they won't have to pay me?

"Nobody in today's sports seems to care about what the others did years earlier to help them get those big million-dollar contracts they have now. There's no respect or appreciation for the past."

But there will be plenty of appreciation for the past this weekend. And Webster wants it known he holds an equal amount of gratitude for the present.

NOV. 9, 1998

Spartans pull together and pull off huge upset

COLUMBUS, Ohio — The man skeptics have denounced as being devoid of emotion and incapable of motivating young men suddenly found himself sitting atop the college football world. But the moment following Michigan State's 28-24 upset of top-ranked Ohio State was far from complete for coach Nick Saban. He couldn't find his teammate, the one person whose belief in his vision and principles never wavered.

"I've got to find Terry," Saban said, referring to his wife. "Where's Terry?"

An Ohio state trooper escorted Saban through a maze of media and delightfully stunned MSU athletic department officials to outside Ohio Stadium, where he was serenaded with screams — though, this time, not for his head. After hugging his mother, Mary Saban, he finally found Terry, tears streaming down her cheeks. Saban dropped his head on his wife's shoulder as they embraced. The aloof public facade faded, washed away by the magnitude of beating the nation's No. 1 team.

This was as pure and genuine as it gets in this business.

Unranked, unhealthy and usually unreliable, the Spartans weren't supposed to have a chance against Ohio State. The Buckeyes perceived the Spartans as nothing more than an appetizer before their annual season-ending feast against Michigan. And the Buckeyes swallowed hard and gagged. Their national championship dreams were dashed once again by competitors from north of the border. But this time, the party crashers wore green and white rather than maize and blue.

"I had to keep looking at the final score on the scoreboard for a couple minutes because I just couldn't believe it," said receiver Gari Scott, one of many major contributors. "We were already down by four touchdowns before we even took the field," receiver Plaxico Burress said of the point spread. "And then we wind up pulling off the biggest upset in the last few years against the No. 1 team in nation."

And on Ohio State turf, as well. Only twice in the 1990s had an unranked team upset the No. 1 team on the road. And Michigan State did it both times — the first coming at Michigan in 1990.

The Spartans (5-4) had toppled the kings, fully entitling them to the spoils that accompany such a coup. For at least one day, there wasn't a bigger football team anywhere in the country than Michigan State.

"This wasn't about vindicating ourselves," Terry Saban said. "This was about believing because we knew that we were doing this the right way. Criticism from fans and media is part of the business. But Nick and I have never stopped believing that something like this was possible."

Sniping at his critics would have been perfectly justifiable, but Saban played down his role, contending he did nothing to inspire this triumph. This was the players' victory.

"They won because they wanted it bad enough," Saban said. "They weren't going to let all the pregame predictions about how badly Ohio State was supposed to beat us affect their attitude. They weren't going to let the people we lost earlier affect their attitude."

Where did this inspired performance take seed? Go back two weeks to the Monday following an embarrassing loss in Minnesota, when co-captains Sedrick Irvin and Sorie Kanu called a players-only meeting before practice. As is usually the case with teams teetering on the verge of collapse, the locker room was split into factions. Fingers of blame pointed recklessly.

"We told them that the only football teams that are successful are the ones that conduct themselves like a family," Irvin said. "Like a group that loves each other and would do anything for the other. It's never 'you and I.' It's always 'we.' We needed to build a fence around ourselves, and we couldn't let anybody break through that fence. Not even our coaches."

Many will take away emotional souvenirs from one of the most special days in the 102-year history of Michigan State football. Perhaps it will be the 250 fans who greeted the team plane when it returned to Lansing, or the delirious students who blocked traffic outside the Duffy Daugherty Football Building while awaiting the players' arrival.

Irvin's memento is a piece of turf from one of the Ohio Stadium end zones. He's going to put the grass in a little vase. It will be a tiny keepsake of a dream realized and an even more important reminder that nothing's unattainable if, together, you want it badly enough.

SEPT. 2, 1999

MSU's Amp Campbell tackles fear head-on

EAST LANSING — Competitiveness sometimes blurs the already thin line separating courage from craziness. For some, adrenaline clouds common sense. But often there comes an epiphany, a moment of clarity when questionable actions seem justified. That moment for Amp Campbell came when he saw replays of Chris Spielman's neck injury.

But rather than scare him into having second thoughts about playing football again, it crystallized his commitment to see his comeback all the way through. Campbell will run onto the field in Michigan State's season opener against Oregon, nearly a year to the day after he suffered a serious neck injury against these same Ducks. He will start at left cornerback, his customary position.

Who knows how well Campbell will play, or how long his comeback from cervical fusion surgery will last? But his return is accomplishment enough.

Spielman, a former Lions linebacker, is the latest football player forced to retire because of a neck injury. He suffered a bruised spinal cord when he collided with another player in a Cleveland Browns exhibition game.

"I didn't want to see the replay of his injury on television at first," Campbell said, "because it was a frightening thing to watch. It made me think about what I'm doing. But I later told myself to look at it because I can't let myself get scared about something happening to me again."

Surgeons fused Spielman's third and fourth vertebrae in 1997. After sitting out the 1998 season to care for his wife, who was diagnosed with breast cancer, Spielman attempted a comeback. But his latest injury Saturday left him motionless on the field, with momentary paralysis.

"You have to accept your mortality," Spielman said. "And my mortality is today. I would love to keep playing, but I can't jeopardize my arms and my legs."

Campbell didn't want to hear those words, either. He underwent spinal fusion surgery in 1998.

"I know that it's hard for other people to understand why anybody would take a chance like this," Campbell said. "But I wouldn't be trying this if the doctors hadn't told me that physically I was 100 percent. The area that they operated on is even stronger now than it was before I got hurt. It just means a lot to me to try and play football again."

The strength in question is mental. Cornerbacks act on reflex. When they see a running back charging around the corner with a full head of steam, instinct tells them to put a helmet on him. There usually isn't time to think about hitting him the right way, with the head up.

As much as Campbell deserves applause for his heart, the temptation is to have his head examined. God already has smiled upon him once. Why take the chance that He might not be so forgiving the next time?

The answer lies in the essence of a competitive athlete. When the end finally comes, he wants it on his own terms. That's why Magic Johnson came back after his HIV-positive diagnosis, even though he was never the same player. That's why numerous other athletes keep competing despite the obstacles of age and injury.

Last season's most stirring moment in East Lansing came just before the Spartans took the field against Notre Dame in a prime-time national showcase. Campbell slowly walked into the locker room, his balance encumbered by a heavy brace that extended to his stomach. The Spartans were 0-2, and Campbell told them never to surrender.

There was hardly a dry eye among player or coach when Campbell finished. There might be tears again tonight, but it will be a festive outpouring.

"That's when it's really going to hit me," Campbell said. "When they introduce me to the crowd, I'm probably going to lose it then. At that time, I'll probably think about everything that I've gone through and my family has gone through in the last year."

His parents won't attend tonight's game because they were unable to get an inexpensive flight from Florida. But they will huddle around their television in Sarasota with relatives and friends, watching on ESPN. Campbell plans to find the nearest phone as soon as the game ends.

"My family and I have always been close," Campbell said, "but this whole experience has made us even closer. My injury made you appreciate everything in your life a lot more."

Campbell doesn't harbor any serious NFL aspirations. He already has earned his undergraduate degree. But he's assuming a risk most wouldn't take because he wants to prove to himself and others that refusing to let fear control his life makes perfect common sense.

In the fourth quarter, Campbell recovered an Oregon fumble and returned it 85 yards for the game-winning touchdown. He never made it to the NFL but returned to MSU and worked as a graduate assistant in the football program.

DEC. 25, 1997

Marshall celebrates victory of spirit in Motor City Bowl

Too often lost amid the materialistic trappings of Christmas is the true spirit of the day — family and faith. Marshall's football team is a testament to the resuscitative powers of both.

Dealt the cruelest hand of fate ever in American sports, Marshall could have disappeared from the football landscape in 1970, reduced to a tragic footnote. But a university and a community's indomitable will have taken the Thundering Herd to heights unequaled in the 1990s.

Thousands of Marshall fans at the Silverdome will celebrate the school's first bowl appearance in 50 years. Making the occasion even more special will be the appearance of one fan in particular.

Former assistant coach Red Dawson has attended only one Marshall game since 1970, but he will be on the sideline when the team plays Mississippi in the inaugural Motor City Bowl. Dawson has kept his distance, fearing he's a reminder of Marshall's darkest day.

A plane carrying 70 Marshall players, coaches and supporters and five crew members crashed while returning from a game Nov. 14, 1970, killing all aboard and making it the worst disaster in history involving an American sports team. Dawson, only 27 then, could have been on the flight, but head coach Rick Tolley wanted him to make a couple of recruiting visits. So Dawson drove — and heard the tragic news on his car radio.

"The worst part," Dawson told Time magazine, "was trying to tell the parents of players I recruited, people who had welcomed me into their living rooms, how sorry I was that their sons were on that plane."

The pain remains, seared into the psyche of Huntington, W. Va., a close-knit town of 60,000. Many residents experienced a personal loss that day, whether family or friend.

"This game is probably the biggest moment in Marshall's football history," said Marshall coach Bob Pruett, a former Thundering Herd running back, "and I told Red that he needed to be here, standing right beside me on the sideline. He's as responsible as anybody for the success Marshall has enjoyed. He's my good-luck charm."

And what a reversal of fortune Marshall has enjoyed. No football team in NCAA Division I-A or I-AA has been more successful in the 1990s than the Thundering Herd. It has 89 victories, four more than Florida State. That's especially impressive considering that Marshall had the worst record of the 1970s — only 22 victories — and ended the decade by losing 28 of its last 30 games.

"It's not farfetched to say our success was born from that tragedy," athletic director Lance West said. "It gave us the focus, commitment and sense of purpose to build a program that they would have been proud of. But nothing can ever completely erase the memories of that terrible day. Nor should it."

The driving rain that greeted the Marshall contingent at the Greenville, N.C., airport was indicative of the team's mood. The Herd had just lost to East Carolina, 17-14, its sixth defeat in nine games that season. The crew of the Southern Airways DC-9 had never landed at Huntington's Tri-State Airport, a tiny field that rested on a narrow plateau in the Appalachian hills.

The winds turned tricky and blew the plane slightly off its proper approach. It missed the runway and slammed into a hillside. Nine-year-old Keith Morehouse, the youngest of six children, was home with his family, watching "The Newlywed Game" on television, when the first bulletin hit the air.

"The memory remains so vivid," said Morehouse, a Huntington television sportscaster who doubles as the Thundering Herd's play-by-play announcer. "I remember hearing my mother letting out this horrifying shriek. And then it hit me. My father was on that plane."

Gene Morehouse was Marshall's sports information director.

"Initially, the only thing that registers in your mind is your own personal loss," Morehouse said. "But the older I got, the more I understood the gravity of the tragedy. It devastated the entire community, but at the same time, it galvanized it."

Morehouse was greatly tempted to flee Huntington and the constant memories. But, like Dawson, Morehourse realized Huntington was family — emotional scars and all — bound together by a terrible accident.

Morehouse met his future wife, Debbie, while in South Carolina a year after his high school graduation. Debbie had gone to another high school in Huntington. She lost both her parents in the plane crash.

"The whole experience bonded us all," said Pruett, an assistant at Marshall in 1979-82. "There was talk late in the '70s about us giving up. But had we thrown in the towel at that point, then those 75 people would have died in vain. We would have been remembered only for that tragedy rather than how a university, a football program and a community grew from that tragedy."

Thanks to an NCAA exemption that permitted the Herd to play

freshmen, who were then ineligible elsewhere, Marshall fielded a team in 1971. It won only two games but drew scores of accolades. One admirer wrote coach Jack Lengyel before the opener against Morehead State, saying that whatever the team's record, "you have already won your greatest victory by putting a varsity squad on the field."

It was signed by President Richard Nixon.

But the pain and guilt were too much for Dawson to bear. He left the team after the 1971 season. His love for Marshall football remained strong through the years, but it wasn't a passion displayed publicly. He stayed in contact with many of the families who lost sons in the crash. But he would rather concentrate on Marshall's present and future than fixate on the past.

At Pruett's insistence, however, he will walk the Silverdome sideline during the Motor City Bowl.

"We all would love nothing more than for Red to see a victory over Ole Miss," Pruett said. "That would be a great gift for him and for all of us if we can give it to him."

Sometimes the best Christmas present isn't found beneath a tree but in someone's heart.

DEC. 28, 2000

Black quarterbacks owe debt to those who have passed

Neither the name nor the historical significance registered with Byron Leftwich. Jefferson Street Joe Gilliam? Didn't he once fight Sugar Ray Leonard?

"Didn't I hear something or read something about him recently?" the Marshall quarterback asked.

Yes, it was his obituary. The former Steelers quarterback, 49 years old, died of an apparent heart attack Christmas Day, news ordinarily tossed aside except that it marked the passing of a trailblazing passer, one of the first black starting quarterbacks in the NFL, in 1974.

"That was a big thing back then," Leftwich said. "But it doesn't seem to be that big a deal now with so many black quarterbacks out there and doing well."

And though it's more timely for promising young collegians like Leftwich to look to guys like Donovan McNabb, Daunte Culpepper, Steve McNair and, yes, even Charlie Batch for inspiration and motivation, it's more important they recognize those a generation earlier who knocked on the door that the quarterbacks of today are knocking down.

It wasn't too long ago when pro scouts would longingly envision a 6-6, 240-pound physical specimen with quick feet and a strong arm like Leftwich as an NFL tight end or a heat-seeking linebacker.

"By the time he's done here," Marshall coach Bob Pruitt said, "he could be the best quarterback we've ever seen here. And you remember, we had (Chad) Pennington here the last three years. Byron's just scratching the surface of his ability. You've got to remember that he's only a sophomore."

But he was named most valuable player in the Thundering Herd's 25-14 Motor City Bowl victory over Cincinnati, their third straight victory at the Silverdome.

"I was forcing everything early," Leftwich said, "trying to do too much. Coach Pruitt told me at halftime that I needed to relax and let the game come to me and take what the defense was giving. I was a lot more comfortable in the second half."

Pruitt went to the no-huddle in the third quarter to limit Cincinnati's defensive substitutions, and Leftwich ably ran the offense, completing eight of his 11 third-quarter passes for 89 yards. He also displayed his athleticism, eluding two tacklers to gain 15 yards on a busted play that should have lost several yards. And on a big third-and-10 late in the third quarter, the pocket collapsed but Leftwich scampered free for 18 yards and a crucial first down.

The makings are there for Leftwich to become a first-round NFL selection, like Pennington in 2000. And this is but another reason to remember Gilliam. The gods gave him a thunderbolt for a throwing arm but, tragically, he wasn't equally disciplined.

He received death threats in 1974 when he started in place of Terry Bradshaw, who was holding out in a contract dispute. And then drugs dimmed what could have been a promising career in just two years. Wasting such gifts doesn't make Gilliam a hero, but if future players learn from his tribulations, his self-inflicted despair wasn't in vain.

Ironically, it was little more than a week before his death when Gilliam assembled with many of his former Steelers teammates for the final game at Three Rivers Stadium. Sober for three years, Gilliam counted his blessings after having recommitted himself to the game he never knew he loved so much until it was too late. When asked about Gilliam that day, Steelers president Dan Rooney remarked how those quarterbacks who followed in Gilliam's often unsettled footsteps owe him a debt of gratitude for helping break down a barrier.

History will unfold in the 2000 NFL playoffs when an unprecedented five of 12 starting quarterbacks will be black. Another, Baltimore's Tony Banks, is the Ravens' backup after losing his starting job to Trent Dilfer midway through the regular season.

Leftwich, who fancies himself as another Culpepper, is right in one important aspect. It isn't that big a deal these days seeing black quarterbacks grow in number and success, and that's perhaps the truest sign of progress. But you hope Leftwich and other up-and-comers like him never take for granted those who endure in anonymity, those who helped make their dreams possible.

Even those whose star barely flickered, like Joe Gilliam.

FEB. 13, 1999

Hot seat doesn't bother NASCAR champ Jeff Gordon

DAYTONA BEACH, Fla. — NASCAR novices aren't easily tolerated at Daytona. This is racing's high holy weekend, and the slightest suggestion of disrespect or lack of interest is sacrilege. The lesson is learned quickly if you're not careful.

As I picked up my rental car, the attendant asked who I thought would win the race. Mistakenly, I expressed my indifference, which produced a scary reaction not seen since the last time I told my wife that I forgot to take out the garbage before coming to bed. On second thought, how about that Jeff Gordon kid? It would be nice to see him win.

Mistake No. 2. It was about time to notify airport security in case fisticuffs ensued.

"Where are you from?" the attendant barked.

"Michigan."

"Figures then you'd like a Northern boy."

Why does Gordon inspire such animosity? He has been branded more style than substance, the beneficiary of a great racing team rather than great racing skill. His boyish good looks not only have made him a mainstream marketing presence — he has shared Pepsi commercials with Shaquille O'Neal — but also snared him a Miss Winston, NASCAR's annual reigning beauty queen, for his wife.

Gordon, 27, spent his teenage years in southern Indiana, which is about as good ol' boy as it gets. But it might as well be the North Pole for some NASCAR diehards. Gordon started racing go-karts and quarter-midgets when he was 5 in (perish the thought) California. His family moved to Indiana when he was 13 so he could further pursue racing.

But NASCAR historically is about family and tradition, a love that's passed down through generations. Many of the drivers have stock car racing ancestries, which give them royal bloodlines of sorts. Gordon is considered an outsider, an opportunist who aligned himself with the sport's top owner, Rick Hendrick, and crew chief, Ray Evernham.

He tries not to let the resentment bother him.

"I've always thought of it as flattering," Gordon said as he walked back to his garage at Daytona International Speedway, stopping frequently to satisfy autograph seekers. "It's a sign that you've been successful. Everybody wants to go after the guy on top, and we've been fortunate to have a lot of success.

"I'd rather deal with being the team to beat rather than the team that doesn't do anything. When we hear things from other teams, that's what we want to hear. That's what you want to be. You want to be the team to beat."

Dominance is certainly one cause for envy. Gordon had won nearly a third of his races in the last four seasons — 40 victories in 127 starts. No one else came close. In 1995, he became the youngest Winston Cup champion ever at 24. He was also the youngest three-time champion. And in 1998, Gordon tied Richard Petty's modern-era record of 13 victories.

Gordon said he's still looking for the perfect race — winning the pole, leading every lap and taking the checkered flag. And when he looks back to last year's historic season, he shakes his head in disbelief.

"I don't think we necessarily look at how can we win more than 13 races this year," he said. "I'm telling you, in this sport, if you win one race, you've done something. If you win five or more, then you're having one heck of an awesome season. Last year has made me more of a target this year, and I accept that."

Derisive signs were sprinkled through the speedway infield. Draped from one camper were two messages, one that read: "Forrest Gump drives the 24 car" — which is Gordon's. The other message implied that Gordon was better at a certain act than Monica Lewinsky. One person, who walked around with a T-shirt bearing an offensive reference to Gordon, was greeted with high-fives when he passed some members of driver Ken Schrader's crew.

For every person pulling for Gordon to win his second Daytona 500, probably two others want anybody but Gordon to win.

"They've got the best team and the best equipment right now," said Petty, a living legend who was the Gordon of his time. "But nobody stays on top all the time. The guy that beats Gordon, if he's not here now, he will be here.

"I've been there. I've been up and I've been down. (Dale) Earnhardt has been up and been down. Nobody stays on top for very long. Time takes care of it. The good Lord has a way of balancing everything out. Nobody gets to be a super-human forever."

The next great hope is the next branch of the Earnhardt racing tree, 24-year-old Dale Jr., who will race in five Winston Cup events this season, preparing for his full-time entry in 2000. So anticipated is the junior Earnhardt's arrival that track promoters already are hyping his impending rivalry with Gordon — young gun vs. young lion.

It doesn't surprise Gordon. Earnhardt has the lineage that drives NASCAR fans to look beyond their prejudices. For some fans, it's not just about winning. It's winning their way. As far as they're concerned, Gordon will always be on the outside looking in. But if 1999 is anywhere close to 1998, Gordon won't mind the view.

Gordon won the 1999 Daytona 500 and six other races that year but finished sixth in the points standings.

JAN. 3, 2002

Stardom eludes son, but Walter would be proud

PASADENA, Calif. — The father is never too far removed from the son.

Every day, Miami (Fla.) running back Jarrett Payton crystallizes the words of the late, great Walter Payton in his mind. Every day, people watch how the scion of the NFL's all-time leading rusher conducts himself, and then they appreciate how the elder's quiet dignity lives on in the next generation.

Jarrett Payton is an afterthought in the big picture of the Bowl Championship Series title setting. He doesn't play much for the top-ranked Hurricanes. That's hardly an indictment because this Miami squad might be one of the most talented collections ever assembled in college football.

But Payton is staying true to his father's memory. And if indeed a memorable moment awaits us when the Hurricanes play Nebraska in the Rose Bowl, let's hope it will be Payton shedding tacklers as his father did and finding the end zone. The loudest roar would be the one only Payton himself could hear.

"I know that my father is still inspiring me," he said. "You never lose that. Football has been an important part of keeping that spirit of him inside of me. He was my hero. He was a warrior the way he always kept coming back. It always seemed like he got beaten up after every game. But he'd always come right back."

Payton, or J. P. as he likes to be called, has endured more than his share of torment, as well. He escaped serious injury in an automobile accident, but he once badly cut his foot on a coral reef after jumping from a boat. He has rushed for only 26 yards this season and was elevated to backup fullback for the Rose Bowl only after the starter suffered a broken foot during Miami's bowl preparations.

Payton was one of the nation's most sought-after high school recruits before arriving at Miami in 1999. That was no surprise considering his rich pedigree. Living in such an immense shadow can often become intimidating, but Payton relished his heritage. He was ready for the challenge of living up to being Walter Payton's son on the football field.

But he wasn't prepared for the tumult off the field that would soon send his safe, secure world into a free fall.

Walter Payton developed a rare kidney disease that required a transplant. Ever protective of his privacy, Payton kept the news out of public reach for as long as possible. But then came that emotional news conference in February 1999 when Payton revealed the depths of his physical deterioration. Unable to finish, Payton broke down in tears, collapsing into Jarrett's arms.

Before a suitable kidney could be found, Payton developed cancer of the bile duct. As the end drew near, Jarrett took a leave of absence from Miami and returned to Chicago to be at his hero's side. He was there when his father passed away at age 45 on Nov. 1, 1999.

"It was difficult trying to concentrate on football with everything else that was going on," Payton said. "I thought it was best to get away from the game and get my thoughts together. But I knew that my father would want me to keep working hard and keep striving for my goals."

Payton returned to the Hurricanes later that freshman season, changing his No. 32 to his father's 34. And when he scored his first collegiate touchdown, against Rutgers, he dropped to his knees and pointed to the heavens.

Payton redshirted in 2000. A position shift to fullback in 2001 didn't improve his playing time. But if Payton has learned anything from the last three years, it is maintaining perspective.

Minutes aren't exactly gifts on teams as talented as the Hurricanes, but Payton never wanted to transfer. He could have followed his father's path to smaller Jackson State, but walking away from challenges feared too great was something his father never tolerated. If Jarrett's football star was ever to shine, it would be with the Hurricanes.

There's a reason the kid with the name perseveres in a nameless role, struggling with a quiet resolve and an unfaltering work ethic. In simple terms, it's gentlemanly class.

Jarrett Payton already has filled his famous father's most important footsteps.

APRIL 2, 2002

Brothers share title, against all odds

ATLANTA — Juan Dixon already knew pressure, and this wasn't it. A tie score with 12 minutes left in the national championship game can't compare to watching your parents wither before your eyes, ravaged by drug-induced AIDS.

The Maryland All-America glanced over to the Terrapins' cheering section behind the bench and briefly locked stares with his older brother Phil before joining his teammates in a time-out huddle.

"That told me everything I needed to know," Phil Dixon said. "When he doesn't look at me, then I get worried. He didn't have to say a word. He was telling me, 'Don't sweat it, bro. Everything's under control.' And he put the team on his shoulders."

And when the little brother delivered on his assurances, leading Maryland to its first national championship, he raced into the crowd to put his championship commemorative T-shirt over Phil's shoulders. They shared a hug, joyous tears and painful memories.

Juan Dixon was a young man with no business dreaming big considering the internal and external forces working against him since childhood. His parents died within 16 months of each other in the mid-1990s. And the odds were against him because few emerged from his financially depressed Baltimore neighborhood unscathed from drugs' nefarious lure.

But there Dixon stood, all 160 pounds of him, atop the college basketball mountain. And he wanted his idol to know that it wouldn't have been possible without him.

"This is Phil's moment as much as it is mine because he set the example for me to follow," Dixon said. "We went through a lot of tough things in our life, and we got through them together. And that's what makes this that much sweeter."

Dixon delivered a performance consistent with the recent pantheon of senior-willed champions. His tournament most-outstanding-player recognition placed him alongside Michigan State's Mateen Cleaves in 2000 and Duke's Shane Battier in 2001. To the seniors go the spoils.

The NCAA tournament's brightest star is again the one who chose to remain in the constellation until his light flickered out in the fully allotted time. And justifiably so, Maryland got the Juan Shining Moment it deserved.

"I am so proud of everyone on this team," Dixon said. "Lonny (Baxter) and me beat the odds and led our team to a title. I can't put it into words how excited I am now. Coach Williams took a chance on me when nobody else would, and I thank him for that. This has been a great experience."

He made sure it ended on the appropriate note. After Indiana took its only lead, 44-42, Dixon drilled a three-pointer. Two possessions later, he hit an awkward-looking fadeaway jumper that seemingly sucked the spirit out of the Hoosiers. It was a good show. Too bad Phil Dixon didn't have the heart to watch.

"I was sitting here with my head in my hands," he said. "I couldn't bring myself to look. I just gauged what was going on by what the crowd did. Juan had that determined look about him. After he hit those last free throws, then I started to relax a little."

Relaxing can cost you against the Hoosiers. Just ask Duke and Oklahoma. The fifth-seeded Hoosiers' modus operandi through their unlikely run to the championship game was lulling opponents into a sense of overconfidence. Once again, the Hoosiers trailed early by double digits. And once again, they averted a blowout.

The Terrapins didn't score for five minutes, unable to take advantage of the physical edge they enjoyed under the basket. It was just as it had been all season for Maryland: If its dream was to be realized, Dixon would have to be the Juan.

"He had done it for us all season, so this shouldn't have been any different," senior forward Byron Mouton said. "He wanted the ball in his hands when the game got close. You got to have those kind of guys who aren't afraid to take the big shot or have the ball at the big moment."

And when the seconds ticked away toward the biggest moment, Dixon wanted the ball in his hands again. And his teammates happily obliged.

APRIL 12, 2002

Like an old general, Arnie knows it's time to fade away

AUGUSTA, Ga. — The army of thousands has shrunk to a modest brigade of devoted loyalists, mindful of the unfathomable odds against a trademark late charge, yet hopeful for one last memorable snapshot for the archives. It doesn't require much to satiate this appetite. One par putt finding the bottom of the cup would do it.

It's sad that the man who was once the lord of golf has been reduced to a pitiable figure in his last hours as a Masters competitor. It hurt to watch Arnold Palmer's first-round 89 unravel amid the dogwoods and azaleas that were once his kingdom. It yanked at the heart to see him bounce toward the first green after reaching it in regulation, only to slump after knocking his first putt over the back of the green. He wound up four-putting the hole.

He already knew the end was coming. That moment solidified it.

"That's it," he said afterward. "I'm done."

The four-time Masters champion, the man who surprised every doubter who questioned whether a low-ball hitter could win at Augusta National, had played his next-to-last round at the Masters. But many would contend that Palmer's game retired 10 years ago. It had been almost 20 years since he made a Masters cut.

"Who's he?" asked one little boy who didn't understand why a 72-year-old was deserving of a long and sweet standing ovation from the crowd surrounding the 18th green.

When told "That's Arnie!," the boy still looked like somebody searching for an answer.

Tradition flows through this sport's bloodstream, and, as a result, golf doesn't easily let go of its ghosts. But parading them as frayed links to an illustrious past is quickly taking the form of comedic parody. Initial applause for 89-year-old Sam Snead on the ceremonial first tee shot turned into snickers when he sliced his shot into the crowd, bouncing the ball off the forehead of an unsuspecting patron.

Nobody laughed at Arnie. Worse, they felt sorry for him. He sensed it. Choosing his words carefully, Palmer said the galleries were "very protective" of him.

"They were very, whatever you want to say," he said. "Just the whole way around. It was one hole after the other and, of course, that made me feel good. On the other hand, as someone said to me, 'How do you account for this large gallery when you're not playing worth a damn?' And I said, 'Hell, the ones I don't know by their first names are relatives.' "

Before Tiger Woods became the game's newest Pied Piper and even before Jack Nicklaus, there was Arnie's Army. A few enlistees proudly displayed their buttons as they followed their leader.

"What they ought to do," said one lady at No. 17, "is give every Masters champion over 65 four strokes a round for each green jacket they've won. That would've given us 16 shots today, and we'd be one over right now. Why not? They've changed everything else on this course."

And what's frightening was that she looked serious.

Let it go, everyone. Let him go. Let him quietly sign off with the class and credibility that still make him one of the most sought-after product endorsers in the sports realm.

"We owe a debt to Arnold," said Masters chairman Hootie Johnson, "and he will always have a very special place in Masters history."

Palmer joked that it was time to stop because he didn't want to get the same letter tournament officials sent to former champions Gay Brewer, Billy Casper and Doug Ford, telling them their shadows of a golf game weren't welcomed any longer.

Maybe he'll take Snead's place on the ceremonial first tee. It's a safe bet that with Arnie there, hard hats won't be required attire for the gallery.

As Palmer chatted with friends along the ropes on the 17th fairway, a huge roar erupted from a neighboring hole. One of the big guns had made a big shot.

"There was a time when that would have been for me," Palmer said wistfully.

There was a time when the general led his troops into championship battle, but the fight now is keeping sympathy at a minimum. It's a crusade Palmer can no longer win, so he's taking the honorable approach, quietly fading into the sunset.

JAN. 19, 2002

Bill Russell stands tall but doesn't look down on anyone

The path taken by people of substance is too easily forgotten or ignored. Times change, priorities shift.

A basketball fan approached me at the North American International Auto Show, interested in what I thought the Pistons needed to do to make a playoff push. I asked the young man if he knew that Bill Russell was just a few steps away in the WXYT-AM radio booth, sitting for an interview. How often does the opportunity present itself to shake hands with one of the 10 greatest NBA players of all time?

The fan wasn't impressed, suggesting that the Boston Celtics legend was great "back in his day," but he couldn't hang with Shaq.

Russell's legacy is sadly devalued in today's celebrity culture. While winning 11 NBA championships and becoming the first black coach in a major sport, he remained a man of convictions. At 67, he still shines brightly through the perceived superficiality of black superstar athletes. Back in Russell's day, he didn't have the luxury of ambivalence now shown by Shaquille O'Neal, Michael Jordan and Tiger Woods. If you didn't take a stand in the '60s, you stood for nothing.

Sports became a forum for addressing the social and political inequities of the era, which coincided with the evolution of the high-profile black athlete. Russell, Muhammad Ali and Jim Brown composed the Holy Trinity of that period, commanding respect through their athletic prowess and demanding acceptance for who they were away from the game.

"I grew up in a different place in a different time," Russell said. "And what I did has nothing to do with what the guys are doing today."

It's disappointing that Russell plays down his efforts. It was, after all, Martin Luther King Jr.'s birthday weekend, a three-day break from work for some. Unfortunately, that might represent the most important part of King's memory to many.

"Are we forgetting some of the things he stood for? Yes and no," Russell said. "Yes, to the historical facts. It's hard to know where you're going unless you know where you've been. And you can't lose sight of your goals. But everyone has to approach it from their own viewpoint. Nobody can say that one size fits all."

Russell thinks athletes today are no more or less principled than the rest of society. For better or worse, he sees no distinction in the behavior separating a teenage NBA millionaire and a 28-year-old dot-com company founder. Money and success come much faster, but maturity still comes at its own pace. And though the uninformed might belittle the past, Russell doesn't condemn his successors for their public indifference.

Marketing dictates motives these days. Woods and Jordan are not only the two most recognizable athletes, they are also the richest, primarily from the combined $20-million plus they take in annually from commercial endorsements.

Jordan was roundly criticized for not publicly endorsing U.S. Senate candidate Harvey Gantt in a close election with incumbent Jesse Helms in his native North Carolina. Jordan's reasoning for not supporting the Democrat who attempted to become the first elected black U.S. senator from the old Confederacy? He said Republicans bought sneakers, as well.

"One of the things about living here is the freedom to do whatever you think is best," Russell said. "Whether or not guys will take a stand likely depends on how they got to this place. All of us can't have the same view. All I tried to do was live a life as responsibly as possible and set the same example for my three kids that my father set for me."

The greatest winner in team sports still won't compromise. He doesn't sign autographs, preferring to extend a handshake and a few words rather than an impersonal scrawl. More than 30 years after his last game, Russell exemplifies an essence sadly lacking today in sports and the world beyond.

CHAPTER FIVE

You're lucky because you get to know these people

BARRY, TAKE ONE: JULY 28, 1999

Sanders turns his back on teammates and fans

Like the little kid who's not happy when things don't go his way during the neighborhood game, Barry Sanders has taken his ball and gone home.

Take that, Lions.

As stunned as we are, this latest cataclysmic chapter of Lions history shouldn't come as a surprise to anyone who has cried with, and screamed at, this franchise for a generation. Disaster is always just around the corner.

There are no heroes here.

It would be nice to say that Sanders has taken a page from Jim Brown's storied career, leaving while still thriving at his competitive peak. But when Brown left the game, he went with his head held high and didn't hide from anyone. There was no cloak of secrecy, and he didn't leave his team guessing or offer his teammates false signals of hope.

Sanders has taken the selfish way out.

"He has come to a decision that he thinks is best for him," said Sanders' equally shocked agent, David Ware. "What can you do?"

It's certainly within any person's prerogative to call it a career anytime he wishes, but this has a touch of vindictiveness to it. It almost appears that Sanders wanted to punish the Lions as much as possible. And the best way to achieve that goal is to wait until the last possible second to announce a decision that he clearly had been thinking about for months.

Sanders isn't retiring. Sanders is quitting.

He's quitting on his teammates who based their off-season hopes on his return. And he's quitting on his fans who knew that he was the only reason to care even the slightest about the Lions.

He's quitting on Herman Moore, who's probably wondering why he bothered signing a long-term contract extension. He's quitting on Charlie Batch, a second-year quarterback who can't be expected now to progress as many had hoped because he just lost his most valuable offensive weapon.

Sanders is quitting because maybe the strongest statement any superstar athlete can make is that records are irrelevant when looking at the overall picture. If you're not happy and the desire isn't there, then it's best to leave while you're still healthy enough to walk away without the aid of surgically repaired legs.

But despite his problems with coach Bobby Ross and Lions management, Sanders owed them the courtesy of addressing his differences instead of hiding all spring and leaving everyone to believe that Barry was just being Barry and would return. He let his father air his grievances instead of broaching them himself.

But it's also hard to feel sorry for the Lions. They got what they deserve. They have wasted the game's most exciting player. They've now opened themselves to a level of second-guessing and 20-20 hindsight that we've never seen before.

Would Sanders have felt differently had the team committed to Matt Millen, as William Clay Ford Jr. wished? Who knows? All we know is that Sanders is not coming back.

He's taken his ball and his records and he's going home. The team that went 5-11 with him likely will go 5-11 without him. But it won't be as exciting.

The 1999 Lions won six of their first eight games, lost six of the final eight games and were eliminated by Washington in the first round of the playoffs.

BARRY, TAKE TWO: SEPT. 15, 1999

In retirement, Sanders sinks to Lions' level

Although we haven't seen him play in months, it's obvious Barry Sanders still possesses the open-field wizardry that left mouths agape for 10 years. Just observe the spin move he's making on his version of the truth.

Six weeks ago, Barry was tired of playing football. Now he's just tired of playing for the Lions.

What? Do we all have the word stupid written across our foreheads?

It seems Barry is testing our intelligence again by believing he can force the Lions to trade him to a contending team, using the return of $5.6 million in signing-bonus money as bait. But although the Lions have elevated bungling to an art form, it's hard to believe even they can mess up this decision.

If Sanders wants to play football again, he can do it wearing

Honolulu blue. If not, then he can enjoy his retirement years.

This is nothing but an attempt by Sanders' representatives to find leverage where it doesn't exist. Agent David Ware maintains he wants the Lions to have the salary cap relief they deserve for next season by recouping the remainder of Sanders' signing bonus, but the Lions must either trade him or grant him free agency by waiving him this season.

But the Lions are confident they're owed the money through the language of the contract, and an arbitrator eventually will rule favorably. NFL commissioner Paul Tagliabue said as much when he came to town to speak at a luncheon.

Ware even intimated that part of Sanders' motivation to ask for a trade was his displeasure with some of the local commentary following his abrupt retirement. I branded him a quitter in this column because his perfectly understandable anger toward management's history of ineptitude didn't justify his actions. He childishly lowered himself to the Lions' level of buffoonery and thus lost the benefit of the doubt in this dispute.

Sanders' latest volley only further validates the previous argument. Sanders and his representatives asked everyone to take him at his word. He spoke of extinguished passion — not rancor — in his retirement fax. There was no ill will toward the Lions. He was simply tired of playing.

Well, obviously something has reignited the pilot light. Or maybe Barry's equally as guilty of duplicity as the Lions. Maybe, just maybe, he's as much to blame for the disintegration of this relationship as Lions management.

Wagging an accusatory finger at the media is always a desperate resort. But maybe Sanders should point at the NFL Players Association since it created the framework for the collective-bargaining agreement that essentially holds a player hostage to the team that holds his rights.

The blanket escalating pay scale that the union desired came at a costly compromise. Teams have the right to declare one free agent a "franchise player," a designation that guarantees the player a salary comparable to the best at his position. But the player isn't free to leave for another team.

So you resort to every imaginable tactic, short of felony, to convince your employer of your irreconcilable differences in hopes they'll eventually surrender and acquiesce to your wishes for a new home.

Free-agent wide receiver Carl Pickens, a two-time Pro Bowl starter, wanted out of Cincinnati, vowing never to play for the lowly Bengals again. He insulted management. He insulted teammates. He insulted fans. He insulted the city. He said he'd quit rather than suit up in a Bengals uniform again.

Pickens purposely detonated every bridge, believing he was

ensuring his departure from the Bengals. Management had no choice but to trade such a malcontent, right?

Pickens was never more wrong. Today's NFL superstar, though dissatisfied with his management's myopia, has only two options — play with that team or not at all. A week before the start of the regular season, Pickens signed a multiyear deal with the Bengals that makes him one of the highest-paid players at his position.

But he's now about as popular in Cincinnati as a local bar patron wearing a Cleveland Indians cap.

And if through time and divine intervention the Lions become a more effective and successful team without Sanders, he can expect a similar reaction in Detroit. And that would be a shame.

But that's the price you pay for not acknowledging sooner that you were accountable for problems that are acknowledged later.

BARRY, TAKE THREE: AUG. 14, 2000

He talks! 'Can't a man just leave his job when he's tired?'

GRAND BLANC — Barry Sanders talks! In a wide-ranging interview, Sanders — who hadn't spoken at length to the media in more than 13 months — said:

He enjoys retirement and won't play football again.

His sudden departure from the Lions had nothing to do with bad feelings for coach Bobby Ross.

He knows he could have better handled the way he left the team.

He wouldn't be surprised if Tiger Woods one day walks away from golf the way Sanders walked away from football.

Sanders, one of the greatest running backs in NFL history, stunned Lions teammates and fans by announcing his retirement on the eve of training camp in July 1999, and then refusing to expound on why he left. A year later, he seems to have attained an inner peace that 15,269 career rushing yards couldn't create.

Sanders broke his long silence in an exclusive Free Press interview at Warwick Hills Golf and Country Club, site of the Buick Open. He firmly put to rest speculation that he would return to football if the Lions traded his rights.

"I'm done with football, and I'm enjoying it," he said. "I like retirement. If I wanted to play football again, all I'd have to do is just show up in Saginaw or at the Silverdome. My decision has nothing to do with the Lions. I know that you probably don't believe me, but it has nothing to do with the Lions. I played 10 years, and that was enough."

Ross said he did not feel vindicated by comments that he had nothing to do with Sanders' decision to retire.

"I have honestly felt that way all along," Ross said. "That was from my own gut feeling, No. 1, and secondly, he had talked to other people in this organization and had conveyed that very same point a number of times."

Yet many outsiders thought the timing of Sanders' retirement was intended to humiliate and hurt the team, or that he must have been upset with management.

"Can't a man just leave his job when he's tired?" Sanders asked. "It doesn't have to mean anything more than just a person who believes that his career is complete."

True to form, Sanders remains oblivious to external forces. He can't understand all the fuss about his decision. And he remains elusive. In our 30 minutes together, he was as elusive with his words as he was with his legs for 10 pro seasons. What about the comments from his father, William, that Sanders' decision was his reaction to a deteriorating relationship with Ross?

"Did you ever hear any of that stuff from me?" Sanders asked.

"No," I said.

"Then why would anyone automatically assume that other people were speaking for me?" Sanders said.

Well, Barry, perhaps because you remained silent rather than publicly disputing your father's statements. People perceived that as tacit agreement. But Sanders reiterated several times during our discussion that he held no animosity toward Ross or management.

"But, Barry, Ross said he tried to telephone you a dozen times during the off-season because he heard there was a problem between the two of you," I said. "Why didn't you just pick up the phone once and talk with him?"

"But I told you there wasn't a problem," Sanders said. "Why would anyone think there was a problem with me if they hadn't heard it from me?"

"But couldn't you have cleared up any misconceptions by calling Ross?" I countered.

"But as far as I was concerned," Sanders said, "there was nothing to clear up. I had to sort some things out myself."

Sanders said he has remained in Michigan and plans to stay here because "I still consider this to be home." He often attends sporting events, although he said he has yet to attend a Lions game and does not intend to in the near future. Because of his visibility at sporting events, Sanders occasionally has endured the venom of long-frustrated fans. He was booed once at Joe Louis Arena when introduced to the crowd.

"That bothered me at first, but I tried not to take it personally," he said.

"Did you feel that the reaction from the media and fans was a cheap shot?" I asked.

"Well, let me ask you that question," he said. "Since you were the guys writing it and saying it, did you think it was a cheap shot on your part?"

"No," I answered.

"I can live with it if you guys can," he said. "Could I have handled it a little better? Probably. But it all seems so long ago that I've just gotten on with the rest of my life. Why worry about it now? It's over."

Barry Sanders the sports icon is more interested now in becoming Barry Sanders the sports fan. Like thousands of others, he went to Grand Blanc to catch a glimpse of Woods. But Sanders soon became a show all his own.

When two of Woods' security guards heard that Sanders was dining with friends in the clubhouse, they wanted to meet him and came by to say hello.

"Can you introduce me to Tiger?" Sanders said, looking like a starstruck kid. "Tell him I'll carry his bags if he wants."

(No need. Woods and Sanders met later outside the clubhouse and chatted for 15 minutes before Sanders went to watch Woods practice on the putting green.)

Michigan State basketball guard Charlie Bell stopped by to visit Sanders, as well, wearing his NCAA championship ring, a bauble that drew Sanders' attention. Sanders, of course, never made it to the championship game.

"You should come back, man," Bell begged, "and then you could get one of these for yourself. We need you back, man."

"Nah," Sanders said. "I'm an old man. What am I? 31? 32? You see, I can't even remember how old I am."

Despite a newfound penchant for hot dogs, Sanders, 32, looks as steely chiseled as he did in his playing days, still capable of spinning a would-be tackler into a memorable "SportsCenter" highlight. Sanders is happy that he could walk — indeed, run — away from the game while he was still healthy. He looks forward to playing with his son, 6-year-old B. J., for years to come.

But what about the records he could have claimed had he stayed in the game?

"In all the time that people have known me," Sanders said, "has anyone ever heard me talk about the importance of rushing records or finishing with the most touchdowns? So if that's never been important to me, then why would that be a motivation to keep playing?

"My reasons for playing as long as I did, and leaving when I did, were pretty simple for me to understand. Why should it be so difficult for everyone else to understand?"

Well, Barry, it's because nobody wanted to see such a great star dimmed. It's because few things are more frustrating than seeing excellence wasted.

"You know, it wouldn't surprise me if Tiger were to leave the same way I did," Sanders said near the end of our interview. "Gets up one day, believes he's accomplished everything he set out to do, and just moves on to the next phase of his life. It's a good way to go."

How do those lyrics go? "Regrets? I've had a few. But, then again, too few to mention."

In the end, Barry Sanders did it his way.

He has happily moved on with his life. And now that he has freed himself from a self-imposed cone of silence, maybe fans can forget the past and happily move on, as well.

TOM, TAKE ONE: JAN. 8, 1998

Izzo and Mariucci: A friendship strong as iron

The friendship bonds that ultimately prove the strongest are often forged from those moments when we're at our weakest. The emotional low for Iron Mountain junior guard Tom Izzo came in the 1972 Class B regional basketball finals. With Iron Mountain trailing West Iron County, 51-50, Izzo went to the free throw line in a one-and-one situation with two seconds left.

Two free throws, and Iron Mountain would advance to the quarterfinals for the first time in school history. But Izzo missed the first free throw. West Iron County grabbed the rebound and the game. Devastated, Izzo dropped to the floor in tears.

The first to rush to his side with a consoling arm around the shoulder and a helping hand up from the floor was his backcourt mate, Steve Mariucci. Since that day, one has always been there for the other.

Best men at each other's wedding. Godfathers to each other's children. Brothers bound together by the most important tie — the heart rather than blood. Kindred spirits whose mutual coaching ambitions helped fuel each other's passionate drive to pursue their dreams. Those dreams stretched far beyond the confines of Iron Mountain, a town of about 9,000 in the western Upper Peninsula.

"We'd spend hours every night talking and dreaming about what we were going to do and how we were going to become big-time head coaches somewhere," said Izzo, basketball coach at Michigan State. "I'm sure most people there probably thought we were crazy.

"I mean, you're in Iron Mountain. How is anybody going to find you up there? That one of us would be able to live the dream would be incredible. But that both of us are doing what we dreamed about is sometimes beyond belief."

Mariucci, the San Francisco 49ers' first-year coach, is quick to correct anyone who refers to Izzo as one of his best friends.

"Tom is my best friend," Mariucci said. "There are things I can tell Tom that I can't even tell my wife. There are certain things that he'll understand that nobody else will."

Only a coach can appreciate the mercurial winds of the profession. Only a coach knows the right words to say when the inevitable pink slip arrives. Only a coach can provide the sacred confessional where the other can fully bare his soul.

When Mariucci took heat for letting Jerry Rice return this season after major knee surgery, only to see Rice hurt the same knee in his first game back, Mariucci immediately phoned Izzo for reassurance. After the Spartans fell to Detroit Mercy for the third straight season, Izzo phoned Mariucci to vent.

"We may only see each other once a year now because of our schedules," Mariucci said, "but we talk so much on the phone, it's almost like we're roommates at Northern Michigan again. Ours is a very special relationship."

Mariucci, Iron Mountain's football pride, is preparing the 49ers for their NFC championship game against the defending champion Green Bay Packers. And the first person offering support is Iron Mountain's basketball pride — Izzo.

"I may be the only person close to Steve who can truly understand what he's going through right now," Izzo said. "He's experiencing the best feeling imaginable and the worst feeling imaginable at the same time."

But like any good friend at this time on the NFL calendar, Izzo's motives are a tad self-serving.

"I just want to make sure I get Super Bowl tickets," Izzo said, breaking into a hearty smile. "I told him: 'Don't mess it up and lose.' "

Mariucci has received hundreds of requests for Super Bowl tickets, but his best friend gets priority. The tickets will be waiting should the 49ers beat Green Bay. Izzo already is planning his itinerary: a flight to San Diego immediately after the Spartans' home game against Penn State the day before the Super Bowl. A red-eye back to Lansing late Sunday night.

But first, the Niners must beat the Packers, and that means risking consignment to purgatory in Mariucci's hometown. Iron Mountain, about 90 miles from Green Bay, is a Packers town. When Mariucci was named Packers quarterback coach after the team acquired Brett Favre in 1992, he became the proverbial little boy in a candy store.

"He'd call me up at night," Izzo said, "and say that he was having some spaghetti with some of his players and one of them wanted to speak with me. All of a sudden, I hear this deep voice saying, 'Hi, Coach, I just wanted to congratulate you on that victory.' "

The voice was Reggie White's.

"It figures that my first chance to get to the Super Bowl would mean having to beat my childhood team," Mariucci said. "You don't grow up in Iron Mountain and not be a Packers fan."

It's hard not to know everybody in a town as small as Iron Mountain. But Izzo and Mariucci didn't really get to know each other until junior high, when both played for a recreational football team. Mariucci was the quarterback, Izzo the center. They later were roommates during their four years at Northern Michigan and became graduate coaching assistants there at the same time.

A year after Izzo replaced Jud Heathcote at MSU, Mariucci was hired as head coach at the University of California. Mariucci thought he would remain in Berkeley for a while. Then Izzo's hotel phone rang about 3 a.m. one day in January 1997. Mariucci had just been hired by the 49ers.

"I told him that he had better have gotten a job to wake me up at that hour," Izzo said. "He asked me to guess which job he got. After the first 28 guesses, I got the right one."

Mariucci followed Super Bowl-winning coaches George Seifert and Bill Walsh, and he has one of the league's highest-profile jobs.

"You would think that jealousies would become inevitable when you have friends striving for the same goals," Mariucci said. "But one's success has never overshadowed the other's. Nobody's happier for me and the success we've had this season than Tom. And I practically jumped out of my seat when Michigan State went down to Purdue and dominated one of the top teams in the country."

Out of his seat and to the phone.

After Izzo got his biggest victory in three years as MSU coach, the first message on his answering machine was from Mariucci. Unfortunately, Izzo didn't have time to immediately return the call.

"He's big-timing me now," said Mariucci, breaking into laughter. "If he wins the Big Ten championship, I'll probably have to set up an appointment just to say hello. He just better make sure that he gets me tickets for that championship game."

They'll be at the will-call window.

The 49ers lost to Green Bay and never did make it to the Super Bowl under Mariucci, who became coach of the Lions in January 2003.

From Iron Mountain to the mountaintop

INDIANAPOLIS — Each remembers the wager, but time has clouded some of the specifics. What endures is that two teenagers from a little Upper Peninsula outpost dared to dream big. And the payoff might come tonight.

Tom Izzo and Steve Mariucci, brothers of the heart since high school, often visualized the footprints they would make once they made it out of the mining town of Iron Mountain. Both knew they wanted to coach. Both had a drive typical of the blue-collar work ethic indigenous to the community. No obstacle, real or imagined, would stop them.

At first, the ultimate was to become head coach at Notre Dame — football or basketball. But then the bet changed. The first to win a national or world championship would win. And to the victor would go?

"Uh, my memory escapes me at the moment," said Mariucci, with a laugh. "But I'm sure that it was purely nothing more than a gentlemen's agreement, and certainly not something that one would hold over the other's head forever or until we're both residents of the old coaches home."

Don't count on it.

"I'm pretty certain that the payoff was something sizable," said Izzo, with a laugh. "He probably doesn't want to remember it now because I'm sure he thought he had the jump on me when he got the 49ers' job."

The bond between these two extends far beyond their profession. Their relationship is so tight that they're on a last-name basis. Together since childhood through trial and triumph, each was the best man at the other's wedding and each is the godfather to the other's kids.

And on an evening that could end with Izzo standing at the mountaintop, there won't be anyone happier than Mariucci, the San Francisco 49ers' coach. It's as if he had made the climb himself. In fact, he has.

One always has been there for the other, and nothing could keep Mariucci away tonight, when Michigan State plays Florida for the national championship. It's Tom's time, but it's their moment.

Mariucci sat in the back of the interview room with Izzo's wife,

Lupe, as Izzo addressed reporters. A prideful glow splashed across his face when Izzo talked about his origins. Only Mariucci could understand this.

"When he first got into town here, we probably spent an hour together talking," Izzo said. "Actually, we spent the entire time pinching ourselves because it's still hard to believe we've gotten this far. We've tried to instill a family attitude into this program, so it's only perfect that if we can win the national championship, Mariucci can be a part of it. He's more a part of this than most will ever realize."

Their paths first crossed when they were fifth-graders in a basketball league. Izzo played for the public school, Central, while Mariucci played for the Catholic school, Immaculate Conception. Central won the game, and Mariucci recalled that people said his team lost because it didn't have an Izzo.

Mariucci thought to himself: "What's an Izzo?" He eventually found out.

"We played on opposite baseball teams the following summer," Mariucci said, "and one time Izzo was catching. I didn't think too much of him, and do you know that little you-know-what picked me off at third base. To this day, I remind him that the only reason he was a catcher was because he was so short, he didn't have to squat to get into position."

The friendship solidified when they became backcourt partners at Iron Mountain High. One year, Iron Mountain had a chance to win a regional title. All Izzo had to do was make two free throws with next to no time left, but he missed the first. Devastated, Izzo remained on the floor, his head buried in his hands. The first to console him with a hug was Mariucci.

And after the victory over Wisconsin that earned Izzo his first trip to the national championship game, Mariucci was the first to congratulate him in the RCA Dome tunnel with a hearty embrace.

"We have come full circle, and that's another reason why this weekend has been so special with him being here," Izzo said. "Only someone who knows you so well and knows what motivates you can appreciate what's going through your mind when your dream is right within your grasp."

Both have become legends in their hometown. A recreation center is named in their honor. Izzo will be the speaker this year at Iron Mountain High's commencement. But his accomplishments will be a greater inspiration than his words.

Izzo and Mariucci remind us that there always will be room for little guys with big dreams who understand that the only true limitations are self-imposed.

TOM, TAKE THREE: APRIL 5, 2000

Izzo savors 'One Shining Moment'

INDIANAPOLIS — The president was on the phone and wanted to speak with Tom Izzo. Why was he on the phone? Izzo had just talked to him a few minutes earlier on the floor of the RCA Dome.

"I thought they were talking about Peter McPherson," Izzo said of the Michigan State president.

Not exactly, Tom. The President. You know, Hillary's husband. Monica's boyfriend.

Ah, the responsibilities of instant stardom. You're suddenly on everyone's A-list. Only a few years back you couldn't get the lowliest elected official to return your calls and here you are, discussing three-point shots and planning a late spring Rose Garden ceremony with the leader of the free world.

"I was thinking to myself that he probably wasn't even watching the game," said Izzo, the Michigan State coach. "But then he knew all the guys' names and talked about how that Peterson was a great player, so I figured he must have seen it."

But enough chitchat — his limo to the hotel awaits.

A limo?

One day removed from his first national championship, and the little Yooper is big-timing us already.

"This wasn't my idea," a somewhat embarrassed Izzo said. "Somebody get me a cab. Or better yet, somebody get me a yellow Iron Mountain school bus because that's more my speed."

That speed should accelerate tenfold now that Izzo has joined the exclusive fraternity of national championship coaches, a group that has eluded such men as Roy Williams of Kansas and Gene Keady of Purdue. No longer on the outside looking in, Izzo is the guest of honor at the party.

But this is also where another test begins. Getting there is fun. Staying there is tougher. And does he risk compromising the standards he has set to maintain a level of excellence?

We all gushed when Steve Fisher played out another Final Four fairy tale at Michigan in 1989. The unknown assistant, tapped into emergency service on the eve of the NCAA tournament, transfused his spirit into his team and rode it all the way to the championship. The sweetness of the moment was genuine, reminding us of the spell only college basketball can cast.

But winning breeds an addiction that only more and more winning can satiate. It ultimately brought down Fisher. And perhaps because of that, Izzo has a blueprint to ensure that he doesn't follow a similar path. He has a nationally elite team that will have McDonald's All-Americas beating down the door for entry, but he must leave a crack open for the blue-collar warriors like Antonio Smith and Andre Hutson.

He promises he will.

"Some things do change about your program when you win a national championship," Izzo said. "But the coach can still control the personality of his program, and I assure you that's not going to change. Our best players are going to be our hardest workers.

"This isn't going to change me personally. And if it does, I'm sure I can count on you guys to put me back in my place. And I still have Jud (Heathcote) around to chew my butt if I get out of line."

Moments after winning the championship, Izzo stood on the floor of the RCA Dome beside his departing captain, Mateen Cleaves, their arms draped around each other. The mission they had plotted four years earlier was successfully completed. Now they bathed in the warm glow of their "One Shining Moment."

Even the most hardened cynic had a moistened eye watching Cleaves collapse in tears during the song. Could there have been a more fitting exclamation point for a purely genuine occasion?

"I wanted to share that moment with Coach because he knew how special it was for me," Cleaves said. "He's always heard me talking about that song. To have that be the last moment we share as a player and coach is about as perfect an ending as you're going to get."

But the end for Cleaves should be only the beginning for what Izzo is building in East Lansing. He's smart enough not to take anything for granted, though. He knows the future holds no guarantee of presidential conversations or White House visits. So, embarrassed or not, he will make sure he enjoys this moment.

TOM, TAKE FOUR: NOV. 17, 2000

Not all victories come on the basketball court

EAST LANSING — No Florida recount or lawsuit is required. If put to a vote, the most popular sports figure in Michigan is the self-avowed "little you-know-what from Iron Mountain."

Tom Izzo is embarrassed at the implication of his popularity, and he's always mindful of the fleeting nature of fame.

"I still fear getting fired," he said. "I still fear failing. That's why I keep so much of where I've been very close to me because that keeps me grounded and provides me with a very keen sense of the reality of this business."

There's an authenticity in Izzo that transcends the parochialism of college athletics. He's beginning his sixth season as Michigan State coach, and there isn't a more familiar face around campus or a more influential voice. Academia, prone to scoff at the increasing prominence of sports, listens intently when Izzo talks about the erosion of scholastic standards in college basketball. Students do a double-take when they see Izzo wending through the Spartan Stadium crowd on football Saturdays to take his customary seat among them in Section 9, eschewing the comfort of his private box.

Izzo, seamlessly crossing cultural barriers, is at ease in any setting — rural or urban, black or white. And although it's difficult for the die-hard Blue to digest, the man is even liked — within reason — in Ann Arbor.

Around East Lansing, Izzo's name appears on a wildly popular bumper sticker. His follows the crossed-out names of Bush and Gore. Some students in the Izzone cheering section at the Breslin Center have echoed the sticker's sentiment. And the coach acknowledges that some people have asked whether he has any interest in running for Congress, following the lead of former Nebraska football coach Tom Osborne. Running up the score once again, Osborne won election recently with 83 percent of the vote.

"If Tom wanted to in another 10 years or so, he could probably become governor of Michigan," said MSU associate athletic director Mark Hollis, perhaps only half-joking. "It's incredible how well he's liked at so many different levels."

Winning breeds popularity. Sincerity sustains it. So why ruin it by embracing politics?

"It's flattering that I get letters from people even suggesting that," Izzo said. "But I've got to be honest with you. I hate politics. I see a lot of gridlock and compromise. I've always considered myself to be a straight-shooting, no-BS kind of guy. I'll tell you what I think and let the chips fall where they may. If that approach upsets people, then so be it. That's not exactly the formula for a successful politician. With that style, I'd have a hard time getting elected dogcatcher in Iron Mountain."

But Izzo already is playing one form of the political game. Now that he has a high national profile, he has remained loyal to the instincts acquired during his days of anonymity. In the aftermath of Bob Knight's dismissal at Indiana, Izzo's reaction was strongest among his fellow coaches. Izzo said of the university's handling of the matter: "Something smells fishy."

Last spring, when he rejected the Atlanta Hawks' $20-million offer, Izzo was hailed as a symbolic hero, perhaps sending a message to young players in a hurry to claim NBA riches. His decision resonated with freshman Zach Randolph, who might be the most talented basketball recruit to come to East Lansing since Earvin Johnson in 1978. Randolph flirted with entering the NBA draft when the Hawks tried to hire Izzo, who had recruited him for five years and has become a father figure.

"Coach is real," Randolph said. "That's the best thing I can say about him. He just doesn't tell you things just to make himself look good. He tells you something because he feels it's the right thing to do. Coach will fight for you. And that makes you want to fight for him."

Izzo went to bat for Randolph with the NCAA Clearinghouse, which oversees academic eligibility. Randolph has a learning impediment. He didn't score high enough on his college entrance exam to meet the usual standards for playing as a freshman, but he made tremendous strides in the classroom his last two years in high school. Izzo made an impassioned plea to allow Randolph to play this season, and he convinced the NCAA to overturn its previous ruling.

That improved his NCAA appeal record to 2-0. Izzo helped get Jason Richardson's eligibility reinstated a year earlier. Randolph was MSU's student-athlete of the month for October, and his gratitude was evident in his excitement.

"He needed something like a 3.5 in a math class to get it, and the son-of-a-gun got it," Izzo said. "He comes banging on my door, looking prouder of this than anything else he's ever done. And he asks me if we can call his mother and tell her the news. You know what? I told myself then that my season was made right there. It's been a success if you can get a kid, whom everyone has told could immediately jump to the NBA, and have him get excited about doing well in school."

The tears welling in his eyes as he recites the story aren't the emotions of someone overly consumed with image. They are a reflection of passion and sincerity, qualities we crave in our political leaders, yet rarely see.

Thank goodness, they still exist in a few who lead elsewhere.

TOM, TAKE FIVE: OCT. 18, 2001

Class act: Spartans build winning tradition

EAST LANSING — The frenetic pace that Tom Izzo sustains on the bench during a game is nothing compared with the borderline chaos of a normal day in his office. He runs in and out, to and from meetings with assistants, or he makes a little time to say hello to someone who has waited a long while for a brief audience.

Such is the price for a life in demand. Popularity becomes a juggling act, easily collapsible if it tilts ever so slightly out of control. But the Michigan State basketball coach remains firmly grounded, as was illustrated recently when he learned there was someone on hold waiting to speak with him.

Jason Richardson was on the line. Everything else stopped.

Izzo, father of MSU's basketball renaissance, has become more of a friend to his former players. He and Richardson talk at least once a week. Normally, it's Izzo checking up on Richardson, wondering how he's adapting to his new life as a 20-year-old millionaire. But this time, Richardson was concerned about his former coach, and the fifth player selected in the 2001 NBA draft offered a suggestion. He will talk to Izzo's young players at any time, as much as possible, to familiarize them with the expectations attached to MSU's program.

Hearing that reaffirmed Izzo's faith that he is establishing a standard of excellence that transcends individual players — the true mark of a consistent power.

"They're trying to make me feel better," Izzo said. "They're worried about me and what I'm going through, which is kind of funny in some ways. I'm not exactly suffering here. Yeah, we don't have the numbers we once did, nor do we have the experience. But we've built the model of what we want this program to become over the last four years. Those kinds of things endure."

The man's not fooling himself. The Spartans' streaks of four straight Big Ten championships and three straight Final Fours are in serious jeopardy with a team that has only eight scholarship players, with no seniors and just two juniors among them. Izzo has lost 10 players from his last two teams, including a freshman and a sophomore, Zach Randolph and Richardson, who opted for NBA riches.

Some believe those circumstances might have pushed Izzo closer to the NBA, but if anything, they have pulled him even deeper into the college game. Such relationships with former players aren't possible in the pros.

"I'm probably more excited about this season than I have been about any other since I've been here because of the pressure on us," Izzo said.

"The pressure is in not using our inexperience as a crutch against playing the best that we can with what we have. We cannot lower our expectations of ourselves as players, coaches or fans because we may not appear as good on paper at the beginning as we did the last two years."

North Carolina and Duke always think big, regardless of personnel shortcomings, because their traditions wouldn't tolerate anything less. That is Izzo's idyllic vision for Michigan State, but it requires the assistance of departed players, same as with the Tar Heels and Blue Devils.

"People think I should be upset with Zach because he left after just one season, but that's ridiculous," Izzo said. "How can anyone be upset with somebody living out his dream? And we helped him reach that. And now I hear from Zach, and he's telling me how well he's adjusting and how much he wants to help Michigan State."

This is where Michigan messed up by distancing itself from the Fab Five. You can't tell me Chris Webber's and Jalen Rose's dissociation from the program the last eight years didn't hurt the Wolverines during the sloppy transition from Steve Fisher to Brian Ellerbe. The past paves the path for the present. The Spartans are young, but they understand their lineage. Living up to that heritage is the test for Izzo, perhaps his biggest head-coaching challenge in his seven years on the job.

"I didn't worry about pushing them hard in practice before a game in the past because we always had the numbers," Izzo said. "Then I started to think that maybe I should let up a little bit because the depth isn't there. But then I realized that if I changed our approach, then I'm compromising what we've been trying to establish. I would be dishonoring what the past leaders like Antonio and Mateen and J. R. went through."

And perhaps they wouldn't return Izzo's phone calls. He could withstand plenty of disappointment, but losing that rapport with his former players would be something he couldn't bear.

SCOTTY, TAKE ONE: MAY 29, 1999

The golden years will have to wait

The end is inevitable for every coach, and each step closer to that eventual finish line brings with it greater perspective. And in Scotty Bowman's case, it also offers a greater appreciation.

Detroit breathed a little sigh of relief when Bowman announced he would return behind the bench. Our elation is selfish, of course, because it's far more convenient to look at this decision through a parochial periscope. Having Bowman back improves our chances of getting the Stanley Cup back next year, right?

But a larger cause for celebration is the rapport that the winningest coach in NHL history has developed with a franchise and a community.

When Bowman first agreed to share his Stanley Cup insights with the less learned in 1993, he envisioned his stay here would last a couple of years and then he'd likely retire. Little did he realize that his Detroit experience would further fuel the internal fire that has made him peerless among his peers.

There's more behind returning for another season than becoming the first NHL coach to boast five decades and two millenniums of experience. The fashion in which the Wings exited the playoffs didn't steer him in a particular direction, nor would have a record ninth Stanley Cup coaching ring. Quite simply, he's staying because he's happy here. Who needs better justification? The Wings and the area provide Bowman with a comfort level that matches his immense competitive spirit.

"Detroit's just a good fit for me," said Bowman during a conference call. "It wasn't a tough decision to make. I pretty much knew I was going to come back after the playoffs. There were some questions health-wise last year, but I'm feeling great. I have family in Lansing and Chicago, so Detroit just seems like the best situation for me and my family right now."

It's hard enough to freely give up something you cherish. It's torture to think it could be taken from you.

Not too long after the Wings' championship season ended in 1998, Bowman received the stunning news that arteries to his heart were clogged and he needed angioplasty. Adding to his torment was the anguish of losing his brother to heart complications. All of a sudden, he feared all choices were gone.

"Being away from coaching last year really helped me appreciate the opportunities I have now," Bowman said. "You always have your highs and lows, but being away from the team hurts you the most. Coaching gives me a good feeling. I'm not ready to give that up yet. Scouting is for some people. I don't know. But coaching is what I've always enjoyed doing."

It's the scent of the hunt — the lure of battle — that motivates Bowman and slows the clock of advancing age. In that respect, he's a lot like former Pistons coach Chuck Daly, a self-described coaching lifer who stepped down as Orlando coach recently, vowing never to return to the bench. We'll see.

"I don't know if I'm a lifer like Chuck," Bowman said. "I don't know. Maybe I am. I like what I do. I started coaching in 1956, although it wasn't in the NHL. I missed it when I wasn't able to do it. Coaching gets into your system. It gets into your blood. But I don't think it's anything about age. It's about having the desire and the enthusiasm and the love for the job. I've never gotten up in the morning and regretted what I had to do that coming day."

As Bowman reflected on his good fortune, he mentioned his friend, the late Bob Johnson. When Bowman was Pittsburgh's general manager, he hired "Badger Bob," the legendary University of Wisconsin coach, as the Penguins' head coach. Johnson, who was behind the bench for the Penguins' first Stanley Cup in 1991, was nearly 60 years old when he accepted his first NHL head coach position.

"Bob always liked to compare everything to golf," Bowman said. "And when he took the job, he said that he knew he was on the back nine. I know that I feel the same way now. I'm not foolish enough to think that I'll be coaching for years to come. I know the end is coming, but I'm not ready for it right now."

Neither are we.

SCOTTY, TAKE TWO: OCT. 4, 2000

Red Wings prove you can't win 'em all

More myth than mortal during his seven years in Detroit, Scotty Bowman has never been burdened by the lack of confidence and skepticism from the outside that buried other coaches in this town. Bowman — the winningest coach in hockey history and one of the greatest championship coaches ever in professional sports — is the man who finally scratched our 42-year Stanley Cup itch.

But two straight stunning, second-round playoff exits are testing our tolerance. The window of Stanley Cup opportunity is closing quickly.

It isn't an indictment of Bowman as much as it is an inevitability of coaching. Regardless of the greatness of the record and reputation, there comes a time when redundancy proves fatal, and players stop listening. It happened with the Los Angeles Lakers and Pat Riley after four titles. It happened with the Pistons and Chuck Daly just two years after their back-to-back championships.

Is it happening with the Red Wings?

"It's never happened to me before, so I don't worry about it," said Bowman, beginning his eighth season with the Wings. "Usually, coaches don't stay in the same place long enough where that even becomes an issue. Eight years with the same team is abnormal."

Even Bowman's associate coaches, Dave Lewis and Barry Smith, have remained the same through his tenure here.

"This is a big year because this might be the last year that we're all together," Darren McCarty said. "The determination is still there. The passion to win is still there, and the coaches still do a good job of keeping everybody on their toes. Everyone naturally wants to focus on what's happened the last two years, but we know that we're still a pretty good team. A couple breaks here or there could put us back to where we want to be."

But the Wings used to make their breaks. They were branded too old three years ago with wheezers Slava Fetisov, Bob Rouse and Larry Murphy on the blue line, but it was as though Bowman merely had to wave a magic wand and all ills were cured. A little lineup tweaking here, a little subliminal psychological push there, and the Wings would respond.

"That third year we were up and down all year," said general manager Ken Holland, "but everyone had that feeling. And I'm not talking internally as much as I'm talking about media and fans that, come playoff time, they'll flip on the switch and everything will automatically fall into place simply because of who we were and who Scotty was."

But that assumption is slowly fading. It's not a lack of appreciation for what Bowman's done for a championship-starved city but a growing suspicion that advancing age and adversity have slid this team past its competitive peak, perhaps even beyond the reach of the man with the Midas touch.

Bowman drew sharp criticism for dumping Brendan Shanahan onto the checking line late in the Colorado series last spring. Previously, such mind games would deliver the message intended and wake up a sluggish scorer. But Shanahan slumped even further. And, following the Wings' playoff departure, he lashed out at his treatment. For the first time since his much-trumpeted arrival here, Bowman was generally painted as the villain.

"We've set a standard here," Bowman said. "Expectations are high and people aren't satisfied with just getting past the first round. But that's the attitude you want. You don't want anyone happy with not achieving your main goal."

The fire still burns inside the 67-year-old coach. Physically, he's probably healthier than at any other time here in Detroit. His mental acuity is as sharp as ever. But this season might serve as a testament to his ability to motivate through his own iron will.

"You've got to be more aware now because we're coming off two straight years where we haven't gotten out of the second round," Holland said. "When you've won championships back-to-back, there's an aura that you have, and we don't have that anymore. That's a reflection on everyone, myself included. It's possible to get it back, but nobody here's kidding themselves into thinking it's going to be easy."

The Wings will need the usual production from the likes of Shanahan, Steve Yzerman, Sergei Fedorov, Nicklas Lidstrom and Chris Osgood. But perhaps Bowman's biggest task this season is culling sizeable numbers from younger yet experienced role players like McCarty, Martin Lapointe and Kirk Maltby.

"I've heard that tuning out coaches does happen at some point," Maltby said. "But I just can't see that happening here because the coaches still do a great job of knowing when to hit the right button at the right time."

But should that right time not come once again next spring, the myth might erode a little further.

Away from the rink, Bowman likes to putter around

File this under the category "Things You Never Thought You'd See."

Scotty Bowman, gushing like a little boy.

"You've got to see this," Bowman said, quickly ushering me into his Joe Louis Arena office. On the wall amid assorted clippings and keepsakes hangs a framed Golf Digest pictorial spread of Tiger Woods marching up the 18th fairway at Pebble Beach on the final day of his record-shattering 2000 U.S. Open championship.

"That's me right there," Bowman said.

Bowman was one of the tournament officials who remain a few paces away from the golfers. Normally, they're innocuous. But this time the official happened to be a hockey coach with the NHL record for all-time victories.

Bowman sees golf as the best spectator sport because of the close proximity to the action. A friend with the U.S. Golf Association arranged for him to have the best seat imaginable, walking right behind Woods and Ernie Els, assisting the scorekeeper.

The 101st U.S. Open starts soon at Bethpage State Park in Farmingdale, N.Y., but Bowman won't be there because of a prior commitment. He's expected to be coaching his ninth Stanley Cup champion, surpassing his idol, Toe Blake, for the most titles in history.

"The Olympics pushed everything back a little later, so it's not going to work for me this year," Bowman said. "But it should be a good one, though, eh?"

It's a side of Bowman not often seen. But when stripped bare of all his convoluted trappings, Bowman comes across as just another sports fan — impressed by the excellence of others, as others are impressed by his brilliance. But why does golf move him so?

Bowman is a man who appreciates history, and not many sports cherish venues that are a century old. But most of all, Bowman appreciates golf for its mental aspects, which shouldn't be surprising. Bowman is a chess player. He's always trying to outthink his adversary, staying one move ahead.

"Championship golf requires the most mental concentration of any other sport," Bowman said. "Nothing else really comes close. I marvel at the focus that all these guys have and the way they just block everything out with people on top of them. And Tiger — whew — he's just incredible."

Bowman met Woods a few weeks before the 2000 Open at a Sports Illustrated banquet honoring the top athletes and coaches of the 20th Century. Bowman acknowledged a little embarrassment at how thrilled Woods was being in Bowman's company. Both appreciated the history of the occasion that brought them together that evening.

At first, Bowman was apprehensive about accepting the Woods-Els pairing on that final Sunday at Pebble Beach because he didn't want to be a possible distraction. What if Tiger noticed he was walking just behind him?

"He didn't even know I was there," Bowman said. "And there might have been times that I was no farther than three or four feet away from him. He was so focused on his round. And that was one of the greatest rounds ever in a major tournament. He didn't see me until we were in the scoring trailer afterwards to check and verify everybody's scores."

Startled, Woods did a double-take. "Scotty, what are you doing here?" Tiger asked.

"I was helping keep your score the last 18 holes," he answered.

"Well, did you have a good time?" Woods asked, smiling.

"Not as good as you," Bowman said.

Woods presented Bowman the ball he putted on the 18th hole.

"And I've got a copy of the scorecard for that final round that both Tiger and Ernie signed," said Bowman, beaming. His expression resembled those moments of our childhood when we found the baseball card of our favorite player and thought that life couldn't get much better.

"I'm a big collector," Bowman said, "and as you can probably tell, that's one of my most cherished possessions."

His fascination with golf is rooted in his Scottish heritage. His father, Jack, was a blacksmith at what's recognized as the birthplace of golf, St. Andrews. His mother grew up less than 10 miles away from Carnoustie, a frequent British Open site.

Bowman rattles off the names of his favorite golfers and their tournament victories as easily as he would line combinations for the Carolina Hurricanes. He never picked up a golf club until he was 17, always more interested in team-oriented competition. Perhaps now he feels he can learn something from golf that he can use as a hockey coach.

Or maybe he's simply a fan. And what's wrong with that?

SCOTTY, TAKE FOUR: JUNE 14, 2002

Cup clincher ends with stunning news: 'It's time to go'

Steve Duchesne dropped what teeth he had left when the stunning announcement filtered through the celebration on the Joe Louis Arena ice.

"Scotty leaving?" Duchesne said with an incredulous look. "What? When? Why?"

Those were the precise three questions everyone else had when Scotty Bowman turned a Stanley Cup coronation into a farewell waltz with the trophy he has won more than any other coach. Bowman told associate coach and good friend Barry Smith of his decision to retire just before the start of the decisive Game 5. He didn't tell anyone else until the Red Wings took the ice for the trophy presentation.

He went up to owner Mike Ilitch, who brought Bowman to town in 1993, and gave him a hug, whispering in his ear: "Mike, it's time. It's time to go." That was the last thing Ilitch expected to hear.

Bowman then went over to the man he molded into the consummate team leader, Steve Yzerman. The captain thought Bowman was merely offering his congratulations for the third Stanley Cup they have won together. But then Bowman leaned over and told him he had just coached his last game.

"My first reaction was probably shock," Yzerman said. "And then, just as quickly, I found myself to be very happy. Happy for him because he's leaving on his own terms, having won the Stanley Cup in his last game. How can you have a better ending than that?"

Bowman's decision cast a certain melancholy over what should have been a moment of unabated joy. You're happy for him because it's a sign that he understands there's more to life than winning more hockey games than anybody else.

He seemingly is in better health than he was during his first Stanley Cup championship with the Wings in 1997. But his retirement also is a little sad because this is the man who built what the city celebrated. Bowman was Hockeytown's architect.

"Without him," Yzerman said, pointing to the red-and-white confetti on the ice, "none of this was possible. He taught me how to win. He taught us all that the only thing that matters is getting to this point where the only goal — the only objective that you consider acceptable — is winning the Stanley Cup."

Bowman's wife, Suella, knew soon after the Olympics that he wasn't coming back, but she was sworn to secrecy. She was under the impression that he wouldn't announce his plans until the parades and platitudes were finished.

"But I get down to the ice and I find out that Scott had already told everyone," she said. "So when I find him I ask him if I can finally answer questions now about this, and he said it was fine. I'm very happy for Scott, but I'm even happier for us and our family because now we'll have more time together to explore more things in life."

Suella Bowman maintained that health wasn't an issue but rather there was nothing left for her husband to prove — except that a coaching lifer can lead a happy and fruitful existence away from the game.

"It's not that I no longer enjoy coaching because I do," Bowman said. "I just thought that this was the right time to do this. I've had a great time in Detroit. The Ilitches have been wonderful people to work for, and this is a great, great hockey city. I just felt that it was time to move on."

And we thought Michael Jordan had the ultimate flair for the dramatic, sinking the championship-winning shot in the 1998 NBA Finals, striking a pose forever embedded in our minds. And then walking away from the game. Only to come back later.

Bowman has retired before, only to come back because the passion still burned and the mind still clicked. That's why this retirement will be hard to believe until the jut-jawed expression no longer is behind the Wings' bench next season. But if this was the last chapter, then there can't be a better ending.

The scene we will hold dear is of Yzerman as he gave Bowman the first dance with the Stanley Cup for the last time.

SCOTTY, TAKE FIVE: SEPT. 11, 2002

Time is on Bowman's side in retirement

The new coach came to town, determined to change an old mind-set, searching for the right motivational hook. It was laundry day, and the coach paid one of the lower-ranked equipment managers to wash his clothes. When he got them back, he noticed one sock missing and approached the young man.

"Where is it?" he asked.

"What's the big deal?" the kid responded. "It's just one sock."

Sternly, the new coach said mistakes weren't going to be tolerated in this organization and stalked away. Startled, the manager went to the locker room to tell the players that the new coach just might be nuts.

"At that point, I knew I had their attention," said Scotty Bowman, recalling his initial days with the Red Wings with a hearty laugh. "Always keep them guessing. He later found the sock, and I nailed it to the clipboard in my office and it stayed there until I left. It sent the message that I wanted to send to everybody connected with the organization. Things were going to be different."

Life is different now for Bowman. Retirement gives him time.

Time is often a blessing, providing the opportunities a nine-month coaching commitment frequently prohibited. Instead of motivating highly skilled athletes, Bowman can channel his energies by stimulating young minds hungry for the secrets that produce success.

Bowman took part in a leadership symposium recently, sharing the stage with legendary coaches Bill Walsh, formerly of the San Francisco 49ers; Duke basketball coach Mike Krzyzewski; Miami Heat coach Pat Riley; and former Michigan football coach Bo Schembechler. Among the five coaches at the Fox Theatre, there were 16 league championships, three NCAA titles and 13 Big Ten championships.

Yeah, this panel probably knew a thing or two about motivation. But where does Bowman find the motivation now that his coaching days are done?

Surprisingly, he will attend Wings training camp in Traverse City. One would think his presence might be a distraction, diverting attention away from new coach Dave Lewis, who's eager to place his imprint on the defending Stanley Cup champions.

"I'm not there to get in anybody's way," Bowman said. "This is Dave's team. But I do want to see the guys again, and I need to sit and talk with Kenny Holland to discuss exactly what he wants me to do in my role as a consultant."

Bowman and Lewis haven't spoken since Lewis was promoted from associate coach two months ago. Bowman knows that following a legend is delicate terrain, so any advice must be offered carefully.

"The two biggest adjustments for Dave will be organizing practice and working the bench," Bowman said. "We had a great arrangement before because Barry (Smith) was the best at running practice while Dave and I could observe from the outside. That may change now that Dave's the head coach. We'll see. But I think this is a team that handles transition well, so they shouldn't have any problems."

Some think Bowman's absence might invigorate stars like Brendan Shanahan and Sergei Fedorov, who often clashed with Bowman's idiosyncrasies.

"Change is good," Bowman said. "I feel great. I feel refreshed. It's like you're getting a fresh start because you're able to do things you couldn't before. I'm not sure how I'll react when the games begin because I know I'll miss that part of it, but there are new challenges in my life now."

Retirement has been far from relaxing. Bowman got a big scare in July when he was in Muirfield, Scotland, for the British Open. Soon after the second round, Bowman got a call from his wife. Their daughter, Alicia, was critically ill in an Atlanta hospital from complications following bladder reconstruction surgery.

"It didn't look good for a couple of days," Bowman said. "She had developed an infection, and then she suffered a bad reaction to some medication and her body practically shut down. It was pretty tense but, thankfully, she came around."

Bowman wants to keep his retirement low-key. He will return to Joe Louis Arena for the banner-raising ceremony at the home opener, but you won't see him much afterward. He'll spend his time speaking to a few groups and collecting a few awards.

Maybe now he'll even find time to do his own laundry.

Woods crushes Pebble Beach on way to U.S. Open title

PEBBLE BEACH, Calif. — The yellow, wind-snapped flag that marked golf's most picturesque and majestic 18th hole turned white as Tiger Woods approached it late Sunday afternoon. The great Pebble Beach had surrendered — humbly bowing before its conqueror, trembling before the roar of the undisputed premier sportsman on the planet.

True greatness is measured only when the performance matches the setting, and Woods turned golf's grandest stage into the site of an unparalleled virtuoso solo. He broke or matched seven U.S. Open scoring records with a 12-under-par effort that extended far beyond mere excellence, leaving the appreciative who witnessed it scrambling for suitable comparisons.

Are there any?

Don Larsen's perfect game in the 1956 World Series would have had to come in the championship clincher to match what unfolded Sunday. Reggie Jackson's three home runs off three pitchers in Game 6 to win the 1977 World Series would have had to come with the elements working against him, a strong wind blowing in, determined to keep everything in Yankee Stadium that evening. Elgin Baylor's NBA Finals single-game record of 61 points in 1962 would have had to come in a victorious seventh game to equal Woods' feat in magnitude.

Consider this tale of the Tiger:

■ Woods' 272 score matched the lowest in U.S. Open history, tying him with Jack Nicklaus, who set the standard in 1980 at Baltusrol in New Jersey, and Lee Janzen, who matched it at the same venue in 1993.

■ Woods' victory margin was 15 shots — 15 shots! — obliterating Willie Smith's previous Open record of 11 shots, which had stood for 101 years. The previous largest winning margin in all major tournaments was 13 shots.

■ Woods' 12-under finish for the tournament was four strokes better than the previous low of eight under par.

"It's difficult right now for me to place this in any historical perspective because it's just too soon after the fact," Woods said. "That's not up to me to determine how others will choose to look at my performance over the last four days. I'm pleased that I was able to play solid golf for four straight days. That was my objective coming into this tournament."

Solid? How's that for understatement? But that description was indicative of Woods' demeanor following his victory. There weren't the tears from the Masters in 1997. There was no emotionally stimulating scene between father and son, as at Augusta. Earl Woods spent this Father's Day watching his son's achievement from home.

"I can't wait to give this trophy to my dad," Woods said, "and let him rub it a little bit."

There's no mistaking the pride an American feels in winning our national championship, but in some ways Woods appeared bored with the achievement because this day had long since become his destiny.

There was a special symmetry to this tournament, a passing of the torch. About the same time its greatest champion, Nicklaus, walked off the 18th green for the final time at a U.S. Open on Friday, Woods was just stepping onto the first tee to begin another assault on the Open record book and to challenge Nicklaus' distinction as the best ever.

At 26, Nicklaus was the youngest ever to have put all four major titles — U.S. and British opens, Masters and PGA Championship — in his victory column. At 24, Woods is weeks away from possibly taking that distinction, when the British Open returns to storied St. Andrews. Nicklaus' record of 18 major championships, the bedrock of his legacy, can breathe easy for a while. But before he returned home Friday evening, Nicklaus reiterated the obvious.

"Not one record in golf is safe when you consider his combination of physical skill and mental determination," Nicklaus said of Woods.

History now is Woods' sole purpose. Nothing else. He already has made enough money to last 10 lifetimes. But if he wants, Woods can transform golf history into his own personal scrapbook. This final day wasn't about winning. It was about records.

"He already knew he won this tournament after the second round," said Thomas Bjorn, Woods' playing partner in the third round. "His motivation was to win it by more than anybody in history. He wants to bring this course down to its knees."

And after Woods birdied four of the first five holes on the back nine Sunday, hitting an incredible approach shot from the deep, deep rough at 13 that landed two feet from the cup, Pebble Beach cried uncle.

But mercy isn't a quality of those determined to change history. Woods wanted more, as did the throngs watching — even those who weren't following him. Screams erupted throughout the course as the red numbers by his name on the leader board grew in succession, hole by hole.

"I didn't really know that I was 15 shots ahead until I was on the

18th green," he said. "I never really felt unbeatable, but there was a weird feeling of tranquillity and calmness, especially amidst the windy conditions Saturday. I felt very calm and at ease with myself."

Woods' Masters romp was more symbolic. The phenomenon was born. The winds in his face then were cultural, a man of color competitively mocking the hallowed grounds of an institution that serves as a reminder of an exclusionary era. But this weekend was the long-awaited birth of the great championship golfer. You must have every shot imaginable to blow away Pebble Beach, let alone a U.S. Open, by 15 shots.

This was the day that the best scaled an even higher plateau, leaving others shaking their heads in wonderment, and bringing a usually indomitable golf course to its knees in submission.

TIGER, TAKE TWO: AUG. 18, 2000

Playing with Woods, the Golden Bear bows out

LOUISVILLE, Ky. — Side by side, golf's past and future sauntered down the 10th fairway. The game's greatest champion, Jack Nicklaus, did all the talking as the successor to his throne listened intently, nodding. Tiger Woods is as much a student of tradition as he is of technique. He was respectful of the moment.

This is Tiger's tournament, but this was Jack's day — a bitter-sweet occasion further burdened by sorrow surrounding his 90-year-old mother's death. The PGA Championship is the last leg on Nicklaus' four-majors farewell tour. He fired a 77 on Thursday at Valhalla Golf Club, and barring a miraculous second round, the tournament will see the last of its only living five-time champion.

If this is the end, it's fitting that Nicklaus is grouped for the first time in tournament play with the young man who might be the world's most dynamic celebrity at the moment. In some respects, the pairing is symbolic of transition and continuity atop golf.

"Isn't that incredible?" said a woman poised along the ropes by the 10th fairway as the two icons passed. "It's like we're watching royalty."

The King is dead. Long live the King.

"It was an honor to play with Jack," said Woods, who assumed his customary major tournament position, tied for the lead after a six-under 66. "And you could tell that his mind really wasn't there initially, and with great reason, too. It was sad what happened yesterday, and you could tell that he really wasn't into the round."

Nicklaus double-bogeyed the first hole and was four over par after five holes.

"I had no desire to be here, I promise you," Nicklaus said. "But I felt like that is what she would have wanted me to do. I think it was probably the right thing to do because there is not much I can do for her at this point."

Helen Nicklaus was in failing health, confined to a nursing home bed. But she had told her son frequently that if he was to hear of her passing during a tournament, he was not to withdraw. She reminded him during their final visit earlier this week.

His father and mentor, Charlie, told him the same thing 30 years ago as he lay dying of cancer. Nicklaus already had begun the Doral Open when he received word that his father had passed away. Too emotionally taxed to continue, Nicklaus withdrew from the tournament.

"My wife and sister both felt like my mother had always worried about it the last couple of years," Nicklaus said. "Every time I'd see her, she'd say, 'Gee, I hope I don't pass away this week. It's a big week for you, and I don't want to mess up your week. But if it should happen, I want you to play.' "

Honoring his mother's wishes, Nicklaus played through, teeing off at 9:13 a.m. with Woods and Vijay Singh, the reigning Masters champion and 1998 PGA champ. And despite the high-profile company he kept, the loudest and longest ovation at the first tee went to Nicklaus.

"It just tells you what a great competitor Jack still is," Woods said. "I just marveled at how he continued to grind it out despite obviously having some difficulty focusing earlier. I don't know if I could have gone through what he did and still play. I have never lost a parent. I came close once, but if you've never gone through it, you can never know what he's going through."

Tiger's father, Earl, underwent quadruple-bypass surgery in the fall of 1996, a couple of months after Woods' PGA Tour debut. Woods stayed at his father's bedside in the hospital until he said Earl told him: "Get your butt out there so I can watch you on TV."

Nicklaus was just four holes through a practice round when he was notified of his mother's death. His initial impulse was to return to Columbus, Ohio, but he remembered his mother's words. Also motivating Nicklaus' decision to play was the pairing with Woods, a PGA-scripted passing of the torch. Although it lacked competitive drama, it was compelling theater. And when both were done, they stood side by side again — this time during a television interview.

"Tiger plays a game that I am not familiar with," Nicklaus gushed. "Of course, I could say that I played a game today that I wasn't familiar with."

But Nicklaus' 77 was irrelevant when considered in the context of the deeper loss he suffered. But he played, and in doing so he properly honored his mother's memory. That won't make Nicklaus the PGA champion, but it made him the champion of its first day.

TIGER, TAKE THREE: AUG. 21, 2000

Mayday for Woods, but he prevails at PGA

LOUISVILLE, Ky. — The machine is human after all, susceptible to imperfection and vulnerable to that rawest of emotions — fear.

Tiger Woods was scared because he found himself on unfamiliar terrain. He was on the run, within sight of his pursuer and strangely unsure of his footing. Even stranger was that the hunter was a relative unknown in pursuit of his first PGA Tour victory. Together, they provided a scintillating, hole-to-hole test of dueling wills.

Bob May was the anonymous David attempting to slay his Goliath with a golf ball. But Tiger refused to fall, adding the final note to two months of record-breaking championship golf with a successful defense of the PGA Championship. Woods, who earlier won the U.S. Open and British Open, is the first since Ben Hogan in 1953 to win three majors in one year.

But Woods also forever silenced those remaining few who questioned his ability to fight from behind and win a major championship. He'll never be pushed any further than he was on this dramatic final day by May — his former California junior golf partner — who played the round of his life.

Shot-for-shot, birdie-for-birdie, miracle-for-miracle, Woods had an answer for every one of May's challenges. Woods' toughest test came on the final hole of regulation, when he had to sink a five-foot putt to force a three-hole playoff, two minutes after May drained what seemed an impossible 25-foot putt for a birdie.

"There was some nervousness because Bob just absolutely made every shot he had to," Woods said. "But I knew that I had to dig a little deeper. And Bob and I probably gave everyone the greatest duel ever in the last round of a major championship. I mean, we both shot a 31 on the back nine in the last round of a major. That doesn't happen. That was just fabulous to be a part of because you don't see that very often at this heightened level of competition."

Same as we don't see such a model of competitive excellence very often. Woods added a few more entries to the record book Sunday:

■ He is the first to win four of five successive majors.

■ He owns the tournament scoring records in relation to par for all four majors — Masters, U.S. Open, British Open and PGA Championship.

■ He either tied or led outright 11 of the 12 rounds in major championships this year.

"What he did here was more impressive than what he achieved at Pebble Beach and St. Andrews," said Woods' coach, Butch Harmon, "because his game was a little out of sync the last nine holes Saturday and the front nine today. It's one thing to win when everything's clicking, but it's a totally different matter when you gut one out. And he won this one solely on guts — and heart."

And work ethic.

Woods was a solitary figure on the Valhalla Golf Club practice putting green at 9 p.m. Saturday, but darkness couldn't prevent him from taking the time to rediscover the smooth stroke that abandoned him earlier that day.

"I said to him, 'How can you see the ball?' " Harmon said. "And he said he didn't have to see it to know it was right. He could feel it and know it's right. That's amazing. This young man never ceases to amaze me."

Woods called Sunday "probably one of the greatest duels I've ever had on the golf course," and said he hoped the show he and May put on might help the PGA Championship shed the inferiority complex it suffers when compared to other majors.

The PGA Championship is criticized for its less-than-aristocratic pedigree of recent champions. Thirteen of its last 21 winners got their inaugural tour victories in the PGA, so it shouldn't be a surprise that most of Woods' challengers were a veritable who's that of professional golf.

May, Franklin Langham, Greg Chalmers and Scott Dunlap entered the tournament with a total of zero PGA Tour victories. They combined for 11 top-10 finishes this year. Woods had 11 top-10s all by himself.

But golf's majesty, as well as its mystery, is that history provides little support in the tight confines of the present. Woods' reputation meant nothing as May continually dropped approach shots within six feet of the cups on the back nine. This was a man with nothing to lose, and the crowd, sensing the possibility of an incredible upset, threw all its support behind him.

May was asked what would have meant more: getting his first PGA Tour victory at the PGA Championship or beating Tiger head-to-head to win his first major.

"I think you probably already know the answer to that one," he said.

Woods is as much an obsession on the tour as he is to the outside world. And even when he looks beaten, he somehow finds the will and the way to win. May's great round may have been forged in heaven, but it wasn't good enough to dethrone the champion.

"I survived out there," Woods said. "I won despite some erratic play, and that might mean more to me than anything else."

Any questions, skeptics?

I didn't think so.

TIGER, TAKE FOUR: APRIL 9, 2001

Masters championship a grand finale to the Tiger Slam

AUGUSTA, Ga. — As he marched up the 18th fairway at Augusta National and toward golfing immortality, Tiger Woods was joined by the spirit of this national treasure's chief architect.

The azalea-laden splendor was Bobby Jones' inspiration. And his ghost was Woods' principle foe this weekend, not the gold standard of leader board pursuers intent on subverting history. It was 1930 when Jones, the smooth-swinging southerner, established the criterion for excellence, achieving that era's version of golf's Grand Slam.

Woods cleared that yardstick Sunday when he won the Masters and became the first to hold the four modern-era Grand Slam titles at once — the Masters, U.S and British opens and the PGA Championship. His second Masters championship in four years — and his sixth major — put an exclamation point on an unbelievable 10 months. Woods shot four-under-par 68 on Sunday for a 16-under 272, two shots ahead of David Duval (67) and three ahead of Phil Mickelson (70).

And at some point soon, as he promised last week, Woods will savor the sight of all four championship trophies sitting beside each other on his coffee table. And he'll likely laugh at those frowning purists who maintain that a true Grand Slam must come in the same calendar year.

Call it a Tiger Slam.

Why not? He's claiming everything in this game as his own, anyway. He already has changed our definition of competitive superiority, once again leaving heads wagging in wonderment as to how anyone can combine such a supreme level of skill with an equally lofty level of concentration.

Call it anything you want, but what this 25-year-old extraordinaire has achieved is indeed a slam in the grandest sense. Nobody can touch him. Peers wilt in his presence, withering under the burden of what to do when close enough to catch a Tiger by the tail.

Duval and Mickelson dueled Woods through a typical Sunday Masters back nine in which birdies turned precious and few. But in the end, their putters rattled with their nerves, reminding everyone once again what separates Woods from the rest. And once again, we're scratching our heads for a historical parallel. No individual accolade comes close.

"It's hard for me right now to sit here and place this in some type of historical context in regards to all sports," Woods said. "All I'm thinking of right now is that I've won the Masters for the second time, and I've been fortunate enough to win four straight major championships. It is special. It really is."

Adding to the revelry was having his parents, Earl and Tida, waiting for him beyond the 18th green, same as they were after his first Masters triumph in 1997. The tears were missing, but tears usually are reserved for surprises, and there's nothing surprising about Woods now. We've come to expect the perfectly scripted theatrics like his birdie putt on No. 18, when only a par was necessary for victory.

"It hasn't sunk in yet," Woods said. "But I don't think it's my place to comment on whether or not this should be considered a Grand Slam. That's left for others to decide. But you do have to look upon this as one of the great moments for our game."

Jones' Grand Slam in 1930 included the U.S. and British opens and the U.S. and British Amateurs. But Arnold Palmer changed the parameters of the accomplishment in 1960, insisting that the Masters and PGA Championship replace the two amateur events. And Palmer has been the most vehement opponent of calling Woods' achievement a true Grand Slam.

But Woods said last week that he would consider holding the four major championships simultaneously a Grand Slam. And who can argue with him?

If anything, Woods' Masters championship assumes an even loftier stature because he endured eight months of building pressure leading up to this grand moment. But nothing rattles this guy. Not even a muffed three-foot birdie on No. 15 that exposed some rarely seen jitters.

"You know, I have a better appreciation for winning a major championship, and to win four of them in succession, it's just, it's just hard to believe, really, because there are so many things that go into winning a major championship," Woods said. "I've had some very special things happen to me, but I guess to win four consecutive majors is — if you look at my career, I don't think I've ever accomplished anything this great."

The achievement matches the man. He's already a third of the way toward matching his ultimate goal — Jack Nicklaus' 18 major championships.

"I'm not sure there's anything that you can compare it to, especially in golf," Duval said of Woods' slam. "I thought I had played pretty well today, putting myself in pretty good position. But you saw again today why somebody has to play and beat him. Tiger's not going to beat himself."

You're sympathetic toward Duval and Mickelson because they're great players trapped in the wrong time. This is Woods' world, his personal courtship with history. And they can only do like the rest of us — just watch in amazement.

TIGER, TAKE SIX: APRIL 10, 2002

Barkley doesn't know what makes Tiger gr-r-eat

AUGUSTA, Ga. — There's a misconception that silence on social issues and cultural barriers translates into acceptance or — worse yet — indifference. Believing that Tiger Woods doesn't sufficiently use his immense celebrity to address certain issues, Charles Barkley anointed himself the conscience of African-American superstars.

But Barkley sprays his opinions like his tee shots: all over the place. And he hasn't given Woods the respect and appreciation the golfer has earned by winning six major championships before his 26th birthday.

An "unshackled" Barkley, bursting free from iron chains, graced a Sports Illustrated cover recently, and an unfiltered Barkley spoke out on a number of topics in the accompanying story. He blasted Augusta National's decision to lengthen the course as racially motivated, intended to keep his good friend Woods from winning a second straight Masters and third in six years.

Woods shrugged off Barkley's comments, suggesting that, "Charles was just being Charles. He likes to stir things up sometimes."

But Woods should've been angered by Barkley's reckless generalizations. Perhaps Barkley didn't realize the tone of his remarks, but all he did was further perpetuate an age-old stereotype — that black athletes' physiological superiority compensates for their psychological shortcomings.

Woods wins because he's smarter than everyone else. He wins because he's more emotionally resilient than Phil Mickelson and David Duval. And lengthening Augusta National doesn't diminish that advantage. It heightens it.

"The alterations put a premium now on holding greens," Hal Sutton said. "Augusta is still all about the short game. Regardless of your drive, you had better attack the green from the proper angle and keep your ball below the hole if you want to have a chance. You've got to have the right shot at the right time. So tell me, exactly how does that hurt Tiger?"

If Barkley had thought a little more before opening his mouth, he would have understood that the changes in the course eliminated 70 percent of the tournament field from title contention before the first swing off the starting tee this morning. The added distance reduced the likelihood that relatively modest hitters, such as 1998 Masters champion Mark O'Meara or two-time champion Jose Maria Olazabal, could sneak up on the pack and snatch the title.

If Barkley had researched more, he would have discovered that Augusta National twice added bunkers in the hope of trapping a hard-charging bear by the name of Jack Nicklaus. The changes didn't slow him down — only those feverishly chasing him.

If Barkley looked at the evolution of the African-American athlete from a broader context, he'd understand that Woods is winning the fight on the most important battleground — the corporate boardroom. True empowerment isn't relying on others to bestow managerial or head-coaching jobs, but in putting yourself in a position to make decisions and set the agenda.

Merely categorizing Woods as the most compelling sports personality on the planet is an understatement. He's potentially the catalyst for a future wave of minority entrepreneurial involvement that could result in blacks owning professional sports franchises.

And that's where the real power is.

Does Augusta National embody some Old South attitudes? You bet. Some of the old guard here still raise an eyebrow at people of color who are not in subservient roles.

I had the high honor of walking these hallowed fairways and leaving a few divots after the 2001 Masters, having won the annual media lottery for an opportunity to play the course. You would have thought I was trying to sneak a nail clipper onto a commercial airliner, with the scrutiny I endured while trying to get into the Augusta clubhouse.

But Barkley's suggestion that the added 285 yards off the tees was intended to keep Woods down was a shanked drive into the woods. The color Augusta National cares most about is the red bleeding off the leader board from all the rounds under par.

"The longer hitters do have an advantage on the par-fives," Woods said of the alterations. "They can get there in two a little easier than the shorter hitters. But they still have to putt."

Woods broke into a Cheshire cat grin. It's his way of reminding everyone that the mental demands of championship golf still outweigh any physical requirements. It's his edge. It's what sets the master apart from the mortals.

It's what Barkley should have realized.

TIGER, TAKE SEVEN: APRIL 15, 2002

Foes fall by the wayside when Woods makes up his mind

AUGUSTA, Ga. — Two hours before his scheduled tee time, Tiger Woods already was in combat mode. He departed the champions' locker room in the clubhouse and headed purposefully for the driving range. A CBS cameraman wished him good luck. His response? Silence. Several patrons offered either an extended hand or an encouraging word. His reaction? Not the tiniest acknowledgment.

Not even the presence of a strikingly beautiful blonde woman standing beyond the ropes could disturb this already fabled level of concentration. Tiger's a big boy. It wasn't a time when he needed his nanny.

New girlfriend Elin Nordegren — formerly the baby-sitter for Jesper Parnevik's children — is discovering what every challenger already understands: Woods is all business when the scent of a major championship is in the air. Intimidation grows from attitude as much as execution. So don't waste his time with amenities. Don't attempt to divert his focus from the bigger picture.

His latest portrait? Leaving world-class players on the Masters leader board crying for their mommies.

The tears came not because of what Woods did with his shots but how he beat the others with his head. One by one, aristocratic challengers Ernie Els, Vijay Singh, Retief Goosen and Phil Mickelson crumbled under the demands of chasing the master. Their communal collapse left many wondering if there's anybody out there with the internal fortitude not to quake in Woods' wake.

This was a deflating afternoon for those who anticipated a heartstopping Augusta finish. History suggests the battle for the green jacket doesn't start until Sunday's final nine, but this time it was over before Woods made the turn. Who's kidding whom? It was over when Woods stepped out of the clubhouse.

"It makes no sense hoping that Tiger will stumble," Mickelson said, "so if you're chasing him, you're going to have to go out and get birdies. That means you're going to have to take chances. That means the possibility of mistakes increases. I think that explains what was happening to some of the guys out there."

The diagnosis is that these guys have Tiger on the brain. And that's exactly how the first back-to-back Masters champion in 12 years likes it. Woods didn't even play his Sunday best. But it wasn't necessary. He played to the level of his pursuers, giving this third green jacket more of an off-the-rack feel than the first two.

Woods figured he'd get pushed for his seventh major championship, considering he was among six of the world's seven highest-ranked players atop the leader board entering the final round. But when Woods leads on Sunday, strategies change. Challengers become more aggressive, a little too daring on an Augusta National final-round setup that demands delicacy. Els wasn't a factor following his snowman on 13. Singh sank one step deeper, scoring a nine on the par-five 15th after twice landing in water.

A nine? That's one of my scores!

The players can talk all they want about how playing with Woods is irrelevant to their performance. But Woods has outscored his playing partners in 27 of 30 Masters rounds. Is that mostly talent? Certainly. But is it also intimidation? You'd better believe it.

Goosen was a dead duck as soon as they approached the first tee. And he isn't easily ruffled. When Goosen muffed a 15-inch gimme, forcing a playoff at Southern Hills in last year's U.S. Open, he recovered, thanks in part to a heart-to-heart telephone conversation with South African compatriot Els later that Sunday evening. He beat Mark Brooks in an 18-hole playoff the following day for his first major championship. He was also the world's hottest player, winning six of his past 24 tournaments, with an equally torrid putter.

But he put his drive off the first tee into serious trouble, a harbinger of heartache to come. Goosen bogeyed two of his first four holes, giving himself — in his own indicting words — "no chance of catching Tiger." Another victim rendered helpless and sucked into the vortex of Woods' pursuit of golfing immortality.

There's nothing anyone can do. Lengthen the course to the county line? It won't matter. Force everyone to use a less lively ball? It won't matter. Tie the guy's right arm to his waist, and it still wouldn't affect the inevitable outcome.

Woods wins because he has his competition convinced they're going to lose. It's that intimidating, war-like mentality that maintains the sizable gap between the world's best and the wanna-bes. The man was ready for the battle of the final nine Sunday, but there was nobody around willing to fight.

TIGER, TAKE EIGHT: AUG. 12, 2002

Be thankful Woods keeps opinions to himself

GRAND BLANC — Somewhere amid the sea of humanity stood the quarry. It just required some creative navigation to find him. There he is! See him? You can't miss him. Get up high on your toes and look just over that guy's right shoulder two rows ahead and then peer just left of that lady's hat and then just underneath that fella's chin, you'll see a patch of red.

That's Tiger Woods.

Isn't that special? You've gotten to see the Nike polo he wears, up close and personal. And, trust me, many left Warwick Hills Golf and Country Club honored even if all they caught was a quick glimpse. Just being in the same area code was enough, although it seemed as though those in the back of the pack were more than a long-distance call away from reaching their man.

A gallery of thousands saw what they wanted — that is, if they could see anything at all. But hearing a Tiger Woods victory can prove equally rewarding.

"There's a rumor that he's out there," one young woman said facetiously, trying without success to find an opening through the crowd on the No. 2 fairway. "But just knowing that I'm this close to somebody that great is excitement enough for me."

All that matters is that they were there when Woods won his first Buick Open, a four-stroke triumph. Their attraction wasn't Tiger Woods, the political advocate. It was purely Tiger Woods, the rock star. He has won 33 PGA Tour events in six years, but this was the first one in our own backyard.

He took home, ho-hum, another championship trophy. He didn't kiss this one, an honor reserved only for the major tournaments. Another winner's check — $594,000. Only tip money. And the Buick of his choice. He's already a spokesman for the company, so he can have his choice of Buick dealerships if he desired.

Redundancy invites boredom, but the Buick Open gallery numbers, as well as its fervor, suggest that Tigermania isn't close to subsiding. Despite outside attempts to tarnish his image with his benign response to the issue of female membership at Augusta National Golf Club, Woods' stature as a once-in-a-lifetime athletic phenomenon surges on. It doesn't matter that his critics believe he has other obligations.

In their eyes, Woods must not only win majors but the Nobel Prize, as well.

What good is powerfully wielding a driver unless it's also used as a sickle to slice through injustice and inequities? How wasteful is it to have a disarming personality and not use it to effect change? Because he has become a modern day Pied Piper, why shouldn't he carry the message for the masses to follow?

But the day Woods turns his putter into a political sword, he risks becoming a caricature who arrogantly inflates his importance. When he speaks, people will listen and may ultimately act. But he should wait until he comfortably finds his voice instead of satisfying the timetables of others.

Before those critics make demands, they should examine what Woods has done. Woods is influential. It's unavoidable. Exposure creates role models, and as long as it remains his choice to chase Jack Nicklaus' record of 18 major professional championships, Woods will be watched, heard and emulated. Every step will be chronicled, every action dissected.

His hesitancy to champion females' fight with Augusta National was cast as disrespectful to women. Disrespectful?

Has he kicked any naked women out of his home? Has he physically abused any women? Has he fathered children out of wedlock, only to toss aside the mother with a token cash payoff? Where's the evidence of the all-too-prevalent male superstar mentality that adoring women are disposable trophies?

Yet somehow he's lacking substance and spine because he possibly possesses no strong emotions either way regarding rich CEOs having the opportunity to commingle with others of their own ilk at Augusta? Aren't there more meaningful public exclusionary practices where Woods' special gifts would be better put to use?

But losing perspective is easy when we're talking about an athlete who usually doesn't lose when he gets the lead. He remains steady while those around him crumble. Just ask Esteban Toledo about his collapse after Tiger's lead shrank to one shot after 12 holes. He's equally steady away from the golf course, not giving away too much while revealing very little.

That's his choice. That's his right.

That also makes him a refreshing alternative in an easily corruptible and contemptible superstar landscape.

CHAPTER SIX

St. Patrick in Game 7, eh, you #@&% genius!

MAY 14, 1998

Osgood answers the Blues and then his critics

ST. LOUIS — Just when you were prepared to embrace him without doubt, ready to lower the beam of the white-hot spotlight focused on him a few degrees, a blunder forces you to continue examining Chris Osgood with a cautious yet optimistic eye.

That hope results from the way Osgood responded after letting Blues defenseman Al MacInnis' center-ice prayer beat him with less than a minute remaining in regulation, forcing overtime in Game 3 of the playoffs. Osgood could have collapsed completely. And how many outside the Red Wings' locker room honestly, truly believed that he wouldn't have, given the circumstances?

"It was my best win," Osgood said. "I haven't had one that was more gratifying, and that includes the 1-0 double-overtime game (in 1996). I was able to bounce back after I made a mistake. Everyone wants to focus on the one I let in, but what about the 10 saves I made in overtime?"

Osgood needs to understand that, fairly or unfairly, questions will remain until he is a Stanley Cup-winning goalie instead of a Stanley Cup-winning backup. Blues players spoke of Osgood's possible vulnerability, despite the fact that he stopped 33 of the 35 shots he faced in more than 90 minutes of playoff pressure. And it's certain that many fans, though obviously delighted the Wings won, 3-2, in double overtime, still took Osgood to task for putting them through such emotional torment.

But the only thoughts and opinions that concern Osgood are in his locker room, an atmosphere that breeds a collective cool, an equilibrium that keeps the players from scaling too high in good times and from falling too low in crises. Darren McCarty describes it as a been-there, done-that mellowness.

"We just looked at each other (after regulation), knowing what we had to do," Osgood said. "We never once thought of ways that we could lose but rather focused on how we were going to win."

That attitude stands as the fundamental difference in this second-round series, one in which the Wings could seize firm control with a victory in Game 4 at Kiel Center. How many other teams could joke about a situation that could have precipitated one of the playoffs' most embarrassing losses?

"Hey, Ozzie," Joey Kocur shouted during practice, "why don't you work on stopping those long shots?"

It's easier to laugh about yourself after a victory, but it's apparent that the intense scrutiny still agitates Osgood. When asked whether he grew weary of defending himself, he snapped back that he wouldn't have to give the same answers if the media would stop asking the same questions.

MacInnis has scored six times off Osgood in seven games this season. Nothing fancy. Each time, MacInnis merely cocked and fired, launching a twisting and turning missile. Osgood flatly denies any intimidation, and anyone possessing a 100-m.p.h. slap shot is certainly a threat to any goalie. But when six of a guy's 21 goals this season have come against you, it's difficult to erase such a ratio from your mind.

"I don't think about him more than I do anybody else," Osgood said. "Hey, the guy's no slouch. He's probably got the most difficult shot to judge in the league. He can drop it. He can curve it. He's like a knuckleball pitcher in baseball. You never know where it's going. You just hope you can get it to bounce off your chest. It's really a scary thought."

The true measure of a goalie is how he responds under attack, when resiliency assumes the utmost importance. Osgood reaffirmed some faith with his overtime performance, but as long as those momentary lapses remain, so too will those annoyingly repetitive questions.

JUNE 18, 1998

Wings provide the Cup, Detroit provides the party

Another championship, another party. And this time we didn't have to wait 42 years. The celebrations began right after the Red Wings' second straight Stanley Cup title, and they will continue with the parade down Woodward Avenue.

Towns all over America love their winners, but in Detroit, professional sports championships bring an emotion, a passion, a sense of history that distinguish our parties from many others. How many pro teams spawn a fleet of flag-waving cars and trucks in an area of more than four million people?

"You can't help but love winning for the fans of Detroit because they live and breathe the game," Steve Yzerman said after the Red Wings completed a sweep of Washington in the Stanley Cup finals. "I can't wait to get back there and celebrate with them."

Party we have, and party we will. Few cities rejoice with the unbridled delirium that we do. It wouldn't surprise anyone if another million red-and-white-clad supporters chanting, "Oz-zie! Oz-zie!" make their way to the parade route or Hart Plaza rally.

Diverse lives remain connected by one common thread in this area — sports. How many other cities can point to a World Series championship as an influence in healing racial wounds opened a year earlier in one of the nation's worst urban uprisings? That happened in Detroit in 1968.

Professor Michael Bernacchi thinks our response to title teams is actually a form of venting, a chance to free ourselves — at least temporarily — from Detroit's negative image in much of the world. It's a way to shout: "Respect us!"

"I've studied this for a while, and we seem to not always have the most favorable opinion of ourselves," said Bernacchi, who teaches sports marketing and trends at the University of Detroit Mercy. "And a lot of that has to do with the image that's fairly or unfairly projected from others on the outside. You know all the comments. 'Detroit's a bad city. Detroit's a dangerous city.' But the notion of pleasant achievement is a confirmation that we aren't to be forgotten. We are a major force."

Having lived here since 1973, Bernacchi has adopted Detroit's teams, but his passion still runs deepest for the Cubs of his native Chicago.

"Sports in general in Detroit, but hockey in particular, is a cultural phenomenon," Bernacchi said. "Hockey holds a special place in metro Detroit hearts. There isn't another of the original U.S. NHL cities that could ever be called Hockeytown. That creates a sense of pride, an attitude that sets you apart from everybody else. These guys are playing for you. And they're winning for you. That's why we consider it our Cup — and why we don't want to give it away."

Bernacchi thinks our culture was long ago shaped by the automobile industry. The blue-collar attitude was forged by the simple creed that hard work breeds success, a mentality that's the basic formula for athletic success.

"It's no coincidence that the average working person is more inclined to live through the fate and fortunes of their sports teams," Bernacchi said. "But the bad side of the blue-collar mentality is that it further fuels the negative image that Detroit may not offer the cultural variety that other large, more notable cities have — which, of course, isn't true. But that gives you another reason to stand up and shout when we know that we're the best."

That national recognition might never come, and the negative images might never vanish. But the fever pitch with which we party when our sports heroes scale the mountaintop seems to indicate that maybe it doesn't matter. Who cares what everyone else thinks about a downsized automobile industry, oversized impoverished pockets in our neighborhoods or other economic, social and political circumstances that occasionally extend beyond the average person's comprehension?

Everyone understands winning. And Detroit is more than delighted to spend an entire summer telling anybody who asks that it's our Cup — and we don't intend to give it up.

MAY 10, 2002

On his 37th birthday, Yzerman zings the Blues

ST. LOUIS — Birthdays become reminders after time. One more year becomes one less opportunity should dreams turn into disappointment. So don't waste the golden chances when they arise.

The Captain turned 37, and blowing out the candles meant blowing away the St. Louis Blues.

Oh, the Blues brought a birthday present for Steve Yzerman — a bull's-eye stitched to his back. The Blues wanted to remind him that he's getting older. Remember when you were a kid and your friends gave you a punch on the arm on your birthday for each year? Well, that's kind of what the Blues had in mind for Yzerman.

But the Captain reminded the youngsters chasing him, hitting him and fighting him for the puck that age often brings the smarts to do the right thing at the right time.

The Blues' captain, hulking Chris Pronger, had Yzerman sized up near the boards for a first-period hit. Yzerman sensed the bruising defenseman was approaching and did the smart thing. He low-bridged Pronger, sending him first into the boards and then into the locker room with a torn ACL.

The game was over then. And, as a result, the series is over now.

The Red Wings withstood their latest challenge, neutralizing the Blues' early fire and force with some good old-fashioned brains. And following their 4-3 victory in Game 4 of the playoffs at the Savvis Center, the smart money is on this series not extending beyond Game 5 at the Joe.

Which is precisely what the Wings want because age makes you wiser, but it also makes you more tired.

Yzerman was tireless. The man was everywhere. When there was a 5-on-3 St. Louis advantage to kill, Yzerman was there. When a Blue chirped a little too much, Yzerman was in his face. When a scrum formed in front of Blues goalie Brent Johnson, Yzerman was there. During one sequence, he took out Johnson's knees after being pushed into the net. And later, when Johnson tried to clear the puck, Yzerman was there. His third-period goal was basically a ricochet off his chest.

Not a bad birthday gift, eh?

But pleasing him more was the overall performance. The defensive leaks from Game 3 were sufficiently plugged until those final frantic moments. The Blues' premier line of Pavol Demitra, Keith Tkachuk and Scott Mellanby was silenced until that last gasp, when the Blues scored twice in the closing four minutes. St. Louis fired 10 shots at Dominik Hasek before the Wings threw their first attempt on net. But the Wings didn't flinch. They maintained their composure while the Blues conceded theirs.

How else can you explain Pronger's mental lapse, going after Yzerman? He cost his team any chance of coming back in this series. Yzerman was a pain in the butt, throwing his rear end at Pronger during their collision.

"Going down like that beats getting run over," Yzerman said. "It was really the only thing I could do. Unfortunately for Chris, when you're a tall guy like he is, you can take a pretty good fall on something like that."

Even at 37, Yzerman doesn't shy away from the scraps and scrapes that epitomize this game. In fact, it almost seems as though he relishes them.

"They play him hard," Darren McCarty said, "but if you look, you'll see that he throws as much as he takes. He doesn't try to avoid anything. They've been coming after him this series, but he's come to expect that."

Look upon the Wings and their Hall of Fame allure as you would a piece of fine china. Everyone wants to admire its intrinsic beauty and unique detailing. But the longer it stays out of the cupboard, the greater the risk a scratch here or a chip there damages the entire piece.

Igor Larionov missed Game 4 with a leg injury, and Yzerman's unstable right knee isn't getting any better. Extending any series longer than necessary exposes the Wings to the ill-timed check to the ice or slam against the boards that further tests their depth. Each additional game the Wings play, every additional hit they take, every additional ounce of energy required, takes a little more out of the tank that they're going to need to fulfill this city's dream of a 10th Stanley Cup.

Why take any additional chances? Get it done! And get it done now!

"Our objective coming in here for these two games was maintain control of the series," Kirk Maltby said.

Mission accomplished.

Both teams resembled their respective captains. The Wings displayed equal parts guts and guile, authoritatively taking charge. The Blues appeared dazed by the suddenness in which this game and this series turned against them, foolishly looking as though they wore Yzerman's birthday cake on their faces.

The Wings took Drew Sharp's advice and finished off the Blues in five games.

MAY 30, 2002

Facing elimination, Wings force showdown in Game 7

DENVER — Amid the occasional cruelties of spirited competition, there are moments when justice is rightfully served. The scales are tipped back and balanced. Regardless of your allegiance or your animosity toward the opposition, you must concede that a true classic deserves to run its full course, ending only when the last possible bead of sweat or drop of blood can fall. Anything less than the maximum seven games for the Red Wings and Colorado would be inappropriate.

"We were due to have a few things go our way," Steve Yzerman said.

Few were owed more than Brendan Shanahan and Dominik Hasek. And, fittingly, that combination — which would have been a popular target for criticism had the Wings' championship aspirations died — was most instrumental in keeping the chase alive.

Shanahan needed a goal. He got it.

Hasek needed a shutout. He got it.

Brace yourself for the much-too-soon ending to a delightfully dizzying ride in Game 7. And this is the way it should be. One night. One game. One chance. To the winner goes the Stanley Cup.

"We all understood the consequences if we didn't come through," Kirk Maltby said. "Everything that we've aimed for since the start of training camp would have come to a disappointing end, but we've bought ourselves one more game."

The Wings staved off playoff execution, delivering their strongest collective effort when it was needed the most. Their 2-0 victory ensured an electrifying climax to a confrontation that hasn't wilted from the hype that so often swells these highly anticipated battles beyond reasonable expectations. Now, if only there's a way the Wings can waive home ice and settle this stalemate where they've played their best — among their friends in the Rockies.

The road remains their friend because they know that it's no place for cuteness. While others panicked at the necessity of getting a win away from home, the Wings found it rather soothing. They play better at the Pepsi Center because they assume nothing there.

No home cooking from the officials. No added jump from the partisan crowd. On the road, they're more inclined to scrap, scratch, poke, pick, whatever's required to get the job done. They're less likely to force the action and more willing to fight for the result they seek.

Ask the Wings if they were a little lucky in Game 6 and they probably wouldn't dispute it. Nor would they care. They got what they came here for — one more breath.

The breaks that worked against both teams through the previous five games tilted a little more in the Wings' favor in Game 6. The officials looked the other way when Steve Duchesne tried to remove Stephane Yelle's Adam's apple without anesthesia.

And then Patrick Roy, clearly out of his element if the gun's not pointed at his own temple, thought he had miraculously swiped a prime Yzerman scoring chance in his glove. But the puck wasn't there, slipping free underneath his pad, and Shanahan punched it through for the gift goal he couldn't collect in the closing two minutes of regulation in Game 5.

"We projected a calm because we were confident coming in here," Yzerman said. "We've felt that we've played well despite being down, 3-2. Just relax, keep your wits about you and we'll get a break."

The Wings got the breaks while the Avalanche collected the bruises. Yelle didn't return because of a bruised neck. Defensive warhorse Rob Blake hobbled off the ice and into the locker room midway through the third period. And there was postgame speculation that Peter Forsberg might have been dinged, though the Avs said he was fine.

The Wings took a series that has already taken an inordinate number of sudden twists down one more winding curve. And this gem may still possess one last stunning jolt. The matchup that everyone wanted has become the grudge match everyone hoped for.

Hasek made his statement, stopping 24 shots. Now it's Roy's turn. Humbling Hasek is the lone missing notch on his stick, the one remaining conquest that would make Roy indisputably the finest money goaltender of this and possibly past generations.

A passionate competitor like Roy probably won't mind that the final passages of this script will play out when both sides have no other choice but to win or wait until next season. And that's the way it should be.

MAY 31, 2002

You heard it here first: Bet on St. Patrick in seven

If you placed a ruler to Patrick Roy's face, you likely would measure a smirk wider than allowable on the day of a win-or-golf Game 7. His record in these situations isn't the greatest — he's 6-5 — but his familiarity with the emotions and expectations makes him a great asset in the final curtain call for the Western Conference championship series. Already in these playoffs, the Colorado Avalanche has won two Game 7s, and Roy finished with shutouts in both, against Los Angeles and San Jose.

"It doesn't mean that we have the edge," Roy said about Colorado's charmed playoff life. "But it gives us the right to feel comfortable."

His confidence should make Hockeytown sweat. After six games between the Red Wings and Avalanche, it's down to one game, a time you never bet against Roy. Not in a Game 7.

Despise him if you choose. Mock him if you must. But never doubt him when survival is at stake.

"He's been proven the best in this situation over the years," said Joe Sakic, the Avs' captain. "We've had two Game 7s already in these playoffs, and Patty didn't give up a goal in either one. That tells you right there what you need to know about the guy."

There are many reasons the Avs shouldn't win, starting with odds and injuries. Their forward lines are depleted, which might leave coach Bob Hartley no alternative but to move someone up from the blue line. No team ever has won three consecutive Game 7s to advance to the Stanley Cup finals. And the Avs are tired and testy over not finishing off the Wings in Game 6. But there's one reason, and one reason only, they will win.

The blessing of St. Patrick. Or if you're a Wings fan, perhaps it's the curse of "Waaaahhhh."

If only the Wings had stopped peppering the poor man with shot after shot, embarrassing him with goal after goal, that Saturday evening in Montreal in December 1995. That rogue Canadiens coach, Mario Tremblay, left Roy out on the ice to absorb the brunt of a 12-1 beating. Humiliated, Roy stormed out of the Forum in a fit, insisting he never would play for Montreal again. He didn't, and he soon was united with his former agent, Pierre Lacroix, the Avalanche general manager. And the rest, as they say, is history.

Roy steps onto hockey's grandest stage for a record-tying 12th time, matching Edmonton forward Glenn Anderson for the most seventh-game appearances. Despite his pedestrian record in Game 7s, few doubt his worth in these moments of desperation, when the mind often dictates the action.

"Goaltending is always important in a Game 7," Wings captain Steve Yzerman said, "because both teams usually try to play a patient game. You're going to wait for the other guy to make a mistake. There might be many good scoring chances, but there will be a lot of importance on the ones that come about."

Experience has taught us never to underestimate Roy. He has kept the Avalanche in a series the Wings probably should already have clinched. Dominik Hasek was the dominant goaltender in Game 6. But until it's proven otherwise, there's no reason to doubt that Roy will conjure one more brilliant moment.

JUNE 1, 2002

No mercy for Roy as Wings humble Avs

Their motives pure, their performance precise, the Red Wings took their sticks and drove them through the heart of their nemesis. Again and again in a 7-0, Game 7 thrashing of Colorado they struck with dizzying ferocity and frequency, ultimately leaving their quarry on its back in a quivering mess.

This was an exorcism. The Wings beat the devil out of Patrick Roy. And what they left behind was neither frightening nor intimidating.

Not only was a season saved, but so was the soul of an impassioned hockey community sorely disappointed over recent failures. In many ways, Roy personified the Wings' playoff aggravation through much of the last four years. He was always the face of the fans' frustration. He was the reason the team aggressively pursued goaltender Dominik Hasek.

And he was the only way Colorado could once again thwart the Wings' championship ambitions. Just as they have so many times in so many similar predicaments, the Avalanche leaned heavily on its anointed savior. Unable to handle the weight, Roy finally collapsed.

Six goals on 16 shots in just 26 minutes not only brought to an end Roy's NHL record-tying 12th career Game 7, it ended the mystifying spell he has recently woven in these climactic moments. He wasn't just mortal. He was mortifying. Give the formerly bedeviled their due.

"A few of us on the bench just looked up at the scoreboard in disbelief when we got those goals that quickly," Brett Hull said.

Disbelief? Shocking might best describe a game that basically ended in the first three minutes.

" 'Shocking' might be a little strong," said Hull, who scored the fifth goal against Roy. "He's also human. But when we had success getting our first two shots past him, we told each other to keep after them. Don't let up. Keep pouring it on."

They did until Colorado was buried under an avalanche.

The Wings return to the Stanley Cup finals after a four-year hiatus, but you couldn't tell that by their demeanor after the game. They graciously accepted their Western Conference championship caps and shirts, but nobody dared model them. After Steve Yzerman was presented the Clarence Campbell Bowl, he whisked it off the ice and placed it in a corner of the locker room, where it sat ignored the rest of the evening. Let's face it. It's like the ugly cousin. You don't kiss that thing. You kiss it off.

"It's not what we want," Hasek said. "We want the Stanley Cup. That's the next step."

And to get there the Wings stepped over what had been their toughest obstacle. Sweetening the triumph was the embarrassment of Roy, whom they drove to the bench after Fredrik Olausson made it 6-0, sending the Joe Louis Arena crowd into a frenzy.

A series filled with pivot turns in momentum had one final surprise. And who thought it would be the image of Roy draped in a white towel of surrender six minutes into the second period? It marked the first time he had been pulled from a Game 7.

"Yeah, I think we're as surprised as anyone," Steve Yzerman said. "We thought that it would be a 1-0 game or go into overtime. We're still thinking after the first period that this isn't the way it's supposed to be. You can't plan on getting four goals against him in the first period in a game like this."

No sweat was needed or created in this one. General manager Ken Holland had brought a couple of extra dress shirts with him just in case the mounting tension drenched his clothes. In a way, it's a pity this scintillating series ended with such a dog. Roy apparently spent so much time swatting away fleas that he couldn't see the shots the Wings threw his way.

There are no excuses for the man. He blew it. The greats are entitled to their off-nights, but not in a Game 7 against your most despised rival. The Avs needed him to kick it into a higher gear. Instead, the Wings kicked him right where it hurt most.

Roy couldn't help but hear the crowd chanting "Has-ek! Has-ek!" as time dwindled in the final period. This battle of the lords between the pipes went to the guy thirsting for his first sip from the Stanley Cup. Hull offered Roy a few consoling words during the final handshake afterward.

"I told him to hold his head up high," Hull said. "I've got the utmost respect for him. He's one of the best, if not the best, goalies in the history of his game, and nothing that happened tonight can take that away. He's still the best."

But the aura that has followed him, particularly since the 2001 playoffs, has dimmed somewhat in the aftermath of this disaster. The Wings proved that Roy doesn't have exclusive rights to Game 7 magic. They turned the trick on him this time, ensuring for Roy a hellish summer similar to those the Wings have endured the last few years.

JUNE 10, 2002

Destiny calls, and Red Wings answer in triple-OT

RALEIGH, N.C. — Fate is mystifying. There's neither rhyme nor reason for its timing when it puts a reassuring arm around a shoulder and steers the chosen down the inevitable road. It waited until the 115th minute to make itself known in the third-longest Stanley Cup finals game in history. And it graced the oldest player on the oldest team in the league.

Igor Larionov's triple-overtime game-winner in Game 3 shares company with Nicklas Lidstrom's center-ice knuckler past Vancouver goalie Dan Cloutier in Game 3 of the first round, Chris Pronger's season-ending pratfall over Steve Yzerman in Game 4 of the second round and Patrick Roy's ill-fated Statute of Liberty showboat in Game 6 of the Western Conference finals. They are those unexplainable plot twists that are often the bedrock of dreams fulfilled. Sometimes, things are just meant to be.

"There's no question that they're a great team," Carolina winger Jeff O'Neill said of the Red Wings. "But it just looks like they have a way of getting the right break at the right time. Just when you think you might have them — bam! — they get what they need. I mean, we were a minute or so away from leading this series, 2-1, and then. . . ."

And then — bam!

The wind was knocked out of the Hurricanes, fate slamming the door in their faces. Carolina coach Paul Maurice proudly refers to his players as "mongrels." Sorry, y'all, but this puppy is over.

The Wings stand confidently near the top of the mountain. They knew this would be a tougher championship series than many predicted. They knew there would be frustrating moments during the eight-week playoffs, brought on by misfires and mistakes. But they also knew that if they steadfastly believed in their purpose, they ultimately would persevere. They have won every way possible against every style imaginable, clearing every obstacle conceivable.

The last was a five-hour marathon that so physically depleted the much-younger Hurricanes that some needed to replace fluids intravenously during intermission after the second overtime. As for the Gray Wings, they dined on bananas and oranges. And in perhaps the funniest twist, the magic mixture for the older team was a children's drink that replaces minerals lost when a 6-year-old is fighting the effects of diarrhea.

Pedialyte: The official drink of the Stanley Cup champions. Think of the marketing possibilities.

"Hi, I'm Igor Larionov. And when my teammates and I run out of Geritol, we drink Pedialyte. It's great for the long run, as well as a long case of the runs."

Why not a standard sports drink? Wings trainer John Wharton said there are more electrolytes in the kids' drink and a faster rate of absorption.

"I've given it to my little girl when she's gotten sick," forward Kris Draper said. "And now we've found another use for it. It's strange how these things work out. But if we should win the Stanley Cup, maybe we should pour Pedialyte in there before any champagne."

"I don't look at it like somebody is smiling down on us," said Lidstrom, who played a game-high 52 minutes, three seconds, the equivalent of two games for most players. "We've had some weird things go our way at times in the playoffs, but everyone knows that you're going to need some breaks to stay in the playoffs this long. But it's more about having the confidence in knowing that those breaks are going to come. All through that overtime, we kept telling ourselves that if we stay patient and keep at it, it's going to break our way. That's not waiting for luck. That's working toward it."

Confidence is an acquired trait. Surround yourself with self-assurance, and it's bound to rub off. Steve Yzerman stood up in the locker room during intermission after the second overtime and told his teammates: "Don't forget that this is a lot of fun."

Fun? What kind of sadist is he?

The game fell 27 seconds short of breaking the record for the longest championship series game in NHL history, held by the first game of the 1990 finals between Edmonton and Boston. Guys lost teeth and gained stitches dropping to block overtime shots at the net. But not once did they think their sacrifices would go unrewarded.

Fate has been the Wings' ally. And now they're two victories shy of taking those first precious sips from the Stanley Cup.

Pedialyte might never taste better.

JUNE 11, 2002

Cup comes at a steep price, but it's worth it

RALEIGH, N.C. — The quest for the Stanley Cup is defined by the sacrifices made. What are you prepared to do? What are you willing to give up?

Steve Duchesne spent the afternoon in a dentist's chair, having a root canal. Nerves were removed from what remained of the two natural teeth he lost when he took a puck in the mouth in the third overtime of Game 3. He also lost four teeth from a bridge. But that didn't stop him from falling face-first to try to block a shot in Game 4.

Mercifully, the shot missed him.

Duchesne's willingness to throw himself into the firing line without regard for his deteriorating dental health underscored the significance of the moment. The Red Wings are so close to their 10th title that they can taste it, even if some of them can't chew.

"I've still got my bottom teeth, so I figure I'm all right," Duchesne said. "Besides, guys said I look better than I did before. And it hurts a little trying to say words that start with the letter 's.' But I don't mind it when you think about the excitement of being in this position."

The countdown to the Stanley Cup is one. One more lost tooth. One more stitch to the face. One more ice bag administered to the bruise of your choice. One more victory, and the motivation for the physical torture these guys have endured crystallizes in the form of a shiny silver trophy.

It's over. It's only a question of when. The Wings seized control of the Stanley Cup finals in Game 4, leaving Carolina on the ropes after their 3-0 victory. A 3-1 series lead has reduced the Hurricanes to a harmless whisper.

What seemed far away when this odyssey began nearly two months ago is within reach. When Brendan Shanahan delivered the death knell, flipping a shot past Arturs Irbe with 5:17 left in the third period, Dominik Hasek jumped for joy at the other end. He's one victory away from the one trophy that has eluded him.

But don't forget normally forgettable role guys like Duchesne, who wasn't even drafted and bounced around the NHL for 16 years, thinking he might never have the chance to have his name inscribed on the Cup. The toughest part now is trying to contain himself.

"I try to," Duchesne said. "It is difficult. But during the finals you forget about all that, and you don't think. You just react. It's awesome, and you have to keep it going."

Even when it hurts to smile.

These Wings have kept it going, methodically taking over Game 4 the same as they did in numerous other road games during this ride. They're 8-2 on the road in this playoff season, perhaps the strongest testament to their resolve.

"We came out and might have played our best defensive game of the playoffs, and that's what we knew we would need," said Nicklas Lidstrom, whose consistent brilliance makes him a Conn Smythe Trophy candidate for playoff most valuable player. "We got plenty of contributions from a lot of guys. And when you see Steve play the way he did after knowing what he's been through since that last game, you see how much everyone wants this."

After Duchesne took the puck in the mouth in Game 3, he missed only one shift. He later set up Igor Larionov's game-winner late in the third overtime. Even knowing the cosmetic price paid, Duchesne said he would do it all over again. That is what winning the Cup means to so many players. And it's why there's a greater appreciation for the bumpy and bruising road these guys endure to get those 16 victories.

And now it's down to one more.

"I'm going to try not to think about what might happen," Duchesne said, "but that's going to be hard. I'll have a lot of family with me, and they'll be talking about it, and you guys aren't going to let us forget about it the next couple of days."

The Wings won't publicly concede the inevitable — that they will win their third championship in six years. Understandably, they can't. But deep down, they certainly realize that the potentially threatening Hurricane winds of Game 1 have diminished to a sigh. The energy generated by the home crowd gradually evaporated as the Wings continually applied pressure, wearing down their opponent.

"We've got the opportunity to take some control over the series," Boyd Devereaux said. "If a team looks like they're feeling down, you don't want to let them back up and give them another chance. You've got to take it to them."

You have to do whatever it takes, regardless of the physical toll. And when the reward is finally attained, there will be smiles all around — especially from those who don't have any teeth to show off right now.

JUNE 12, 2002

Lidstrom is the man of the hour for Red Wings

It would be a test of wills, waiting to see which happened first: Nicklas Lidstrom getting tired or getting mad.

"That would take too long," Red Wings forward Kirk Maltby said. "I don't think anybody's that patient. No, I take that back. There's probably only one person that patient."

And that's Lidstrom himself.

Teammates are hard-pressed to cite an instance of his temper, provoked or otherwise. He isn't a physical player, but that doesn't exclude him from taking punishment. Discretion is the better part of victory in his mind. He casually deflects praise as though it were a wrister off an opponent's stick. Lidstrom is as smooth in a locker room of superstars as he is in his own defensive zone.

He's too modest and soft-spoken to spout his virtues. So permit me.

The man has earned the Conn Smythe Trophy, a tribute to playoff consistency as much as excellence.

With the Red Wings on the brink of eliminating the Carolina Hurricanes and claiming their 10th Stanley Cup, Lidstrom should get the award because of his headline-worthy goals. He should get it because he deserves the recognition from others that he declines to give himself.

"I don't think about those things," he said when a reporter futilely tried coaxing a little self-acknowledgment from the Swede. "You can't lose sight of the team objective."

Lidstrom would make history winning the Conn Smythe, becoming the first European player to receive the award. Perhaps it should be called the Cann Smythe, since it's gone to a non-Canadian only once in its 37-year history. American Brian Leetch won it with the New York Rangers in 1994.

"We're a team of great players," Maltby said, "with guys who are very valuable. But you look at these playoffs and the guy we could least afford to lose for an extended period of time would be Nick. And that's because he logs so much time."

Lidstrom played more than 52 minutes in the Game 3 triple-overtime thriller won by the Red Wings, 3-2, and he has quietly left huge footprints throughout the championship march. Evidence of his icy cool and unflinching discipline: For all his time on the ice and in the thick of the action, he's taken only one penalty in the playoffs, for tripping.

There are many deserving Wings candidates for the Conn Smythe, such as Dominik Hasek, Steve Yzerman, Brett Hull and Sergei Fedorov. But Lidstrom best symbolizes the defensive stability that has made life relatively easy for Hasek the last two months.

"You can't just look at one person and say that's why we've played well," Lidstrom said. "The credit goes all around. Cheli (Chris Chelios) was healthy all season and had a great year. He's a finalist for the Norris Trophy. Freddie (Olausson) and Stevie (Duchesne) were consistent all season, and the young guys like Jiri (Fischer) stepped up with big contributions."

How ironic that a team assembled for its offensive prowess sits one victory shy of the Stanley Cup primarily because of its defensive stinginess. Hasek's save percentage isn't even ranked in the top five among playoff goalies, but it doesn't have to be. Funny, isn't it? He was brought into town to compensate for perceived defensive shortcomings.

"This was the best defense I've ever had in front of me," Hasek said. "I don't want to say that it takes the pressure off the goalie, but it makes you feel more comfortable.

"Knowing that I'll have guys like Lidstrom and Chelios out there for a combined total of 50 minutes for each game helps you. There have been times in these playoffs where I haven't gotten much work because the defense wasn't giving up many good scoring chances."

The Wings' defense has reflected the attitude of its leader. Its efficiency is underappreciated, but it shouldn't go unrewarded.

The Wings won the Cup, of course, and Lidstrom did indeed become the first European to take home the Conn Smythe Trophy.

JUNE 14, 2002

Wings realize ultimate goal with Hasek in goal

On the morning of the biggest day of his competitive life, Dominik Hasek was told to take it easy. Why bother with the optional morning skate? Stay at home. Relax. Lie low and avoid distractions.

But there was Hasek on the ice, preparing, simulating what he might encounter later, existing in his own world, which insulated him from the peripheral theatrics. This is how the man relaxes. One individual's obsession became a team's objective.

Hasek has answered the soldier's call ever since the Red Wings stunned the NHL with his acquisition in July 2001. He was all business because he knew that time was running short for removing the asterisk from his career — no Stanley Cup title. He was no-nonsense because he might not want to endure another excruciatingly long season.

And then the collective mission became his singular moment as a joyous city counted down the final seconds. The weight of unfulfillment finally removed, Hasek screamed in delight. But only after he sighed in relief. His long wait was finally over, his brilliant career finally validated.

In-Dom-itable!

When Brendan Shanahan drove home an empty-net goal in the final seconds, Hasek at last could let loose. He raced up the ice, desperate to join the celebration, but he couldn't go past the red line or he would risk a penalty. So he waited for the party to come to him. And when it did, he piled on top. This was one occasion when nobody minded that he wandered from the net.

Hasek made what might have been the Conn Smythe-winning save in the second period when Rod Brind'Amour centered a perfect opportunity onto Bates Battaglia's stick. Hasek recovered quickly, throwing out a leg to stop what should have been a Carolina goal.

But the Conn Smythe Trophy, given to the playoffs' most valuable player, went to the deserving Nicklas Lidstrom. And do you think Hasek cared for one minute that he didn't get another individual award? He already has a closet full of them. What he lacked was what was brought out next — Lord Stanley's pride and joy.

This title was about the restoration of an organization's vision, as well as redemption of an individual's career. Steve Yzerman thought this was the best of the three championships he has because the Wings were the favorites from the beginning. And there's no greater pressure than the burden of high expectations.

But you couldn't get past the first sip of champagne without wondering if Hasek's initial taste will sufficiently quench his thirst for competition. The job of selling Hasek into staying another season in Detroit began in the closing minutes when the raucous crowd repeatedly chanted his name. The Wings already have lost a coach. How close are they to losing a goalie, as well?

"I don't want to say, 'Yes, this was my last game,' right now," Hasek said. "I will make my final decision in the next three or four days. I will sit with my wife and talk about it."

Scotty Bowman said he made up his mind after the Olympic break. It's hard to believe that Hasek doesn't already know his next move. But if it's to retire, it's a good thing he didn't tell anyone on this night. This town couldn't have handled two retirements in one hour.

"Why keep playing is the big question for me," Hasek said. "The truth is I want to go back to the Czech Republic with my family, but the biggest dream was to win the Cup, and I have done it. So there's the question of if I want to do it one more time."

Hasek owes neither the Wings nor its fans another season. All the Wings got what they were after this season. Nobody is kidding anybody here. Hasek, 37, retired once before, only to return because the Stanley Cup void left him incomplete. He thought the Wings provided the best shot at glory, so he took a little less money and the Wings agreed to rent his services on a year-to-year basis. Incidentally, Hasek gets a $1 million bonus for winning the Stanley Cup.

But everyone needs to understand that the mental edge that makes Hasek stand out is perhaps the reason he might opt for retirement. The man is such a perfectionist, paying attention to every minute detail, that it might be impossible for him to reach the high level of concentration he developed this season, now that his name is etched on the Cup. As prideful as he is, Hasek might think it better to leave on the ultimate high note.

Hasek already is a hero in his native Czech Republic. Game 5 was televised live there — at 3 a.m. That wouldn't have stopped folks from converging in front of their televisions. Compatriots Jiri Slegr and Jiri Fischer expected it would be the most-anticipated sports event in that nation since the 1998 Olympic hockey gold medal game, when Hasek was deified after willing his country to the championship.

We've seen that unbreakable resolve unfold during a remarkable drive toward immortality. And if this is the end, there should be resounding gratitude that Hockeytown provided the exclamation point to a wonderful career.

JUNE 26, 2002

Dom's a consummate pro, right to the end

The romance proved nothing more than a quick fling. Wham, bam, welcome back, Stan.

Dominik Hasek liked his short time in Detroit, but he loved his priorities and principles more. He fought off the intoxicating flirtations of another championship run, staying true to his word. He promised his family when he was traded to the Red Wings that if he won the Stanley Cup, he would retire.

Hasek is Czeching out, returning to his homeland. The goalie's one-year, one-Cup-and-out Wings career was hardly surprising, but that didn't stop a couple of young fans standing outside Joe Louis Arena from making one final, desperate lunge for Hasek's heart.

"Please don't go, Dom," pleaded one little fella draped in Hasek's No. 39 sweater.

That appeal was echoed by thousands more over the past two weeks. But the only call Hasek felt obliged to answer came from his conscience. His emotional tank drained, his competitive flame extinguished, Hasek didn't believe it right to take another $8 million or more for a performance he didn't believe could reach his high standard of excellence. So he walked away. And he should depart to a round of applause for proving in this jaded sports climate that principles still stand for something.

Only the selfishly shortsighted would think that Hasek, 37, shortchanged an organization and city by staying only one season. His efforts aren't tarnished, nor are his intentions questioned. All parties got what they wanted from this association. All parties knew from the beginning that the makings were there for a short-lived relationship.

"That's it," Hasek said. "I won't put Red Wings jersey on again. But I feel good about the decision. I don't want to disappoint all those people, but I need to do what I feel is best for me and my family. I'm very happy that I had this opportunity to play in Detroit. This is great city."

Give Hasek credit for showing his face and delivering the expected news in person. He could have Barry-ed us. His agent could have faxed over a retirement statement while he was on his way to the airport, like Barry Sanders did in 1999. Hasek faced the media the same as he did a breakaway: He didn't back down.

Hasek first read a prepared statement, thanking the Ilitch family and general manager Ken Holland for bringing him to town and conveying his gratitude to coaches and teammates for helping him realize his final competitive dream. The statement concluded with his declaration that he was "and will be a Red Wing forever."

Neither money nor melodrama could sway him into another season here. Such unwavering devotion to personal loyalties is rare in sports. The dollar too often dilutes commitment, but there was no price tag on Hasek's soul.

"An athlete unwilling to accept anything less than the best possible from himself should be the rule rather than the exception," Holland said. "But that's Dom. He's the exception in many ways. That's why, although we're disappointed that our relationship didn't last longer, we're appreciative for everything that Dom gave us this season."

Hasek had told Holland twice since the Stanley Cup clincher that he was retiring, and each time Holland hoped something might change the goalie's mind. Holland had dinner with Hasek, his agent, Rich Winter, and captain Steve Yzerman, with the intent of making one last push. But Winter whispered in Holland's ear that Hasek's decision was unyielding.

The Wings knew when they made the trade with Buffalo that they were getting the goalie for a 12-month lease.

"He held up his end of the bargain," owner Mike Ilitch said. "We know the type of effort he put out, and we're appreciative. As far as I'm concerned, we couldn't have won it without him. But we were prepared for something like this. Dominik has been up front with us from the very beginning about his future. We wish him the very best and thank him very much."

Perfectionists cannot tolerate even the tiniest compromise. The Wings proposed he play just half a season, but that insulted Hasek's sensibilities. This is a man who was in full gear practicing, while others slept, just a few hours after the Wings' five-hour marathon against Carolina in Game 3 of the Stanley Cup finals.

"There were times when I told Dom to take it easy and just show up for the game," Yzerman said. "But he wouldn't hear of it. If he can't do something all-out, then he's not going to do it. You've got to respect that attitude."

Yzerman stood in the back of the room as Hasek explained his motives. In two weeks, Yzerman has lost his coach and his goalie, and he's a few weeks away from major surgery on his ailing right knee. He didn't have the look of a leader facing upheaval but rather someone who was grateful for the short time shared together.

"I never really got to know Dom as a person," Yzerman said. "But what we got to know of him as a player and teammate is something we can take and teach to our younger guys. He wanted to come here because he wanted to win, and he never let up for one second the whole season. Dom set a pretty good example for everyone to follow."

The best example of that professionalism came at the end.

CHAPTER SEVEN

Where's the sofa? Where are the matches?

MARCH 22, 1999

Spartans take first step toward national prominence

ST. LOUIS — "Show 'em your heart, baby! Show 'em your heart, baby!"

And with each word, Valarie Peterson thumped her chest, reassuring her son in one of those high-pressure moments that usually tighten the throats and soften the spines of most 21-year-olds. Heart is what Michigan State has been about all season.

Morris Peterson drained six free throws, each one driving one more nail into the perception that the Spartans shrivel physically and shrink emotionally when the intensity is the hottest.

"We've been cool under fire all season," Peterson said, "but nobody's given us credit or has really taken notice. But that all changes now. It's Fi-nal Four, ba-by!"

The team that has had to apologize for winning 22 straight games had something to say to those who drooled over the prospect of a Duke-Kentucky national showcase in the Final Four.

Sorry, folks.

"This is the greatest day of my life," a weepy coach Tom Izzo said after MSU defeated Kentucky, 73-66, in the Midwest Regional final. "The only day that comes close was when I was in the hospital when my daughter was born. I'm just so happy for these guys, and I'm so proud that we were able to give our Michigan State family a Final Four."

And practically the entire family was there. Magic Johnson and his 1979 national title teammate, guard Terry Donnelly, were there. Football coach Nick Saban sat beside his predecessor, George Perles. And when the time came for Izzo to climb the ladder and cut the last of the twine, he wanted Antonio Smith with him. Smith was Izzo's first recruit in 1995. He brought him to MSU, and now Smith was taking Izzo to the Final Four.

That family spirit was evident earlier in the day, too. As the team prepared to leave for the Trans World Dome, more than 500 green-clad, fanatical supporters created a human passageway to the team bus. Somebody covered their route with a Kentucky flag, and the Spartans walked on it on their way to the bus. An appropriate precursor to what would unfold later, when the Spartans refused to fold after falling behind by 13 points.

It was the fans' way of saying, "We're proud of you. We love you.

We thank you."

"Man!" Mateen Cleaves said. "It sure wasn't like this last year."

There were few believers when the Spartans met their tournament demise against North Carolina in 1998 — even among their fans. No one knew what to think then. Was their surprising run to a share of the Big Ten regular-season championship another of those agonizing, one-year flirtations with success that have become so customary in East Lansing?

"We've always been about family and sticking together, and that's what makes this so special," Cleaves said. "The only ones who kept believing in ourselves was us."

Before the Spartans' tournament run began in Milwaukee, Smith's mother, Debora, gave all the players little footprint pins that each attached to his varsity jacket, right over his heart. The idea came from the inspirational poem "Footprints in the Sand."

Margaret Fishback's religious verse concentrates on the various journeys we take. A man reflects on his life and how there were always two sets of footprints — his and God's. But whenever the man was tested the greatest, he saw only one set of footprints. And he asked God why He abandoned him in his most challenging hour. Wasn't He supposed to always follow him?

God tells him that the single set of footprints wasn't a sign that He left the man but rather reflected the occasions when He carried the man.

"I've always kept a copy of that poem in my coat pocket," said Peterson, named the Midwest Regional's most outstanding player. "I always read it before every game to remind me that you never go through anything in life alone. Someone's always looking out for you, whether it's God, your family, your coaches or your teammates."

And sometimes, vindication is the guiding light.

As the team left its locker room following a third-round victory over Oklahoma, the players stopped to watch some of Kentucky's dismantling of Miami (Ohio) on a television. And they heard CBS's Jim Nantz tell the nation how the college basketball world was a step closer to a dream Duke-Kentucky confrontation.

"You see that?" assistant coach Mike Garland told his guys. "Don't forget that when you step out onto the floor Sunday."

Nor did they forget former Kentucky star Sam Bowie's arrogance following that victory when Bowie, the Wildcats' radio analyst, assured his bluegrass listeners that Kentucky would have the opportunity to defend its championship because he questioned Michigan State's heart and desire. When reminded of Bowie's comments, Peterson broke into a sly grin.

"People have been underestimating us all season," he said, "even though all we've done is keep winning."

No apologies necessary, guys.

MARCH 26, 1999

Lupe Izzo — 'I'd be lost without her,' coach says

EAST LANSING — The wispy frame, perpetual smile and whispery voice are deceptive. A stranger might think Lupe Izzo can be easily overmatched by the moment. But organization, attention to detail and pushing for maximum efficiency were principles she regularly applied to her Lansing water purification franchise for 20 years. Little did she know those experiences would toughen her for another role: Wife of a Final Four coach.

"I'd be lost without her this week," said her husband, Michigan State coach Tom Izzo. "Properly managing time in a week like this is similar to properly managing a business, so she's well-prepared."

The objective is making sure her husband stays fresh and focused, eliminating the distractions that can divert attention and concentration. Whether it's coordinating endless ticket requests from family and friends or rubbing her husband's chest with Vicks VapoRub at night to fight off a cold, Lupe Izzo has taken charge of the home so Tom can take charge of the team.

"I knew what I was getting into when we married," she said. "There are a lot of demands on a coach's wife, particularly in these situations when your husband's playing for the national championship. But this is what Tom and I had hoped and prayed for, and we can share this together."

Their marriage was born from a blind date. Lupe is the sister-in-law of MSU basketball secretary Beth Marinez, who orchestrated plenty of behind-the-scenes maneuvers to bring the two together. Like a good businesswoman, Lupe did a little investigating before deciding whether Tom would be worth the emotional investment. And she didn't like what she saw initially.

"I kept him at arm's length for a while," she said. "He'd call, but I might not immediately call back. I wasn't sure at first. You'd watch him on the bench those days, and it looked like he was crazy and not exactly under control."

Tom didn't exactly endear himself to Lupe on what amounted to their first date — the Spartans' regular-season finale against Purdue in 1990, a victory that clinched the Big Ten title. Tom, an assistant coach then, hadn't heard from Lupe before the game. Somewhat peeved, he gave Marinez two tickets and told her to give one to Lupe and the other to her "boyfriend."

"When I heard that, I couldn't believe that he actually said that," Lupe said. "So I went to the game. And I brought my date with me just like he requested. It was my nephew, Dylan."

Tom's face still reddens a shade when he reminisces about their beginning.

"She should have taken that as a clue," he said, laughing. "She had the chance to get away from me and keep running. And that might have been the best move instead of getting involved with me."

Lupe didn't think there was much of a future, but that changed after a conversation with her mother. Her mom suggested that she look a little deeper at Tom. Underneath the hardened coaching exterior lay a person who shared Lupe's religious convictions and family values.

She gave him another look. They soon were engaged. They got married in 1992.

"I had started to wonder if Tom would ever get married," said his mother, Dorothy Izzo of Iron Mountain. "It all started for him late in life because he was always so focused on his ambitions to get into coaching. And I'm just so pleased that Lupe came into his life when she did. She's been a blessing to him and our family."

But Lupe knew her new life in high-stakes college basketball wouldn't come without sacrifice. When it was announced in 1993 that Tom would replace Jud Heathcote, she knew that meant many late nights and absent nights while Tom trekked the lonely recruiting trail. She sold her water-purification franchise so she could provide an anchor at home.

"At no point have I ever felt that I've lost Tom in any way because of all the demands on his time," she said. "No matter how hectic it gets, we always manage to find some moments, here or there, for the three of us to spend together."

Lupe is certain that 4-year-old Raquel understands the insanity whirling around her, although she has been known to doze through a few games. But when she sees her father after a game, her first question is: "Did my boys win?"

But she has given her father a better appreciation of winning and losing. Raquel smiles regardless of the outcome.

"It's impossible to overstate their importance in helping me maintain some degree of sanity through all of this," Tom said. "I had always thought that I could never be in this business for 20 years because the tensions and the pressures would just eat away at me. But your family helps replenish you daily. You don't survive in this business without a strong support system at home."

He needed the support last season, when some people publicly questioned his coaching aptitude after his third straight loss to Detroit Mercy.

"Tom knows that the love from his family isn't based on wins and losses," Lupe said. "We'll always be there for him."

MARCH 29, 1999

Title hopes dashed, and season goes up in smoke

ST. PETERSBURG, Fla. — There were no cameras or notepads around when Michigan State University president Peter McPherson introduced himself to Duke coach Mike Krzyzewski, so neither gentleman was bound by decorum or professional courtesy, creating an occasion for sincerity. Duke had just eliminated MSU in the national semifinal, 68-62.

"You have one great program there and one heck of a coach," Krzyzewski said. "Watching a team like yours is what makes me love college basketball. They're very classy young men, and I told them that. You should be very proud of them."

But McPherson's pride turned to shame five minutes later — the time it took to return to the Michigan State locker room, where he learned the grim news.

"They're rioting in East Lansing."

Nobody thought much about it initially. Interpretations are occasionally more exaggerated than reality. What could it really have been? Another defenseless piece of furniture engulfed in flames? A handful of inebriated idiots testing the limits of police tolerance?

But as the ugly descriptions of lawlessness filtered into the locker room, a season of tremendous achievement sadly dissolved into an excuse for moronic malcontents to flex their stupidity and once again turn MSU into a national embarrassment at what should have been one of its most glorious moments.

And coach Tom Izzo couldn't hide his disgust. "Everything we did this season," he said, the rioters "undid to a certain extent."

There's no way of knowing whether those who initially lit the fuse were MSU students, but that's irrelevant in the smoldering aftermath. It's obvious by the sheer numbers of those involved in the unruliness that some students participated, and those mental midgets weren't deserving of a basketball team that so gallantly represented their university and their state.

"I've never been more angry or embarrassed about anything in my years at Michigan State," Izzo said as he turned his head and stared directly into a television camera. "And if any of them are watching me right now, and if they're students or fans of Michigan State basketball, I don't want you as a part of my program any longer.

"If you're a season-ticket holder, I will personally buy your tickets next year because I don't want you as a fan. I don't want you in the building. I don't want you as a part of my program. I don't understand that kind of behavior. We try to give them something to be proud about, something to be happy about, and this is how they thank us. What happened was ridiculous. It was sick."

Izzo tried to cool the emotions from 850 miles away. He asked Mateen Cleaves to go on live television to call for calm.

"Coach pulled me and Antonio (Smith) to the other room and told us about what was happening," Cleaves said. "And I just thought it was just a few people who got a little carried away. But then when we heard about them setting cars on fire and breaking windows and stuff like that, it made us feel pretty bad. People shouldn't be acting this way."

The rioters tried to set fire to a Taco Bell. And this was after a loss! What would have happened had the Spartans upset top-ranked Duke? There is no justification for such wanton disregard for property or such disrespect for the efforts of a group of dedicated young men who never listened to those all season who said they couldn't or shouldn't win.

The Spartans were a team that should have been embraced. Instead, they were slapped in the face.

"What angers you the most is that it wouldn't surprise me at all if most of the rowdies or the instigators weren't even Michigan State students," athletic director Merritt Norvell said. "But there's a perception that you can come to Michigan State and act crazy if you want because of what's happened before. Other folks come into town and act like fools, and it's our reputation that takes the hit."

These Spartans won more games in a single season than any Big Ten basketball team. They won the hearts of fans and the admiration and respect of opponents through their toughness and class for 38 games.

It's a damn shame their achievements were dampened because some of their fellow students couldn't exhibit a little class for one night.

DEC. 2, 1999

Spartans win one for Mateen and football brethren

CHAPEL HILL, N.C. — Following one of the biggest moments for Michigan State basketball, coach Tom Izzo went on national television and dedicated the Spartans' victory over North Carolina to the Spartans' football team.

"This one's for them," Izzo said.

Nick Saban's abrupt departure to Louisiana State confirmed what many already believed — Izzo is the poster boy of Michigan State athletics. Before he left for North Carolina, Izzo talked to a football team somewhat dazed over the loss of its head coach. Izzo asked the team to gather together to watch his team meet the challenge of facing the nation's No. 2-ranked team on its home floor. He also talked about toughness and perseverance.

Sounds like his basketball team listened, as well.

Non-conference opponents don't come into the Dean Smith Center expecting good fortune. The Tar Heels had a 55-game non-conference home winning streak and a 70-year winning streak in home openers. That is, until Morris Peterson came calling. His career-high 31 points stole the spotlight in the Spartans' 86-76 victory.

"Michigan State is like a Rolls-Royce without the engine," the nation's No. 1 college hoop-aholic, Dick Vitale, said before tip-off. "It just won't be the same without Mateen Cleaves."

But the Spartans got an All-America effort from Peterson, who convinced a skeptical college basketball nation that the Spartans aren't in a holding pattern until Cleaves returns from a stress fracture in his right foot. But, perhaps more important, they set an example for a school fighting off old insecurities.

"They lost their leader, and we've lost ours," guard Charlie Bell said, "but that doesn't mean you still can't succeed if you want it bad enough. We all learn from each other. That's what an athletic program's supposed to be all about. I'm glad we were able to put some smiles back on some Michigan State faces."

But the biggest smile was reserved for the fallen captain. Missing this game hurt more than his foot because Cleaves had dreamed about this night ever since the schedule came out. Cleaves appreciates history more than his teammates. That was evident when the Spartans first walked into the Smith Center for practice. While his teammates looked straight ahead, Cleaves looked straight up. Up to the rafters. Up to the championship banners and retired names and numbers of former Carolina greats.

"It's almost like there are thousands up there," Cleaves said. "There's a lot of tradition here. That's what makes this hurt so much, not being out there."

This was the first time Cleaves' inactivity moved him to tears. He got so worked up following his Dean Dome visit that he spent an hour on the exercise bike later in the evening, pushing himself harder in the hope of accelerating his progress.

"He wants to get back as quickly as he can," Izzo said, "because he sees what we can become when he's back to full strength."

The Spartans weren't so bad without him. But can you imagine what they can be with him? How would Dickie V call it?

Awesome, baby!!! With a capital A!!!

"I'm happy that we gave the university and the football team something that everybody can be proud of," Cleaves said. "It's been tough for everybody the last couple days, but these guys showed a lot of toughness and character. Man, the way they played tonight, they probably don't have any use for me anymore."

Hey, Mateen, maybe LSU's looking for a point guard?

DEC. 8, 1999

Hair apparent, Bell steps in for ailing Cleaves

CHICAGO — The look just doesn't fit the normally conservative Charlie Bell fashion motif. He fancies himself an old-school throwback, more substance than style. He's high socks and an Afro. But then Bell showed up at practice wearing short socks and his hair in cornrows.

"When I saw him come in," MSU basketball coach Tom Izzo said, "I pulled up the collar on my jacket because I thought Latrell Sprewell was in the building."

If Bell keeps playing like he has of late, Izzo might even let Bell clutch the coach's throat.

Spre-Bell displayed an offensive flair against Kansas rarely seen since his high school days, when he was the most prodigious scorer in Flint prep history. It has been awhile since Bell carried a team. But his game-high 21 points, efficiency at the point and customary defensive tenacity were the lift the fourth-ranked Spartans needed in a 66-54 victory over the No. 5 Jayhawks.

Bell tolled, and the Spartans rolled.

"Man, if he keeps playing like that," Mateen Cleaves said, "I'll braid his hair for him."

The United Center hadn't been the home of shooting accuracy for the MSU backcourt. Cleaves had laid enough bricks at the arena in the past two seasons to build an annex. Even though he didn't play because of injury, it wouldn't have surprised anyone if the official scorer had slapped an 0-for-10 next to his name out of habit.

But Bell looked comfortable from the start, scoring the Spartans' first five points. This has become his team, a distinction that extends only to the New Year, when Cleaves is expected to return from a stress fracture. Bell's point-guard capabilities leave plenty to be desired, but he's more willing to take charge. The new hairstyle is an example of that aggressiveness.

"I'm usually old school, but I just wanted to try something different," Bell said. "It's kind of the new look, and it didn't look bad, so I thought I'd keep it for a while. But I couldn't wear the long socks with it. That's old school. And you can't have two schools clashing."

Is an earring or tongue stud next?

"I don't know what I'm going to do," he joked. "It all depends on what I feel like."

The Spartans won't care as long as he plays like he did against Kansas. Bell tied Jayhawks point guard Jeff Boschee in knots. Boschee was a 65 percent three-point shooter, but Bell helped hold him to one trey — and one basket — for the game. And once again, Bell's biggest supporter was his fellow Flintstone, Cleaves.

"It's great because everyone in the country's now getting to see all the things that Charlie can do," Cleaves said. "I guess I've become kind of an unofficial assistant coach. So if I have to grade Charlie as a coach, I'll give him an A-plus. He put us all on his shoulders tonight."

Winning without Cleaves can only make this team stronger when he returns.

"They're showing great character in that different guys step up each game to deliver for them," Kansas coach Roy Williams said. "You've got to like the way Tom has them playing. They're aggressive and physical defensively, and they make you work for everything that you get."

They're an old-school basketball team. Consider Morris Peterson. He's that rarity in college basketball, a talent willing to return for his senior season. Peterson struggled on offense, but he found other ways to contribute, getting 10 rebounds, three assists and two steals.

The Spartans win with no flash, little dash. But just in case Bell has stumbled onto something, perhaps Cleaves should consider a new look when MSU returns to Chicago for the Big Ten tournament.

MARCH 13, 2000

Family feud sharpens resolve for the battle ahead

CHICAGO — Families aren't immune to bickering. Even brothers, born from the heart rather than the blood, go at each other's throats once in a while. And often it's the father who must make peace.

Seniors Mateen Cleaves and Morris Peterson exchanged unprintable pleasantries as they sat beside each other during a first-half time-out in the Big Ten tournament championship game. Head coach Tom Izzo cooled the tension by suggesting that if they didn't shut up, he'd have freshman behemoth Aloysius Anagonye silence them.

Cleaves and Peterson cracked up — and it was back to business, back to focusing on the bigger picture. It's all about getting to the mountaintop, the ultimate destination that barely eluded Michigan State in 1999.

The Spartans' second straight conference tournament title — a 76-61 victory over Illinois — was an exercise of been there, done that. They've grown accustomed to No. 1 NCAA tournament seeds, championship caps and T-shirts. It's no big deal to the veterans such as Cleaves, Peterson and junior center Andre Hutson.

But freshman Jason Richardson was enjoying his first dip into the ecstasy. He joyously hugged his teammates before the awards presentation. But when he got to Hutson, he was met with an intimidating, emotionless stare. The look told the youngster that this wasn't the goal but merely the first step. And this is Cleaves' and Peterson's last chance, and anything short of a national championship will be an extreme disappointment.

These are the times when emotions burn so raw that they ignite at the slightest provocation. It's when experience usually prevails. And that's why many believe the Spartans — No. 1 seed in the Midwest Regional — might be the team to beat in a wide-open NCAA basketball tournament.

"I'll tell you this," Izzo said. "How long we stay in the tournament won't be a factor in how proud I am of what this team has done, especially this senior class. I'm not going to be able to relish the remaining time that I have with these guys, but I hope people watching will. They're so special, and we should savor them because we may not see the likes of a senior class like this again."

Applaud them because the senior class of Cleaves, Peterson and forward A.J. Granger is just two victories from becoming the first 100-win class in MSU history. Appreciate them because Cleaves and Peterson are an anomaly in today's world of get-me-to-the-NBA-as-quickly-as-possible college basketball. They were possible first-round draft choices last year but stayed in school, bound by one common goal: tearing down the only nets that really matter, the ones from the national championship game.

"When I was younger," Cleaves said, "I always dreamed about being in the Final Four or the championship game, the clock running down and you're down by a point. You always dream about making the big shot and winning the game and having everybody going crazy around you. That's why you play the game. The money's fine, but you play because you like winning."

That's what separates Cleaves from so many other players in the NCAA tournament. Cleaves is motivated through collective goals, not individual statistics. The Spartans (26-7) didn't need to beat Illinois to become a No. 1 seed. The NCAA eventually revealed the top seeds were determined two hours before tip-off. This was solely about pride.

"You can't tell Mateen and MoPete a game doesn't matter," Izzo said. "That's what I mean when I say they've created a standard for the younger guys to follow when they're gone."

That's why the No. 1 seed doesn't mean as much as it did last season. Then, the Spartans were still proving themselves. Now, they realize they belong among the national elite. They reacted somewhat indifferently when told they were the first Big Ten team to earn successive No. 1 seeds since the tournament expanded to 64 teams in 1985. Yeah, it's nice. But we've still got a climb before the summit. And if they get there, making it special will be that they got there together as a family.

"The team that doesn't let their emotions get in the way is going to have the best chance to win it all," Peterson said. "We've been through all this before. It's not that winning ever gets boring. There will be time for celebrating and thinking back on where we fit with all the great teams to ever play in the Big Ten later. But right now, we've got a job to do."

When Peterson heard his name announced as the most valuable player of the Big Ten tournament, the first congratulatory hug came from Cleaves. It wasn't hard reading Peterson's lips. "I love you," he told his basketball brother. Cleaves responded in kind but reminded Peterson that dreams remain.

MARCH 31, 2000

They're from Flint and proud of it

Urban squalor, exemplified by the plywood-covered windows on seemingly endless rows of vacant buildings, bears witness that this decaying automotive town never received the memo that prosperity's upon us. But there is pride here, stamped on the arms of an increasing number of local teenagers.

"Anytime you go around the city, you see a lot of kids wearing their Flint tattoos," said Flint Northwestern junior Kelvin Torbert, one of the top high school basketball players in the country. "Or the hot one now is getting a Fred Flintstone face on your arm. And all they talk about is going to play for Michigan State when they get older. They want to be a Flintstone."

And that may include Torbert. He hasn't gotten a tattoo yet, but he concedes that it's probably just a matter of time. Especially if he commits to Michigan State, where a Flint tattoo is regarded as a badge of honor.

"What the Flintstones have done is tell people that there's a lot more to Flint than crime and unemployment," Torbert said. "We're proud of the basketball players that have come from here."

And MSU coach Tom Izzo might have exclusive rights to that pipeline. Back when Chris Webber, Jalen Rose, Juwan Howard and company made baggy shorts and black socks chic, many assumed the Fab Five would have far-reaching ramifications at Michigan. But the only championship of relative significance in the six years since the bulk of the Fab Five bolted was one Big Ten conference tournament.

But the marriage between Michigan State and Flint basketball should bear fruit long after the last of the original Flintstones, Charlie Bell, leaves in 2001.

"It's really amazing when you think about the impact that we've had on a city," Bell said. "And every time I see another kid with a Flint tattoo, I know we're having a positive effect on him. They're always coming up to me or Mateen (Cleaves) or MoPete (Morris Peterson) and telling us how they're going to keep the tradition going. I think that's great."

But the imprint they're leaving is more than basketball. It's about elevating self-esteem and establishing a sense of community and camaraderie.

Following the Spartans' last home game, three of the mother Stones — Frances Cleaves, Valarie Peterson and Belle Bell — wanted to take a group picture with Izzo as a present for the coach. Izzo joked that if they really wanted to give him a gift, they each could nurture another tough-as-stone son.

But the mothers assured Izzo that they wouldn't leave the program just because their kids are leaving. They're already pitching Michigan State to the next generation of Flintstones, like Torbert.

"This isn't the end," Frances Cleaves said. "This is just the beginning. Flint is about strong family roots, and that's what Izzo's building with this program. Mrs. Peterson and I are still planning on traveling with the team next year, and we want to help the mothers of the new Flint kids here adapt. This could be a new kind of assembly line for Flint, with MSU being GM."

The city's Berston Fieldhouse is to Flint what St. Cecilia's is to Detroit. If you have game, this is where you get your sternest test. All you see around there these days are green and white jerseys bearing Cleaves' No. 12 or Peterson's No. 42.

"The success of this program is connected to attracting the Flint guys," said Mateen's father, Herbert Cleaves, who does social work for the Flint public schools. "And they're winning because they're tough. Coming back in the final five minutes of a basketball game doesn't scare these kids with the stuff they had to overcome on the streets. That's something that translates positively to the young kids in Flint, and that's what the tattoos are all about. They don't have to be ashamed of telling people where they're from."

Cleaves said Torbert already has told him that he's coming to MSU. But Torbert, a leaper who makes MSU freshman jumping jack Jason Richardson look like he's wearing lead shoes, was more evasive, saying he was leaning toward the Spartans but also considering Cincinnati. The allure of the Flintstones is obvious, however.

Mateen Cleaves telephones Torbert weekly, reminding him to avoid the temptations that have tragically diverted many a promising young Flint basketball talent.

"There's so much bad that goes around on the streets in this city that he wants to make sure that I'm staying on the right path," Torbert said. "He's looking out for me because he knows how tough it was for him at my age. But I don't think that he's doing that because he's Michigan State. He's doing it because he's from Flint." And the two have become inseparable.

MARCH 30, 2000

Odd couple follows bumpy road to the Final Four

EAST LANSING — The Final Four is about snapshots, memories provided from that instant of impending victory forever frozen in our thoughts and our hearts. It's the "One Shining Moment" sung about on CBS in its championship ode during the epilogue of its NCAA tournament title game coverage.

And if that moment belongs to Michigan State, the visual stamp of the occasion will be the reaction when Mateen Cleaves walks off the court for the final time as a Spartan and greets his coach, combatant and confidant of the last four years, Tom Izzo.

"Win or lose, it's going to be an emotional moment because it'll be the end of a long road for us," Cleaves said. "I'm sure there's going to be some tears because we've both been through so much together. But, man, if we win, he's going to get the biggest bear hug he's ever gotten in his life."

And thus provide the appropriate symbolism of what both parties describe as a peculiar alliance, two comparably volatile personalities from diverse cultural backgrounds embracing each other's ambitions to build something memorable from the mediocrity that was Michigan State basketball when Izzo took over in 1995.

The road there wasn't without potholes. Cleaves' occasional off-court transgressions made him an easy target for the overly judgmental and Izzo a target for accusations of disciplining by double standard. Their mutual stubbornness clashed often, one challenging the limits of the other's tolerance to see how far he could push before the other pushed back. But each learned from the other, ultimately forging a respect that grew in direct proportion to the success of the program.

"But we've had our moments," Izzo recalled with a rather devilish leer.

One came in the aftermath of the Spartans' loss at Kentucky on Dec. 23. Cleaves believed he was ready to return from his fractured foot and demanded to play sparingly in the Spartans' last two non-conference games. Izzo thought otherwise, believing it was best that Cleaves wait another week. Angry, Cleaves told Izzo that if he didn't let him play, he would stop going to class.

Through the years, Cleaves learned the right buttons to push to ignite Izzo's internal volcano, and blowing off class was one of them. But Izzo didn't bite. There was no eruption this time. Instead, he used an argument Cleaves couldn't rebut — winning above all else. How would Cleaves feel if a premature return in meaningless December cost his team in all-important March?

"He knew Mateen was frustrated over not being able to play, so he made him understand the importance of making sure he was completely healthy," said Frances Cleaves, Mateen's mother. "And then he got into Mateen's face and told him he was going to class or else."

Or else what?

"Or else Mateen was going to have to tell me that he wasn't going to class anymore," his mother said.

Cleaves jokes that he has to listen to Izzo for only one more weekend "and then I'm free," but humor serves as a defense mechanism. He's going to miss the jousting of equally strong wills. He's going to miss a relationship that every father wishes he had with his son, a juggling act of being demanding one minute, loving another minute and forgiving the next. He's even going to miss those frequent late-night — or, rather, early-morning — telephone calls.

"Coach is the kind of guy that whenever something comes into his head, he's telling me about it," Cleaves said. "The phone rang one time at 1 in the morning and he was calling to tell me about something he read about people taking shots at our program. He kept saying to me: 'It's time, Mo. It's time.' And I told him, 'It is time, Coach. It's time for me to get back to sleep.' "

But the end is coming, so Izzo savors these last few days, his eyes turn misty and his voice melancholy when waxing nostalgic because he knows he'll never have a similar rapport with future stars.

"Mateen has taught me that if a coach expects his players to go to the wall for him when things get tough on the court," Izzo said, "then the coach had better be prepared to go to the wall for his players when things get tough for them off the court. Our relationship has helped make me a better coach, and, more important, a better person because it made me understand the importance of looking beneath the exterior to see what's really important deep down."

What's important is that such cultural opposites as rural Iron Mountain and urban Flint aren't really as far apart as we think when bonded by a mutual objective.

"Theirs is a relationship that bridges cultural and racial differences to find that common ground of attaining a level of excellence," MSU President Peter McPherson said. "That's precisely the image we want to convey about Michigan State beyond athletics, and they've created an expectation that everybody at the university should strive to emulate."

And should that partnership culminate in a national title, their shining moment will be indelibly etched in our minds.

APRIL 2, 2000

MoPete spirits Spartans to national title game

INDIANAPOLIS — One game. One win. One dream. A season-long mission has been reduced to its simplest form.

"It's hard to imagine that we're just one away from achieving something that you've dreamed about ever since you were a little kid," said a still bubbly Morris Peterson more than an hour after Michigan State's 53-41 national semifinal victory over Wisconsin. The buzz hadn't worn off. "It always seemed so far away, but it's so close now that you can practically taste it."

Michigan State is one win away from sipping the sweet nectar of champions.

The dream began following last year's national semifinal. The Spartans fell to Duke, and it was in those moments following defeat that the resolve that has forged this drive toward college basketball supremacy took shape. It was then that Mateen Cleaves knew he was definitely returning for his senior season. The NBA could wait. And it was then that Peterson made up his mind that if he were fortunate enough to get another chance at a Final Four, he would play more aggressively.

"I knew Pete was going to have a great game after I saw him sky for that offensive rebound off the first shot of the game," Cleaves said. "He just soared for the ball. I knew he was charged up then. His intensity was up, and he was going to give us the emotion we needed."

Peterson credited his late grandmother's spirit for providing the jolt that was personally lacking early in the Spartans' previous two tournament games. For a change, it was he who awakened his slumbering teammates with a blistering second half against Wisconsin, scoring 16 of his game-high 20 points in the final 20 minutes. He also snared seven rebounds.

"It's been a difficult last couple of days for me," Peterson said. "I think that's why I was so fired up. But my teammates have been great. They just told me to go out and play hard. It's been an emotional time, but I was determined to be as aggressive as I could."

Peterson, who attended his grandmother's funeral in Mississippi two days before the semifinal victory, often pointed a finger toward the heavens to salute her after making a basket.

"Yeah, I pointed to her just to let her know that I knew she was watching me," he said. "She's always going to be with me, and I wanted to make that extra effort to let her know that I feel her presence."

Peterson was reminded of reality's cruelties in the past week. There are no guarantees in either life or basketball, and you must take advantage of the special opportunities when they present themselves. He figures the best way to honor his grandmother would be to win the national championship that she always heard him talk about growing up.

"I wanted the ball," Peterson said. "Just like Mateen was saying last week in the Iowa State game and the Syracuse game, I needed to be more aggressive and take charge of the situation. I was getting open, and I felt like I could make something happen."

"We knew that this was going to be a battle because that's the way Wisconsin plays," said Tom Izzo, who will coach in his first national championship game in his fifth year as a head coach. "I'm sure it wasn't a pretty game to watch, but at this point, it doesn't matter how nice they look. All that matters is winning."

All that matters is that the Spartans' yearlong mission has been reduced to 40 minutes.

APRIL 4, 2000

Storybook finish for Cleaves and the national champs

INDIANAPOLIS — For five frightening minutes, it looked like Michigan State would have to end the season the way it began — without its leader. The Spartans all saw the tears in Mateen Cleaves' eyes and the anguish on his face as he writhed on the floor after his right ankle rolled beneath him. Tom Izzo leaned over him, trying to console him while deep down fearing the worst.

"It's broke," Cleaves yelled. "I know it's broke."

The dream couldn't die this way. This was Cleaves' moment. The reason he put the NBA on hold for another year. And until now, the national title game against Florida had been his show.

But the toughness of a town and its basketball heritage was

there for a national TV audience to see as Cleaves returned in a scene reminiscent of Willis Reed hobbling from the locker room to lead the New York Knicks to victory in Game 7 of the 1970 NBA Finals. This was what put the "stone" in Flint.

"I told the trainer that they were going to have to amputate my leg to keep me out of this one," Cleaves said. "I went back to the locker and shed a few tears. But I told myself, 'not now.' I wanted to get back in there. I wanted to win this game."

Adversity has molded this team since two weeks before the season, when doctors inserted screws in Cleaves' foot to repair a stress fracture. So it was only fitting that they finally scaled the mountaintop against forces trying mightily to keep them down.

The Spartans are the champions of college basketball after an 89-76 victory over Florida.

They yabba dabba did it!

"This doesn't get any more storybook for Mateen," said a teary-eyed Izzo, still somewhat stunned that he has reached the pinnacle after critics called for his head only three years ago.

"He not only comes back for a senior year, he comes back from an injury. And then to have everything seem to turn on him like it did when he went down tonight only to come back. I don't know if I'm more emotional right now for myself or for him."

Much happier tears streamed down Cleaves' cheeks when he was surrounded by the three things that moved and motivated him more than anything else — his mother, Frances, his father, Herbert, and the NCAA championship trophy. The three of them swung with the rhythm as "One Shining Moment," Cleaves' personal anthem for as long as he has played college ball, was played with a video on the RCA Dome's screens.

Afterward he buried his head, softly sobbing onto his mother's shoulder, washing away all the slams he took because he couldn't hit any shots and the snide remarks regarding some of his less-than-astute off-court moves.

"Oh, God, this is just the greatest feeling you can think of," Cleaves said. "This has been the goal ever since last year when we walked off the floor after losing to Duke. We said we were coming back here and we were going to win it. And we did it! We did it!"

"We" is certainly the appropriate word. The Spartans didn't fold when they lost their captain. When Izzo told the team that Cleaves' ankle might be broken, Morris Peterson looked to everyone and said, "Then let's just get it done for him then."

The Spartans got contributions from reserves who were largely absent through the tournament. There was Mike Chappell, who replaced Cleaves and immediately nailed a crucial three-pointer to offset any momentum shift. There were freshmen Aloysius Anagonye and Jason Richardson, snaring a clutch rebound or blocking a shot.

When Cleaves returned five minutes after he left, Florida knew it was done. He didn't take another shot. He didn't have to. The Gators knocked him down, but they couldn't knock him out. He was named the tournament's most outstanding player, and it could have been as much for his courage and composure.

"That's why he's the leader," Peterson said. "I knew he was coming back even when they were saying he had broke it. Nothing was going to keep him out of this. This just meant too much to him."

You'd think that Cleaves was beyond proving himself after 103 career victories, three straight Big Ten regular-season championships, two consecutive conference tournament titles, two straight Final Fours and one national championship game. You'd think that a battle-tested senior, possessing the mettle made for these moments, was beyond answering to a legion of doubters following a sloppy semifinal effort against Wisconsin.

And when he drilled his first three-pointer midway through the first half, he wagged his tongue as if to say, "Take that!"

Until the title game, Florida held opposing point guards to a seven-point average and 27 percent shooting through the tournament. Cleaves scored 18 points and shot 7-for-11 from the floor.

Any more questions?

"But I've been hearing that stuff so much throughout my career that it doesn't matter anymore," Cleaves said. "People are going to keep talking about my shot or that I can't do this or do that. But I've always said that when my career was over at Michigan State, I just wanted to be remembered as a winner."

It's over, and he will be.

APRIL 6, 2000

The happiest ending of all

EAST LANSING — Thousands of students took advantage of what was, in effect, a university holiday. Some instructors canceled afternoon classes so that many could gather along the Parade of Champions route as it entered the Michigan State campus.

Crowds were three-deep along West Circle Road. Music blared out of dormitory windows. Some flung Frisbees or tossed basketballs, while some imbibed a few adult beverages. It's not often you get to celebrate a national championship, so you make the moment as memorable as possible.

But heading out of Landon Hall was a solitary figure armed with a backpack. Christina Alves had to go to class.

"Unfortunately, they didn't cancel my Math 202 class," said Alves, a 19-year-old freshman from Muskegon. "It's too bad because I really wanted to be a part of all this. It's just so cool that we've got a championship basketball team and to show them how much everyone's proud of them."

This was a family reunion, stretching from the steps of the state Capitol to the grounds of Spartan Stadium. But this celebration was as much for the students as the players. They won something, as well. They won back their good name.

They partied heartily after the Spartans' national championship victory over Florida. More than 30,000 revelers converged on the streets, with nothing out of the ordinary tainting the occasion. Now maybe that's due to the rising cost of gasoline, which made it economically infeasible to burn innocent furniture. Or maybe the students took ownership of their university, the same as the basketball players took control of their team.

"I think more students got involved this year to make sure that we didn't have a repeat occurrence of what happened last year," said Alves, who wore a button bearing coach Tom Izzo's face and his statement: "Spartans Act With Class." "It was embarrassing, and we didn't want to do anything that would take away from all the great things the basketball team was doing."

Last year's Final Four loss to Duke was followed by a riot, which resulted in numerous arrests and property damage. Although most of the instigators weren't affiliated with the university, MSU became identified with drunken lawlessness. Izzo e-mailed all students, asking them to represent the university as proudly as his players did. He echoed a similar statement in 30-second spots that local television stations aired frequently during the NCAA tournament.

And often along the parade route, Izzo applauded the students as they applauded him. He remembers his disgust the day after the loss to Duke, when he angrily blasted those students who took part in the unruliness or looked the other way, giving MSU a black eye nationally.

"What's so exciting about what we've done as a basketball team the last three weeks, what the football team did to Florida in the Citrus Bowl and what the student body did over the weekend is that we're all starting to work from the same page," Izzo said. "It's all about pride, pride in yourself and pride in what you're doing. How can you not succeed when you have that working for you?"

Izzo opened his mouth in amazement when he walked through the stadium tunnel and saw about 25,000 celebrants.

"Wow!" he said. "I've always been a football kind of guy, so it's only fitting that we have this here."

Coach Bobby Williams wanted his football players to get a taste of the aura that has followed the basketball team. Before practice, he brought his team to the stadium to congratulate its basketball brothers. But Williams also wanted his players to watch and listen. See the euphoria. Hear the passion. This is how Michigan State embraces its champions.

"And who wouldn't want to be a part of that?" Williams said. "We're proud of them because they represent us when they play, and we try to represent them when we play. We hope some of that magic rubs off on us because we're all in this together. We want the best for Michigan State."

Williams was in the crowd at the championship game, as were hockey coach Ron Mason and five other MSU head coaches. Rarely have the various university factions coalesced so nicely. And Izzo should get a lot of the credit. Izzo always has espoused family, loyalty and hard work, understated virtues that were the foundation for the Spartans' excellence of the past three years. He thinks those values attracted national support for the heavily favored Spartans through the tournament, negating the natural instinct to pull for the underdog.

"This team has become a reflection of the university, a standard of pride, excellence and commitment that others wish to emulate," said MSU president Peter McPherson, who also voiced his pleasure with the students' conduct at the celebration. "I want to thank you for celebrating the Spartan way."